TOKYO

TOP SIGHTS, AUTHENTIC EXPERIENCES

Rebecca Milner,
Thomas O'Malley, Simon Richmond

Contents

Ueno & Yanaka
Tokyo's most famous museum, a sprawling park and well-preserved historic neighbour-hoods. *(Map p254)*

Tokyo National Museum
Ueno
Sensō-ji

Kanda & Akihabara
Swathe of central Tokyo that includes a former geisha district and a pop-culture hub. *(Map p254)*

Akihabara
Ryōgoku Kokugikan

Narita (60km)

Asakusa & Ryōgoku
Riverside district of ancient temples, old merchants' quarters and Tokyo's sumo sta-dium. *(Map p254)*

Imperial Palace
Tokyo

Suntory Museum of Art

Kabukiza Theatre

Tsukiji Market

Marunouchi & Nihombashi
History meets modernity where the grounds of the Imperial Palace meet the skyscrapers of downtown. *(Map p250)*

i Art eum

Toyosu Market

teamLab Borderless

i & Around
ry for its
this area
e place for
dge art and
Map p252)

Ginza & Tsukiji
Ginza is Tokyo's most polished neigh-bourhood; Tsukiji is synonymous with its famous food market. *(Map p250)*

Odaiba & Tokyo Bay
Waterside museums, amusement parks and shopping malls plus pleasure-boat cruises.

Rikugi-en

0 — 2 km
0 — 1 miles

Welcome to Tokyo

Rather than any particular sight, it's Tokyo itself that enchants visitors. It's a sprawling, organic thing, stretching as far as the eye can see. Its diverse collection of neighbourhoods is always changing, so no two experiences of the city are ever the same.

Some neighbourhoods feel like a vision from the future, with ever-taller, sleeker structures popping up each year; others evoke the past with low-slung wooden buildings and glowing lanterns radiating surprising warmth. Elsewhere, drab concrete blocks hide art galleries and cocktail bars and every lane hints at possible discoveries. In Tokyo you can experience the whole breadth of Japanese arts and culture, from centuries-old sumo and kabuki to cutting-edge digital art.

When it comes to Tokyo superlatives, however, the city's food scene tops the list. Wherever you are, you're usually within 100m of a good, if not great, restaurant. It's a scene that careens nonchalantly between the highs and lows: it's not unusual for a top-class sushi restaurant to share the same block with an oil-spattered noodle joint. Tokyoites love dining out; join them and delight in the sheer variety of tastes and experiences the city has to offer.

Tokyo may seem daunting at first: its subway map is a tangle of intersecting lines and is often compared to a bowl of noodles. But once you get out there, you'll be surprised how easy it is to navigate. That subway can take you everywhere you want to go; trains are frequent (though sometimes uncomfortably crowded) and almost always on time, and stations are well signposted in English.

In Tokyo you can experience the whole breadth of Japanese arts and culture, from centuries-old sumo and kabuki to cutting-edge digital art.

Graffiti Flower Bombing, teamLab Borderless (p78)
TEAMLAB BORDERLESS, ODAIBA, TOKYO ©

★ TOKYO ★

Shinjuku & Ikebukuro
Shinjuku has the world's busiest train station, city hall and nightlife galore; grittier Ikebukuro is a student haunt. *(Map p253)*

Golden Gai ◎

🚇Shinjuku

Kōenji & Kichijōji
Neighbourhoods loved by locals, who appreciate the vintage mid-20th-century look and bohemian spirit.

Ghibli Museum (6km)

◎ **Meiji-jingu**

Harajuku 🚇

National Art Center Tokyo
🏛

Shibuya & Shimo-Kitazawa
Shibuya is the heart of Tokyo's youth culture; Shimo-Kitazawa is a beloved, bohemian haunt. *(Map p246)*

Shibuya Crossing ◎🚇

Shibuya

Mo
Mu

🚇Ebisu

Harajuku & Aoyama
Nexus of tradition and trends with Tokyo's grandest Shintō shrine, shops galore and stunning architecture. *(Map p246)*

Ebisu & Meguro
Broad collection of hip neighbourhoods with fashionable boutiques, (relatively) quiet streets and great dining. *(Map p246)*

Roppon
Legenda
nightlife
is also *t*
cutting-
design.

*Haneda ✈ (10km);
Kamakura (60km);
Mt Fuji (150km)* ↓

Plan Your Trip
This Year in Tokyo

2020

Tokyo

From pop culture events to festivals that have been taking place for centuries, there is always something going on in Tokyo. Like elsewhere in Japan, the seasons have special meaning and every new bloom is a reason for celebration.

Clockwise from left: Chidori-ga-fuchi in cherry blossom season (p9); Sumida-gawa Fireworks (p12); Kōenji Awa Odori (p13); Sanja Matsuri (p10)

2020

★ **Top Festivals & Events**

Hatsu-mōde, January (p6)
Cherry blossoms, April (p9)
Sanja Matsuri, May (p10)
Sumida-gawa Fireworks, July (p12)
Kōenji Awa Odori, August (p13)

Plan Your Trip
This Year in Tokyo

BROSTOCK/GETTY IMAGES ©

January

01

Tokyo is eerily quiet for O-shōgatsu (the first three days of the new year), but picks up as the month rolls on. Days are cold, but usually clear; sights are generally uncrowded.

✿ Greeting the Emperor   2 Jan
The emperor makes a brief – and rare – public appearance in an inner courtyard of the Imperial Palace (p98) to make a ceremonial greeting.

🛍 Lucky Bags   early Jan
While lots of shops close for *Shōgatsu*, others stay open for *hatsu-uri* – the first sale of the New Year. Shops compete for customers with *fukubukuro* (lucky bags) containing unknown, but heavily discounted, goods. Quantities are limited and serious shoppers are known to queue for them.

☆ Sumo Tournament   13–27 Jan
The January *bashō* (grand sumo tournament) is the first chance of the year to see Japan's top wrestlers have at it. It's held at Ryōgoku Kokugikan (p68). Tournaments also take place in May and September.

✿ Hatsu-mōde   1 Jan
Hatsu-mōde, the first shrine visit of the new year, starts just after midnight on 1 January and continues through O-shōgatsu. Meiji-jingū (p226) is the most popular spot in Tokyo; it can get very, very crowded, but that's part of the experience.

✿ Coming of Age Day   13 Jan
Seijin-no-hi (Coming of Age Day) is the collective birthday for all who have turned 20 (the age of majority) in the past year. Many celebrants wear formal kimonos and gather at shrines for photos.

🛍 Setagaya Boro-ichi   15–16 Jan
Boro means 'old and worn'. At this market, held for centuries in residential Setagaya ward, hundreds of vendors converge to sell antiques and other sundry secondhand items. A second market is held on 15 and 16 December.

Above: Sensō-ji (p72)

2020

02

February

February is the coldest month, though it rarely snows. Winter days are crisp and clear – the best time of year to spot Mt Fuji in the distance.

⚜ Shimo-Kitazawa Tengu Matsuri
Feb 1–2

On the weekend nearest to Setsubun, Shimo-Kitazawa celebrates the turning of the seasons with a parade of people dressed as *tengu* (a specific kind of devil with a long red nose).

⚜ Setsubun
3 Feb

The first day of spring on the traditional lunar calendar signalled a shift once believed to bode evil. As a precaution, people visit Buddhist temples on Setsubun (pictured above), to toss roasted beans, and shout, '*Oni wa soto! Fuku wa uchi!*' ('Devil out! Fortune in!').

⊙ Plum Blossoms
late Feb

Ume (plum) blossoms, which appear towards the end of the month, are the first sign that winter is ending. Popular viewing spots include Koishikawa Kōrakuen and Yushima Tenjin.

Plan Your Trip
This Year in Tokyo

LEUNGCHOPAN/SHUTTERSTOCK ©

03

March

Spring begins in fits and starts. The Japanese have a saying: sankan-shion – three days cold, four days warm.

🏃 **Tokyo Marathon**   1 Mar
Tokyo's biggest running event (www. marathon.tokyo) happens on the first Sunday of March. Sign up the summer before; competition for slots is fierce.

☆ **Anime Japan**   late Mar
Tokyo's biggest anime expo, Anime Japan (www.anime-japan.jp) has events and exhibitions for industry insiders and fans alike.

☆ **Tokyo Haru-sai**   Mar–Apr
This month-long classical-music festival (www.tokyo-harusai.com/index_e.html) is held at venues around Ueno-kōen (p54).

🎎 **Hina Matsuri**   3 Mar
On and around Girls' Day, public spaces and homes are decorated with *o-hina-sama* (princess) dolls in traditional royal dress.

ZIGGY_MARS/SHUTTERSTOCK ©

2020

KEIMA YAMADA/500PX ©

04

April

Warmer weather and blooming cherry trees make this quite simply the best month to be in Tokyo.

🎎 Buddha's Birthday   8 Apr
In honour of the Buddha's birthday, Hana Matsuri (flower festival) celebrations take place at temples. Look for the parade of children in Asakusa, pulling a white papier-mâché elephant.

🎎 Kannon-ura Ichiyo Sakura Matsuri   11 Apr
This annual spring event takes place along the backstreets behind Sensō-ji (p72). The highlight is the procession of women dressed in the finery of Edo-era (1603–1868) courtesans.

👁 Azalea Blossoms   mid-Apr
From mid-April to early May the city's azaleas bloom bold shades of pink. Nezu-jinja is the place to see them.

👁 Cherry Blossoms   early Apr
From the end of March through the beginning of April, the city's parks and riversides turn pink and Tokyoites toast spring in spirited parties, called *hanami,* beneath the blossoms.

🎎 Earth Day   18–19 Apr
Tokyo celebrates this international event over the nearest weekend to Earth Day (22 April) with a festival at Yoyogi-kōen (p41) that includes organic food stalls, live music and workshops for kids.

🎎 Nakizumo   late Apr
At Sensō-ji (p72) sumo wrestlers pull faces to make babies cry, and the one who cries first, or loudest, is the winner – because in Japan it's believed that crying babies grow big and strong. It's usually held on the last Saturday of the month.

Plan Your Trip
This Year in Tokyo

PATARA/SHUTTERSTOCK ©

05

May

There's a string of national holidays at the beginning of May, known as Golden Week, which can make it hard to secure accommodation. Otherwise, with festivals and warm days, this is an excellent time to visit.

🎏 Children's Day   5 May
For the celebration also known as *otoko-no-hi* (Boys' Day), families fly *koinobori* (colourful banners in the shape of a carp), a symbol of strength and courage.

☆ Sumo Tournament   12–26 May
Another chance to see sumo live, at Ryōgo-ku Kokugikan (p68).

🎏 Sanja Matsuri   16–17 May
The biggest Tokyo *matsuri* (festival) of all, put on by Asakusa-jinja (p75), attracts around 1.5 million spectators. Both days feature parades of *mikoshi* (portable shrines); Sunday's parade is bigger.

🎏 Tokyo Rainbow Pride   early May
Usually over Golden Week, Japan's LGBT+ community comes together for the country's biggest pride event (www.tokyorainbowpride.com), some years followed by a parade. It's not London or Sydney, but it's a spirited affair just the same.

🎏 Design Festa   mid-May
Weekend-long Design Festa (www.designfesta.com) is Asia's largest art festival, featuring performances and thousands of exhibitors. There is a second event in November.

⊙ Roppongi Art Night   late May
A weekend-long (literally, venues stay open all night) arts event with large-scale installations and performances takes over the museums, galleries and streets of Roppongi (www.roppongiartnight.com).

2020

06

June

Early June is lovely, though by the end of the month tsuyu (the rainy season) sets in.

🍺 BeerFes Tokyo   6 & 7 Jun
Sample over 100 different craft beers from around Japan and the world at Yebisu Garden Place. Tickets often sell out; get them early at www.beerfes.jp.

❀ Sanno Matsuri   mid-Jun
This centuries-old festival (pictured above) takes place at Hie-jinja. There are ceremonial rites and traditional music performances but the highlight is the parade of *mikoshi* (portable shrines) that happens only on even-numbered years.

◉ Japan Media Arts Festival   mid-Jun
The innovative Japan Media Arts Festival (www.j-mediaarts.jp) celebrates the year's top animated, digital and virtual works of art and entertainment.

◉ Late Spring Blooms   Jun
Rainy season in Tokyo can be a drag, but it does result in some glorious late spring blooms. June sees irises bloom in gardens around Tokyo. Meiji-jingū Gyoen (p41) is the most famous viewing spot. You'll also spot star bursts of hydrangea around town.

Plan Your Trip
This Year in Tokyo

MAHATHIR MOHD YASIN/SHUTTERSTOCK ©

July

07

When the rainy season passes in mid-to late July, suddenly it's summer – the season for lively street fairs and hanabi taikai (fireworks shows).

🎿 Mt Fuji
Climbing Season   Jul–Aug
The most popular hiking route up Mt Fuji, the Yoshida Trail, opens 1 July. Other trails open 10 July. All are open until 10 September.

🎇 Tanabata   7 Jul
On the day the stars Vega and Altair (stand-ins for a princess and cowherd who are in love) meet across the Milky Way, children tie strips of coloured paper bearing wishes around bamboo branches; look for decorations at youthful hang-outs such as Harajuku and Shibuya.

🎇 Mitama Matsuri   13–16 Jul
Yasukuni-jinja celebrates O-Bon early with a festival of remembrance for the dead that sees 30,000 illuminated *bonbori*

🎇 Sumida-gawa
Fireworks   25 Jul
The grandest of the summer fireworks shows features 20,000 pyrotechnic wonders. Head to Asakusa early in the day to score a good seat. Check events listings for other fireworks displays around town.

(paper lanterns) hung in and around the shrine.

🎇 Ueno
Natsu Matsuri   mid-Jul–mid-Aug
Held from mid-July to mid-August, Ueno's summer festival includes markets and music performances in Ueno-kōen (p54).

🎇 Shinjuku Eisa Matsuri   25 Jul
A parade of drumming and folk dancing in the Okinawan tradition (pictured above; www.shinjuku-eisa.com) takes over the streets of Shinjuku.

2020

CANYALCIN/SHUTTERSTOCK ©

08

August

This is the height of Japan's sticky, hot summer; school holidays mean sights may be crowded.

🎎 Asagaya Tanabata
early Aug

Asagaya holds a Tanabata festival with colourful lanterns strung up in its *shōtengai* (shopping arcade), Pearl Centre, for several days.

🎎 O-Bon
13–16 Aug

Several days in mid-August are set aside to honour the dead, when their spirits are said to return to the earth. Graves are swept, offerings are made and *bon-odori* (folk dances) take place.

🎎 Fukagawa Hachiman Matsuri
mid-Aug

Held in peak summer, this centuries-old festival comes with an appropriate seasonal twist: spectators throw water over the *mikoshi* carriers along the route, which starts at Tomioka Hachiman-gū. The big floats come out only every three years, which will happen in 2020.

🎎 Kōenji Awa Odori
29–30 Aug

Kōenji Awa Odori (pictured; www.koenji-awaodori.com) is Tokyo's biggest outdoor dance party – of the traditional kind (*awa odori* is a folk dance associated with O-Bon). Over 10,000 dancers parade through the streets, drawing upwards of a million spectators.

☆ Comiket
mid-Aug

Twice-annual Comiket (www.comiket.co.jp), also known as Comic Market, is a massive event for manga fans. Here original self-published works are sold and many attendees come dressed as their favourite character. It happens again in December.

☆ Summer Sonic
mid-Aug

The Tokyo area's biggest music festival (www.summersonic.com) is this part-indoor, part-outdoor weekend-long bash at Makuhari Messe that draws big international and domestic artists.

Plan Your Trip
This Year in Tokyo

J. HENNING BUCHHOLZ/SHUTTERSTOCK ©

September

09

Days are still warm, though the odd typhoon rolls through at this time of year.

☆ **Tokyo Jazz Festival**　early Sep

Tokyo's biggest jazz festival (www. tokyo-jazz.com) is held at NHK Hall, near Yoyogi-kōen (p41). The line-up includes international superstars and local talent. New sister event Tokyo Jazz X (www.tokyo-jazz. com/x), at Shibuya's WWW (p190), has more experimental artists.

☆ **Sumo Tournament**　8–22 Sep

The final Tokyo sumo tournament of the year, held at Ryōgoku Kokugikan (p68).

☆ **Tokyo Game Show**　late Sep

Get your geek on when the Computer Entertainment Suppliers Association hosts Tokyo Game Show (http://tgs.cesa.or.jp).

◉ **Moon Viewing**　2 Sep, 2 Oct & 31 Oct

Full moons in September and October call for *tsukimi*, moon-viewing gatherings. People eat *tsukimi dango, mochi* (pounded rice) dumplings that are round like the moon.

HANA/ALAMY ©

2020

KOBY DAGAN/SHUTTERSTOCK ©

10

October

Pleasantly warm days and cool evenings make this an excellent time to be in Tokyo; many arts events take place at this time of year.

☆ Festival Tokyo   Oct–Nov

Tokyo's contemporary theatre festival (www.festival-tokyo.jp) takes place from October through mid-November at venues around the city, featuring works by local and international directors. Some events are subtitled.

◉ Design Touch   Oct–Nov

Held in and around Tokyo Midtown (p160), Design Touch is a series of public exhibitions and events around the theme of design, from mid-October through early November.

☆ Tokyo International Film Festival   late Oct

Tokyo's principal film festival (www.tiff-jp.net) screens works from Japanese and international directors with English subtitles.

◉ Chrysanthemum Festivals   late Oct

The chrysanthemum is the flower of the season (and the royal family). Dazzling displays are put on in Hibiya-kōen and at Meiji-jingū (p226).

✕ Tokyo Ramen Show   late Oct–early Nov

Test your stamina at this annual ramen fair (www.ramenshow.com), where 20 vendors set up shop in sprawling Komazawa Olympic-kōen.

🎃 Halloween   31 Oct

Tokyo goes mad for Halloween with thousands of costumed celebrants converging on Shibuya Crossing (p66). Shinjuku Ni-chōme and Roppongi see action, too.

Plan Your Trip
This Year in Tokyo

IRINA GUSEVA/SHUTTERSTOCK ©

November

11

Crisp and cool days, few crowds and pretty autumn leaves.

✿ Shichi-go-san   15 Nov
This adorable festival (pictured right) sees parents dress girls aged seven *(shichi)* and three *(san)* and boys aged five *(go)* in wee kimonos and head to Shintō shrines for blessings.

◉ Design Festa   mid-Nov
The off-the-wall DIY art fair that is Design Festa makes a repeat appearance this month.

✿ Kagurazaka Street Stage Ōedo Tour   mid-Nov
Traditional music and storytelling in the streets of atmospheric Kagurazaka (http://kaguramachi.jp); there's even a cameo appearance by the neighbourhood's geisha.

☆ Tokyo Filmex   late Nov
Tokyo Filmex (www.filmex.net) focuses on emerging directors in Asia and screens many films with English subtitles.

✿ Tori-no-ichi   2, 14 & 26 Nov
On 'rooster' days in November, 'O-tori' shrines such as Shinjuku's Hanazo-no-jinja hold fairs called Tori-no-ichi *(tori* means 'rooster'); the day is set according to the old calendar, which marks days by the zodiac. Vendors hawk *kumade* – rakes that literally symbolise 'raking in the wealth'.

BENOIST/SHUTTERSTOCK ©

◉ Maple Leaves   late Nov
The city's maples undergo magnificent seasonal transformations during *kōyō* (autumn foliage season); Rikugi-en (p102) and Koishikawa Kōrakuen have spectacular displays.

2020

COWARDLION/SHUTTERSTOCK ©

12

December

Early December is pleasantly crisp, but as the month goes on the winter chill settles in. Commercial strips are decorated with seasonal illuminations.

☉ Golden Gingkos   early Dec
Tokyo's official tree, the *ichō* (gingko), turns a glorious shade of gold in late autumn; Ichō Namiki (Gingko Ave) in Gaienmae is the top viewing spot.

🎎 Gishi-sai   14 Dec
Temple Sengaku-ji hosts a memorial service honouring the 47 *rōnin* (masterless samurai) who famously avenged their fallen master; locals dressed as the loyal retainers parade through nearby streets.

🎎 Winter Illuminations   mid–late Dec
Tokyo loves its winter illuminations (pictured above), and commercial districts like Ginza outdo themselves with extravagant displays. Keiyaki-zaka at Roppongi Hills (p104) is particularly magical.

✗ Toshikoshi Soba   31 Dec
Eating buckwheat noodles on New Year's Eve, a tradition called *toshikoshi soba*, is said to bring luck and longevity – the latter symbolised by the length of the noodles.

SASAKEN/SHUTTERSTOCK ©

☆ Comiket   late Dec
The winter edition of Comiket sees just as many attendees as the summer version – some 500,000.

🎎 Joya-no-kane   31 Dec
Temple bells around Japan ring 108 times at midnight on 31 December in a purifying ritual called *joya-no-kane*. Sensō-ji (p72) draws the biggest crowds in Tokyo.

Plan Your Trip
Hot Spots For...

CULTURE VULTURES

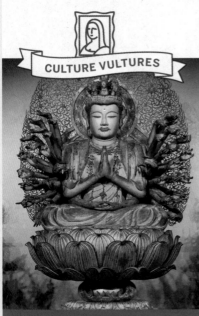

👁 **Tokyo National Museum** Home to the world's largest collection of Japanese art. (pictured above; p52)

🖌 **Toyokuni Atelier Gallery** Learn the art of *sumi-e* (ink brush painting) from a master. (p200)

👁 **Omote-sandō Architecture** See boutiques designed by Japan's leading architects.

🍴 **Sakurai Japanese Tea Experience** Take a deep dive into the world of Japanese tea. (p128)

☆ **Kabukiza** See Japan's signature performing art at Tokyo's leading kabuki theatre. (p90)

GLITZ & GLAMOUR

🍴 **Kikunoi** Go all in on *kaiseki* (Japanese haute cuisine) at this acclaimed restaurant. (pictured below; p137)

♨ **Spa LaQua** Soak away your troubles in this onsen (hot spring) complex. (p84)

🍷 **New York Bar** Lord over the city from a perch at the Park Hyatt's famous cocktail bar. (p115)

🛍 **Shopping in Harajuku** Check out the latest designs from Japanese fashion designers famous and still under the radar.

☆ **Suigian** Traditional Japanese performing arts at a chic dinner theatre. (p192)

FOODIES

⊙ **Toyosu Market** See the morning tuna auction followed by sushi breakfast. (p86)

✕ **Inua** Book a table at Tokyo's hottest spot for the meal of a lifetime. (p144)

🛍 **Akomeya** Shop for packaged foods from around Japan at this beautiful foodstuffs boutique. (p160)

✕ **Ramen** Go on a ramen-tasting spree and devour all the different flavours. (p42)

🥢 **Tsukiji Soba Academy** Get soba-making lessons from a pro. (p200)

ACTIVE OUTDOORS

🥾 **Mt Fuji** Hoof it up Japan's iconic volcano in the summer months.

⊙ **Rikugi-en** Take a morning stroll through Tokyo's most beautiful landscape garden. (p102)

☆ **Tokyo Dome** Cheer on baseball powerhouse the Yomiuri Giants. (pictured above; p198)

🚲 **Tokyo Great Cycling Tour** Explore the city on two wheels. (p198)

✕ **Ohitotsuzen Tanbo** Enjoy healthy meals featuring organic rice from the restaurant's own fields. (p124)

CRAFTY CREATIVES

🍷 **Golden Gai** Clink glasses with local artists and fellow travellers in this bohemian hot spot.

🛍 **Ōedo Antique Market** The city's best flea market. (pictured above; p166)

✕ **Farmer's Market @UNU** Come for the colourful produce; stay for the food trucks. (p146)

⊙ **3331 Arts Chiyoda** Explore contemporary art galleries with a pop-culture twist. (p113)

☆ **WWW** Catch indie bands on this Shibuya stage. (p190)

Plan Your Trip
Top Days in Tokyo

PHOTOGRAPHER2E53/SHUTTERSTOCK ©

West Side Highlights

The neighbourhoods of Harajuku and Shinjuku, on the western edge of central Tokyo, make for a strong first impression: this is the Tokyo of skyscrapers and streets illuminated with many-coloured liquid-crystal lights; of bold architecture statements and even bolder fashion statements; and of just enough tradition to give it all perspective.

Day
01

❶ Meiji-jingū (p38)

Tokyo's most famous Shintō shrine is tucked inside a wooded grove. It's a peaceful haven that feels worlds away from the city – though it is right in the thick of it. (And even more peaceful if you get here nice and early.)

↪ Meiji-jingū to Omote-sandō

🚶 Walk The broad boulevard Omote-sandō starts just across the street from the shrine entrance.

❷ Omote-sandō Architecture (p50)

Stroll down Omote-sandō to see the striking fashion boutiques, designed by Japan's leading contemporary architects, that line this wide, tree-lined boulevard.

↪ Omote-sandō to Maisen

🚶 The restaurant is a five-minute walk down a side street from Omote-sandō.

JIRAT TEPARAKSA/SHUTTERSTOCK ©

❸ Lunch at Maisen (p126)

Maisen is a Tokyo classic, serving up perfectly tender and crisp *tonkatsu* (breaded, deep-fried pork cutlets) plus miso soup and cabbage salad in a cool old building that used to be a public bathhouse. (Bonus: lunch is a bargain.)

○ Maisen to Harajuku

🚶 You're already here! Take the long way back to Harajuku Station via the side streets.

❹ Shopping in Harajuku (p46)

Harajuku is Tokyo's real-life catwalk, where the ultra-chic come to browse and be seen. More than a particular look, Harajuku symbolises an ethos of freedom of expression and (literal) transformation; shopping here is equal parts acquisition and inspiration.

○ Harajuku to the Tokyo Metropolitan Government Building

🚃 Take the JR Yamanote line from Harajuku Station two stops north to Shinjuku, then walk 10 minutes to the government building from the west exit.

❺ Tokyo Metropolitan Government Building (p114)

The government building has observatories at 202m high that stay open until 11pm, so you can come for twinkling night views over the city. And entry is free.

○ Tokyo Metropolitan Government Building to the Park Hyatt

🚶 It's just a five-minute walk from the city hall to the hotel.

❻ Drinks with a View (p115)

Choose between the sophistication of the New York Bar, on the 52nd floor of the Park Hyatt hotel, or the excellent happy-hour deal at Peak Bar, on the 41st floor. If you've still got steam, walk to the eastern side of Shinjuku station, to see the crackling neon canyons of Tokyo's biggest and most colourful nightlife district.

From left: Meiji-jingū (p38); Tokyu Plaza entrance (p50), Harajuku (p46)

Plan Your Trip
Top Days in Tokyo

MATTHIEU TUFFET/SHUTTERSTOCK ©

Classic Sights of Central Tokyo

Start with a morning visit to the fish market and then spend the rest of the day exploring Tokyo's more polished side, in Ginza and Marunouchi (home to the Imperial Palace and Kabukiza). This is a day that puts an extra emphasis on food.

❶ Breakfast at Toyosu Market (p86)

Get up early and head to Tokyo's central wholesale market on Toyosu, an island in Tokyo Bay. Here you can see the morning tuna auction followed by sushi breakfast at one of the shops in the market, like Sushi Dai or Daiwa Sushi.

➲ Toyosu Market to Imperial Palace

🚃 Take the Yurikamome line to Toyosu and transfer to the Yūrakuchō line for Sakuradaimon Station, near one of the palace gates.

❷ Imperial Palace (p98)

While much of the palace grounds is off limits (it's the emperor's home), you can stroll alongside the moats, past tiered keeps and pine groves to the Imperial Palace East Garden, with its old stone walls from the fortress that once stood here.

➲ Imperial Palace East Garden to Chashitsu Kaboku

🚕 Hop in a taxi; it should cost less than ¥1000. Otherwise, it's a 20-minute walk.

Day
02

UGIS RIBA/SHUTTERSTOCK ©

❸ Tea at Chashitsu Kaboku (p140)

Get to know *matcha* (powdered green tea) at this teahouse run by a famous Kyoto tea producer. There are a variety of styles on the menu, served traditional-style with a seasonal sweet.

◉ Chashitsu Kaboku to Okuno Building

🚶 It's a 10-minute walk.

❹ Okuno Building (p160)

The Okuno Building is a rare pre-WWII structure that houses dozens of small boutiques and galleries. It's the perfect starting point for exploring Ginza (a neighbourhood known for boutiques and galleries).

◉ Okuno Building to Mitsukoshi

🚶 The two are five minutes apart.

❺ Mitsukoshi (p161)

Mitsukoshi is a quintessential Tokyo department store, with floors for pretty Japanese-style homewares, gourmet

food products, and local and international fashion brands.

◉ Mitsukoshi to Kabukiza

🚶 It's five minutes on foot to the theatre.

❻ Kabukiza (p90)

Kabuki, a form of stylised traditional Japanese theatre, features stories based on popular legend and an all-male cast in dramatic make-up and decadent costumes. Catch a performance (or just a single act) at Kabukiza, Tokyo's principal kabuki theatre.

◉ Kabukiza to Tempura Kondō

🚶 The restaurant is an 8-minute walk from the theatre.

❼ Dinner Tempura Kondō (p140)

Wrap up the day with a tasting course of exquisite tempura at a classic Ginza restaurant. Reservations essential.

From left: *Matcha* (powdered green tea), Chashitsu Kaboku; Kabukiza Theatre (p90)

Plan Your Trip
Top Days in Tokyo

COWARDLION/SHUTTERSTOCK ©

The Historic East Side

Welcome to Tokyo's historic east side, which includes Ueno, long the cultural heart of Tokyo, with its park and museums; Yanaka with its high concentration of traditional wooden buildings; and Asakusa, with its ancient temple and old-Tokyo atmosphere.

Day

03

❶ Tokyo National Museum (p52)

Start with a morning at Japan's premier museum, which houses the world's largest collection of Japanese art and antiquities, including swords, gilded screens, kimonos and colourful *ukiyo-e* (woodblock prints). You'll need about two hours to hit the highlights.

➲ Tokyo National Museum to Ueno-kōen

🏃 The museum is on the edge of the park.

❷ Ueno-kōen (p54)

After the museum, take an hour or two to explore Ueno-kōen. Wend your way southward past the temples and shrines in the park, which include some of Tokyo's oldest standing buildings, to the large pond, Shinobazu-ike, choked with lotus flowers. There are cafes here, too.

➲ Ueno-kōen to Innsyoutei

🏃 The restaurant is in the park!

MANUEL ASCANIO/SHUTTERSTOCK ©

❸ Lunch at Innsyoutei (p144)

Innsyoutei, in a beautiful traditional structure that's over 140 years old, is one of the
city's most charming lunch spots. It serves
formal Japanese cuisine designed for the
tea ceremony; bookings recommended.

➲ Innsyoutei to Yanaka

🚶 It's a 15-minute walk back through the park, to the
northwest exit, where Yanaka begins.

❹ Walking in Yanaka Ginza (p88)

Yanaka is a neighbourhood with a high
concentration of vintage wooden structures and more than a hundred temples.
It's a rare pocket of Tokyo that miraculously
survived the Great Kantō Earthquake and
the allied fire-bombing of WWII to remain
largely intact. It's a wonderful place to
stroll.

➲ Yanaka to Sensō-ji

🚉 Take the Yamanote line from Nippori to Ueno then
transfer for the Ginza subway line for Asakusa.

❺ Sensō-ji (p72)

The temple Sensō-ji was founded more
than 1000 years before Tokyo got its start.
Today the temple retains an alluring, lively
atmosphere redolent of Edo (old Tokyo
under the shogun). There are lots of shops
selling traditional crafts and foodstuffs
around here, too. Don't miss Sensō-ji all lit
up from dusk.

➲ Sensō-ji to Oiwake

🚶 It's a 10-minute walk from the temple to the pub.

❻ Oiwake (p193)

Get a taste of entertainment old-Tokyo style
at Oiwake, one of Tokyo's few remaining
folk-music pubs. Here talented performers
play *tsugaru-jamisen* (a banjo-like instrument) and other traditional instruments.
Beer and classic pub food (such as edamame) are served.

From left: Yanaka Ginza (p55); Ueno-kōen (p54)

Plan Your Trip
Top Days in Tokyo

Icons of Art & Pop Culture

On the agenda for your final day: culture, shopping and, most importantly, fun. This is a packed schedule, with a bit of running around, but it covers a lot of highlights – and some great souvenirs and photo ops in the process.

❶ Ghibli Museum, Mitaka (p76)

Take the train to the western suburb of Mitaka for a visit to the magical Ghibli Museum, created by famed animator Miyazaki Hayao (reservations necessary; we recommend getting in early at 10am). Afterwards walk through woodsy Inokashira-kōen to Kichijōji.

➲ Kichijōji to Kikanbō

🚃 Take the JR Chūō line from Kichijōji to Kanda (25 minutes).

❷ Ramen at Kikanbō (p45)

Break for lunch at cult-favourite ramen shop Kikanbō, where you get to choose the level of spiciness and amount of noodles (careful: spicy really does mean spicy).

➲ Kikanbō to Akihabara

🏃 It's a 10-minute walk, crossing the Kanda-gawa (Kanda River), or one stop on the JR Yamanote line, to Akihabara.

Day
04

TOMML/GETTY IMAGES ©

❸ Akihabara Pop Culture (p110)

In 'Akiba' you can shop for anime and manga; play retro video games; and ride go-karts – while dressed in costume – through the streets (reserve ahead; international driving licence required).

➡ Akihabara to Mori Art Museum

Take the Hibiya subway line from Akihabara to Roppongi, the nearest stop for the museum.

❹ Mori Art Museum (p106)

The excellent Mori Art Museum stages contemporary exhibits that include superstars of the art world from both Japan and abroad. It's open until 10pm and entry includes admission to the observatory Tokyo City View – so you can sneak in another look over the city.

➡ Mori Art Museum to Shibuya Crossing

You can take the no 1 bus (¥210; 20 minutes), but a taxi will only cost about ¥1500 and is much easier.

❺ Shibuya Crossing (p66)

This epic intersection, lit by giant screens, has become synonymous with Tokyo. It's best seen in the evening when all the lights and signs are aglow. Shibuya is a nightlife centre and there's lots to do here after dark.

➡ Shibuya Crossing to Karaoke Rainbow

The karaoke parlour is a five-minute walk from the crossing.

❻ Karaoke (p116)

End your last night with a time-honoured Tokyo tradition: singing yourself hoarse until the first trains start running again in the morning. Karaoke Rainbow is a popular karaoke parlour with tons of English-language songs from which to choose.

From left: Exhibition at Mori Art Museum (p106) by teamLab Borderless (p78); Akihabara (p110)

Plan Your Trip
Need to Know

Daily Costs

Budget:
Less than ¥8000

- Dorm bed: ¥3000
- Free sights such as temples and markets
- Bowl of noodles: ¥800
- Happy-hour drink: ¥500
- 24-hour subway pass: ¥600

Midrange:
¥8000–20,000

- Double room at a business hotel: ¥15,000
- Museum entry: ¥1000
- Dinner for two at an *izakaya* (Japanese pub-eatery): ¥6000
- Live music show: ¥3000

Top End:
More than ¥20,000

- Double room in a four-star hotel: from ¥35,000
- Private cooking class: ¥10,000
- Sushi-tasting menu: ¥15,000
- Taxi ride back to the hotel: ¥3000

Advance Planning

Three months before
Purchase tickets for the Ghibli Museum; book a table at a top restaurant.

One month before Book tickets online for theatre and sporting events, activities, courses and tours of the Imperial Palace.

When you arrive Look for discount coupons for attractions at airports and hotels; have your accommodation help you reserve seats at popular *izakaya* (Japanese pub-eateries).

Useful Websites

Go Tokyo (www.gotokyo.org) The city's official website includes information on sights, events and suggested itineraries.

Lonely Planet (www.lonely planet.com/tokyo) Destination information, hotel bookings, traveller forum and more.

Spoon & Tamago (www. spoon-tamago.com) Japanese arts and culture blog with great suggestions for cool spots and events.

Tokyo Cheapo (https://tokyo cheapo.com) Hints on how to do Tokyo on the cheap.

Time Out Tokyo (www.time out.jp) Arts and entertainment listings.

Arriving in Tokyo

Narita Airport An express train or highway bus to central Tokyo costs around ¥3000 (one to two hours). Both run frequently from 6am to 10.30pm; pick up tickets at kiosks inside

Currency

Japanese yen (¥)

Language

Japanese

Visas

Visas are generally not required for stays of up to 90 days.

Money

Convenience stores and post offices have international ATMs. Credit cards are widely accepted, though it's still best to keep some cash on hand.

Mobile Phones

Prepaid data-only SIM cards (for unlocked smartphones only) are widely available at the airports and electronics stores. Many hotels now offer Handy phone service.

Time

Japan Standard Time (GMT/UTC plus nine hours).

For more, see the **Survival Guide** (p228)

When to Go

Spring and autumn, when the weather is mild, are the best times to visit. Summer is hot and humid, but also has the most festivals. Winter sees fewer crowds.

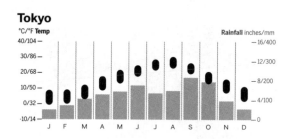

Tokyo

the arrivals hall (no advance reservations required). Taxis start at ¥20,000.

Haneda Airport Frequent trains and buses (¥400 to ¥1200, 30 to 45 minutes) to central Tokyo run from 5.30am to midnight; times and costs depend on your destination in the city. There are only a couple of night buses. For a taxi, budget between ¥5000 and ¥8000.

Tokyo Station Connect from the *shinkansen* (bullet train) terminal here to the JR Yamanote line or the Marunouchi subway for destinations around central Tokyo.

Getting Around

Efficient, clean and generally safe, Tokyo's public transport system is the envy of the world. Of most use to travellers is the train and subway system, which

is easy to navigate thanks to English signage.

Subway The quickest and easiest way to get around central Tokyo. Runs 5am to midnight.

Train Japan Rail (JR) Yamanote (loop) and Chūō-Sōbu (central) lines service major stations. Runs from 5am to midnight.

Taxi A pricey option but the only one that runs all night; easy to hail.

Cycling A fun way to get around, though traffic can be intense. Rentals available; some hostels and ryokan lend bicycles.

Walking Subway stations are close in the city centre; save cash by walking if you only need to go one stop.

What to Take

o Tokyo hotels tend to be tiny, so bring as small a suitcase as possible.

o Japanese pharmacies don't carry foreign medications; local substitutes can be found in a pinch, but it's a good idea to have some stuff from home on hand.

What to Wear

o Tokyoites are smart dressers but are never overly fancy. Only the highest-end restaurants and bars have enforced dress codes, which usually just means no sleeveless shirts or sandals on men.

o Religious sights (Buddhist temples and Shintō shrines) have no dress codes.

o Keep in mind that you may be taking your shoes on and off so slip-on ones are handy. You may also find yourself sitting on the floor, which can be uncomfortable in short or tight clothing.

Plan Your Trip
What's New

New Toyosu Market

In a move years in the making, Tsukiji's famous wholesale market moved to a new location in Toyosu (p86) in autumn 2018. What was formerly known as the outer market can still be visited in Tsukiji (p108).

teamLab Borderless

Tokyo's hottest new attraction is the digital-art museum teamLab Borderless (p78).

Sake & Tea

After years of going all in on craft beer and third-wave coffee, Tokyo is looking to sake and tea. We're seeing more and more craft-sake bars and third-wave-style teahouses.

VR Attractions

Also trending: VR attractions. Our favourite is Sky Circus (p200), where you can experience a simulation of being shot out of a cannon over the city.

More Activities

From kayaking (p199) along Tokyo's old canal system to learning the art of ink-wash painting (p200), there are more and more ways to connect with the city beyond just sightseeing.

Design Hotels

Tokyo's midrange hotels (p206) have long been a bland bunch, but many new properties are incorporating original artwork and creative design.

Improved Ease of Travel

It's never been easier to visit Tokyo: more and more attractions, restaurants and shops have English-speaking staff and signage; there's more duty-free shopping opportunities, and 'hands free' courier services (p234) mean you don't have to lug stuff back to your hotel or the airport.

Above: Sky Circus (p200)

Plan Your Trip
For Free

ESB PROFESSIONAL/SHUTTERSTOCK ©

Temples & Shrines

Shintō shrines are usually free in Tokyo and most Buddhist temples charge only to enter their *honden* (main hall) – meaning that two of the city's top sights, Meiji-jingū (p226) and Sensō-ji (p72), are free.

Parks & Gardens

Spend an afternoon people watching in one of Tokyo's excellent public parks, such as Yoyogi-kōen (p41) or Inokashira-kōen (p59). Grab a *bentō* (boxed meal) from a convenience store for a cheap and easy picnic.

Architecture

Wander the city streets in search of the ambitious creations of Japan's leading architects. Omote-sandō is great for this.

Festivals

Festivals are always happening in Tokyo – way more than we can list here; Go Tokyo (www.gotokyo.org) has a pretty comprehensive list. In the warmer months, festivals and markets, often hosted by Tokyo's ethnic communities and with live music, set up in Yoyogi-kōen (p41). And where there are festivals, there are usually street-food vendors.

24-hour Metro Pass

If you want to cram in the sights in a short stretch of time, Tokyo Metro's 24-hour pass (adult/child ¥600/300) is a great deal. You'll have to be strategic though, as the pass is only good for Tokyo Metro lines.

Discount Cards

The Grutto Pass (¥2200; www.rekibun.or.jp/grutto) gives you free or discounted admission to 92 attractions around town within two months. Also check hotel lobbies and TICs for discount coupons to city attractions.

Above: Sensō-ji (p72)

Plan Your Trip
Family Travel

Sights & Activities

Top sights for kids include the Ghibli Museum (p76), a portal to the magical world of famed animator Miyazaki Hayao (*Ponyo*, *Spirited Away*); and teamLab Borderless (p78), an interactive digital art museum. Odaiba, where the latter is located, is a district with many family-oriented attractions, like the National Museum of Emerging Science & Innovation (Miraikan; p81) and Unicorn Gundam (p218); it has easy meal options in shopping-centre food courts.

Tokyo has lots of great parks for running around in, such as Yoyogi-kōen (p41), Inokashira-kōen (p59) and Shinjuku-gyoen (p59), and amusement parks, including Tokyo Disney Resort (p199) and Tokyo Dome City Attractions (p200). Also fun: seeing a baseball game (p198) or a sumo tournament (p68) and visiting Ueno Zoo (p54). Shrines and temples aren't obviously interesting, but have some hands-on elements, such as writing prayer plaques.

With older kids and teens you have more options, such as cultural activities that include making woodblock prints (p201), and outdoor excursions, such as kayaking (p199) through Tokyo's old canal system. They'll also likely get a kick out of Tokyo's pop culture and neon streetscapes. Young fashionistas will love shopping in Harajuku. Thrill seekers will enjoy the virtual reality attractions at Tokyo Joypolis (p199) and Sky Circus (p200).

Karaoke is often associated with late-night drinking but can be a fantastic family activity. Major chain parlours usually have colourful rooms designed for kids (though regular rooms are fine, too – you can ask for a nonsmoking one). Bonus: karaoke during the day is very cheap. This is a great rainy-day activity.

Eating Out

Big chain restaurants (such as Jonathan's, Royal Host and Gusto) are the most family-friendly eating options: they have large booths, high chairs and children's menus. Unfortunately many central Tokyo restaurants are small, and often just not set up for

ARTRAN/GETTY IMAGES ©

littler ones (you might have to park the pram outside). Finding food kids will love isn't too hard: *gyōza* (dumplings), *okonomiyaki* (savoury pancake) and noodles are usually hits. Convenience stores and bakeries are cheap, easy and ubiquitous sources of sandwiches and snacks.

Getting Around

You won't receive much sympathy if you get on a crowded train during morning rush hour (7am to 9.30am) with a pram. If you must, children under 12 can ride with mums in the less crowded women-only carriages. Otherwise the subway system is fairly child friendly: priority seats exist for passengers who are pregnant or travelling with small children; most train stations and buildings in larger cities have lifts; and children between the ages of six and 11 ride for half price on trains (under-sixes ride for free). Beware that side streets often lack pavements, though fortunately traffic is generally orderly in Tokyo.

Best Spots for Kids

Tokyo Disney Resort (p199)
Ghibli Museum (p76)
Tokyo Joypolis (p199)
Mokuhankan (p201)
Tokyo Dome (p198)

Need to Know

Resources Savvy Tokyo (https://savvytokyo. com) has lots of suggestions for kid-friendly spots and events.

Babysitting Babysitters (www.babysitters. jp) partners with many Tokyo hotels to provide English-speaking childcare workers.

Nappy Changing & Nursing Department stores and shopping malls always have nappy-changing facilities; newer ones have nursing rooms.

From left: Lemur, Ueno Zoo (p54); *okonomiyaki* (savoury pancake)

TOP EXPERIENCES

The very best to see & do

MLENNY/ GETTY IMAGES ©

Golden Gai

Golden Gai – a Shinjuku institution for over half a century – is a collection of tiny bars in low-slung wooden buildings, often literally no bigger than a closet and seating maybe a dozen.

Golden Gai has long been a gathering spot for artists, writers and musicians. Originally many bars here functioned more like clubhouses for various creative industries. Some bars prefer to keep their doors closed to customers who aren't regulars (foreign tourists included) to preserve that old atmosphere; others will welcome you (if there is space, of course). Recently there's been a changing of the guard, as new, younger owners take over, and the exclusive atmosphere of old is giving way to a lively scene of international bar hoppers, instinctively drawn to Golden Gai's free spirit.

The best way to experience Golden Gai is to stroll the lanes and pick a place that suits your mood. Bars that expressly welcome tourists have English signs posted on their doors. Many bars have a cover charge

Great For...

☑ Don't Miss

Finding your favourite spot among the myriad bars, each as unique and eccentric as the 'master' or 'mama' who runs it.

Shinjuku-
S nishiguchi

S Shinjuku

Kuyakusho-dōri

Yasukuni-dōri

**⊙ Golden
Gai**

Gyoen-dōri

Shinjuku-
sanchōme

R Shinjuku

Shinjuku-
sanchōme **S** **S**

❶ Need to Know

(ゴールデン街; Map p253; http://goldengai.
jp; 1-1 Kabukichō, Shinjuku-ku; **R** JR Yamanote
line to Shinjuku, east exit)

✕ Take a Break

Get ramen at any hour at Nagi (p45).

★ Top Tip

Golden Gai is a hard place to visit with
a group, as you'll have trouble finding
enough seats. Go alone, on the other
hand, and you're bound to make friends.

(usually ¥500 to ¥1500), which is often
posted on the door. Note that while Golden
Gai is highly photogenic it is also private
property; do not take photos unless you
have explicit permission.

Open Book
Bar

(Map p253; Golden Gai 5-ban-gai, 1-1-6 Kabukichō,
Shinjuku-ku; ⊘7pm-1.30am Mon-Sat; ⊕🉐;
R JR Yamanote line to Shinjuku, east exit) Part
of the new generation of Golden Gai bars,
the Open Book is run by the grandson of
award-winning novelist Tanaka Komima-
sa (whose collection of well-loved books
line the walls). The house special is an
upgraded take on an old classic, the 'lemon
sour' (shōchū distilled liquor, soda water
and lemon juice; ¥700). Look for the sliding
wooden door. ¥300 cover charge.

Lonely
Bar

(ロンリー; Map p253; 1-1-8 Kabukichō, Shinjuku-
ku; ⊘6.30pm-2am Tue-Sun; **R** JR Yamanote line
to Shinjuku, east exit) Akai-san established
Lonely 50 years ago because he wanted his
friends to always have a place to go. Some
of those friends, like the creator of classic
manga *Ashita no Joe* – you'll see posters
on the wall – also happened to be famous.
Lonely is everything you want a Golden Gai
bar to be: cosy, eccentric and always fun.

Albatross G
Bar

(アルバトロスG; Map p253; www.alba-s.
com; 5-ban Gai, 1-1-7 Kabukichō, Shinjuku-ku;
⊘5pm-2am Sun-Thu, to 5am Fri & Sat; 🉐;
R JR Yamanote line to Shinjuku, east exit) With
chandeliers dripping from the ceiling and
gilded frames on the walls, Golden Gai
haunt Albatross G has a louche decadence
that has clearly struck a chord: the bar is
routinely packed. But with three floors,
odds are you will get a seat. Try to get the
table on the 3rd floor. Cover charge ¥500,
drinks from ¥600.

Meiji-jingū

Tokyo's grandest Shintō shrine feels a world away from the city. The grounds are vast, enveloping the classic wooden buildings and a landscaped garden in a thick coat of green. Meiji-jingū is dedicated to the Emperor Meiji and Empress Shōken, whose reign (1868–1912) coincided with Japan's transformation from isolationist feudal state to modern nation.

Great For...

❶ Need to Know

明治神宮; Map p246; www.meijijingu.or.jp; 1-1 Yoyogi Kamizono-chō, Shibuya-ku; ☉dawn-dusk; ☒JR Yamanote line to Harajuku, Omote-sandō exit; FREE

★ **Top Tip**

The rule of photo taking here is this: if there's a roof over your head, it's a no-go.

Constructed in 1920, the shrine was destroyed in WWII air raids and rebuilt in 1958; however, unlike so many of Japan's postwar reconstructions, Meiji-jingū has atmosphere in spades. In preparation for its centennial in 2020, Meiji-jingū is currently undergoing renovations. Some structures may be under wraps, but the shrine as a whole will remain open.

The Shrine

The shrine is secreted in a wooded grove, accessed via a long, winding gravel path. At the entrance you'll pass through the first of several towering, wooden *torii* (gates). These mark the boundary between the mundane world and the sacred one; as such, it's the custom to bow upon passing through a *torii*.

In front of the final *torii* before the main shrine is the *temizu-ya* (font), where visitors purify themselves by pouring water over their hands (purity is a tenet of Shintoism). To do so, dip the ladle in the water and first rinse your left hand then your right. Pour some water into your left hand and rinse your mouth, then rinse your left hand again. Make sure none of this water gets back into the font!

The main shrine is built of unpainted cypress wood and has a copper-plated roof. To make an offering here (and, if you like, a wish), toss a coin into the box, bow twice, clap your hands twice and then bow again (a ¥5 coin is considered lucky). Time your visit for 8am or 2pm to catch the twice daily *nikkusai,* the ceremonial offering of food and prayers to the gods.

Ema (prayer boards)

To the right, you'll see kiosks selling *ema* (wooden plaques on which prayers are written) and *omamori* (charms). Our personal favourite is the charm for safe travel, naturally.

The Grounds

The shrine itself occupies only a small fraction of the sprawling forested grounds, which contain some 120,000 trees donated from all over Japan. Of this, only the strolling garden **Meiji-jingū Gyoen** (明治神宮御苑, Inner Garden; Map p246; ¥500; ◷9am-4.30pm, to 4pm Nov-Feb; ⓇJR Yamanote line to Harajuku, Omote-sandō exit) is accessible to

> ☑ **Don't Miss**
>
> Festivals, ceremonies and events (all free!) are held here throughout the year; check the website for a schedule.

PABKOV/SHUTTERSTOCK ©

the public. Here there are peaceful walks, a good dose of privacy at weekdays and spectacular irises in June. The entrance is halfway along the gravel path to the shrine.

What's Nearby?

Yoyogi-kōen Park

(代々木公園; Map p246; www.yoyogipark. info; Yoyogi-kamizono-chō, Shibuya-ku; ⓇJR Yamanote line to Harajuku, Omote-sandō exit) If it's a sunny and warm weekend afternoon, you can count on there being a crowd lazing around the large grassy expanse that is Yoyogi-kōen. You'll usually find revellers and noisemakers of all stripes, from hula-hoopers to African drum circles to retro greasers dancing around a boom box. It's an excellent place for a picnic and probably the only place in the city where you can reasonably toss a Frisbee without fear of hitting someone.

During the warmer months, festivals take place on the plaza across from the park (see website, in Japanese, for a schedule). Cherry blossoms draw huge crowds and parties that go late into the night.

Yoyogi National Stadium Architecture

(国立代々木競技場, Kokuritsu Yoyogi Kyōgi-jō; Map p246; 2-1-1 Jinnan, Shibuya-ku; ⓇJR Yamanote line to Harajuku, Omote-sandō exit) This early masterpiece by architect Tange Kenzō was built for the 1964 Olympics (and will be used again in the 2020 games for the handball event). The stadium, which looks vaguely like a samurai helmet, uses suspension-bridge technology – rather than beams – to support the roof.

> ✕ **Take a Break**
>
> Coffee shop **Mori no Terrace** (杜のテラス; Map p246; ☎03-3379-9222; 1-1 Yoyogi Kamizono-chō, Shibuya-ku; coffee & tea from ¥400; ◷9am-dusk; ⊜🌱; ⓇJR Yamanote line to Harajuku, Omote-sandō exit) is near the main gate.

Ramen

Ramen may have been imported from China, but in Tokyo it has developed into a legitimate passion: the subject of profuse blogs, a reason to stand in line for over an hour, and a dream for many to master – in the form of their own shop. By conservative estimates there are over 3000 ramen shops in the capital (some say 4000).

Great For...

ℹ Need to Know

Ramen shops are everywhere, and especially common near train stations. Look for door curtains with ramen (ラーメン) written on them.

★ **Top Tip**

Ramen should be eaten at whip speed, before the noodles get soggy; that's why you'll hear diners slurping, sucking in air to cool their mouths.

Your basic ramen is a big bowl of crinkly egg noodles in broth, served with toppings such as *chāshū* (sliced roast pork), *moyashi* (bean sprouts) and *menma* (pickled bamboo sprouts). The broth can be made from pork or chicken bones or dried seafood; usually it's a top-secret combination of some or all of the above. It's typically seasoned with *shio* (salt), *shōyu* (soy sauce) or hearty miso – though at less orthodox places, anything goes. Many shops also sell *tsukemen*, noodles that come with a dipping sauce (like a really condensed broth) on the side.

Mensho   Ramen ¥

(☏03-6902-2878; http://menya-shono.com/mensho/; 1-17-16 Otowa, Bunkyō-ku; noodles from ¥1000; ◷11am-3pm & 5-9pm Wed-Sun; Ⓢ Yūrakuchō line to Gokokuji, exit 6) The

Mensho chain is known for its innovative ramen recipes and the clean, contemporary design of its shops. At this branch the concept is farm to bowl. The *shio* (salt) ramen is beautifully presented in a seafood broth, with a dusting of golden roe and seaweed-flake-covered scallop on the side of the bowl.

Afuri   Ramen ¥

(あふり; Map p246; www.afuri.com; 1-1-7 Ebisu, Shibuya-ku; ramen from ¥980; ◷11am-5am; ◉🖊📵; 🚆JR Yamanote line to Ebisu, east exit) Afuri has been a major player in the local ramen scene, making a strong case for a light touch with its signature *yuzu-shio* (a light, salty broth flavoured with *yuzu*, a type of citrus) ramen. It's since opened branches around the city, but this industrial-chic Ebisu shop is the original. It now does

Ramen restaurant, Shinjuku

a vegan ramen. Order from the vending machine.

Nagi   Ramen ¥

(凪; Map p253; ☑03-3205-1925; www.n-nagi. com; 2nd fl, Golden Gai G2, 1-1-10 Kabukichō, Shinjuku-ku; ramen from ¥890; ☺24hr; 🖊; 🚉JR Yamanote line to Shinjuku, east exit) Nagi, once an edgy upstart in the ramen world, has done well and now has branches around the city. This tiny shop is one of the originals, and located up a treacherous stairway

---

🛈 Need to Know

Ramen restaurants often use a unique ordering system: a vending machine. Insert your money and select the button with your desired dish; you'll get a coupon from the machine, which you should hand to the cooks behind the counter.

SEAN K/SHUTTERSTOCK ©

in Golden Gai. It's still our favourite...we're clearly not alone as there's often a line. The house speciality is *niboshi* ramen (egg noodles in a broth flavoured with dried sardines).

Kikanbō   Ramen ¥

(鬼金棒; Map p254; ☑03-6206-0239; http:// karashibi.com; 2-10-8 Kaji-chō, Chiyoda-ku; ramen from ¥800; ☺11am-9.30pm Mon-Sat, to 4pm Sun; 🖊; 🚉JR Yamanote line to Kanda, north exit) The *karashibi* (カラシビ) spicy *miso-rāmen* here has a cult following. Choose your level of *kara* (spice) and *shibi* (a strange mouth-numbing sensation created by Japanese *sanshō* pepper). We recommend *futsu-futsu* (regular for both) for first-timers; *oni* (devil) level costs an extra ¥100. Look for the black door curtains.

Harukiya   Ramen ¥

(春木屋; www.haruki-ya.co.jp; 1-4-6 Kami-Ogi, Suginami-ku; ramen ¥850-1350; ☺11am-9pm Wed-Mon; 🖊; 🚉JR Chūō-Sōbu line to Ogikubo, north exit) Harukiya, open since 1949, is one of Tokyo's oldest existent ramen shops. It serves what has since come to be known as classic Tokyo-style ramen: with stock made of chicken and fish, seasoned with soy sauce, and with crinkly, doughy noodles.

Tokyo Rāmen Street   Ramen ¥

(東京ラーメンストリート; Map p250; www. tokyoeki-1bangai.co.jp/ramenstreet; basement, First Avenue, Tokyo Station, 1-9-1 Marunouchi, Chiyoda-ku; ramen from ¥800; ☺7.30am-11.30pm; 🚉JR lines to Tokyo, Yaesu south exit) Eight handpicked *rāmen-ya* operate branches in this basement arcade on the Yaesu side of Tokyo Station. All the major styles are covered – from *shōyu* (soy-sauce base) to *tsukemen* (cold noodles served on the side). Long lines form outside the most popular shops, but they tend to move quickly.

☑ Don't Miss

Classic Tokyo style ramen has a broth flavoured with soy sauce and *niboshi* (dried young sardines); the latter gives it a subtle bitter smokiness.

Ice cream vendor, Takeshita-dōri (p49)

Shopping in Harajuku

Harajuku is the gathering point for Tokyo's diverse fashion tribes – the trendy teens, the fashion-forward peacocks and the polished divas. For shopping (and people watching), there's no better spot in Tokyo.

Great For...

☑ **Don't Miss**

Exploring Harajuku's maze-like (and surprise-filled) side streets.

Harajuku is trend-central for young shoppers. Malls and department stores on the main drags carry international fast-fashion brands alongside home-grown ones. Edgier boutiques are located on the backstreets. Omote-sandō, the boulevard connecting Harajuku and Aoyama, has statement boutiques from pretty much all the famous European fashion houses. Many of the big names in Japanese fashion, such as Issey Miyake, Comme des Garçons and Yohji Yamamoto, have their flagship boutiques in Aoyama.

Arts & Science Fashion & Accessories (Map p246; www.arts-science.com; 103, 105 & 109 Palace Aoyama, 6-1-6 Minami-Aoyama, Minato-ku; ⊙noon-8pm; ⑤Ginza line to Omote-sandō, exit A5) Strung along the 1st floor of a midcentury apartment (across from

the Nezu Museum) is a collection of small boutiques from celebrity stylist Sonya Park. Park's signature style is a vintage-inspired minimalism in luxurious, natural fabrics. Homewares, too.

House
@Mikiri Hassin   Fashion & Accessories

(ハウス@ミキリハッシン; Map p246; ☎03-3486-7673; http://house.mikirihassin.co.jp; 5-42-1 Jingūmae, Shibuya-ku; ☉noon-9pm Thu-Tue; ⑤Ginza line to Omote-sandō, exit A1) Hidden deep in Ura-Hara (Harajuku's backstreet area), House stocks an ever-changing selection of experimental Japanese fashion brands. Contrary to what the cool merch might suggest, the sales clerks are polite and friendly – grateful, perhaps, that you made the effort to find the place. Look for ハウス spelled vertically in neon.

Laforet   Department Store

(ラフォーレ; Map p246; www.laforet.ne.jp; 1-11-6 Jingūmae, Shibuya-ku; ☉11am-9pm; ℝJR Yamanote line to Harajuku, Omote-sandō exit) Laforet has been a beacon of Harajuku fashion for decades, where young brands cut their teeth and established ones hold court. Check out the avant-garde looks at ground-floor boutiques **Wall** and **Hoyajuku**; more mainstream boutiques are on the upper floors.

Comme des
Garçons   Fashion & Accessories

(コム・デ・ギャルソン; Map p246; www. comme-des-garcons.com; 5-2-1 Minami-Aoyama, Minato-ku; ☉11am-8pm; ⑤Ginza line to Omote-sandō, exit A5) Designer Kawakubo Rei threw a wrench in the fashion machine in the early '80s with her dark, asymmetrical designs. That her work doesn't appear as shocking today as it once did speaks volumes about her far-reaching success. This eccentric, vaguely disorienting architectural creation is her brand's flagship store.

Sou-Sou   Fashion & Accessories

(そうそう; Map p246; ☎03-3407-7877; http://sousounetshop.jp; 5-3-10 Minami-Aoyama,

Minato-ku; ⏱11am-8pm; Ⓢ Ginza line to Omote-sandō, exit A5) Kyoto brand Sou-Sou is best known for producing the steel-toed, rubber-soled *tabi* shoes worn by Japanese construction workers in fun, playful designs – but it also has clothing and accessories that riff on traditional styles (including some really adorable stuff for kids).

Musubi   Arts & Crafts

(むす美; Map p246; ☎03-5414-5678; http://kyoto-musubi.com; 2-31-8 Jingūmae, Shibuya-ku; ⏱11am-7pm Thu-Tue; Ⓡ JR Yamanote line to Harajuku, Takeshita exit) *Furoshiki* are versatile squares of cloth that can be folded and knotted to make shopping bags and gift wrap. This shop sells pretty ones in both traditional and contemporary patterns – sometimes in collaboration with fashion brands. There is usually an English-speaking clerk who can show you some different ways to tie them.

KiddyLand   Toys

(キデイランド; Map p246; ☎03-3409-3431; www.kiddyland.co.jp; 6-1-9 Jingūmae, Shibuya-ku; ⏱11am-9pm Mon-Fri, 10.30am-9pm Sat & Sun; Ⓡ JR Yamanote line to Harajuku, Omote-sandō exit) This multistorey toy emporium is packed to the rafters with character goods, including all your Studio Ghibli, Sanrio and Disney faves. It's not just for kids either; you'll spot plenty of adults on a nostalgia trip down the Hello Kitty aisle.

Pass the Baton   Vintage

(パスザバトン; Map p246; ☎03-6447-0707; www.pass-the-baton.com; 4-12-10 Jingūmae, Shibuya-ku; ⏱11am-9pm Mon-Sat, to 8pm Sun;

Ⓢ Ginza line to Omote-sandō, exit A3) There are all sorts of treasures at this consignment shop, from 1970s designer duds to delicate teacups, personal castaways to dead stock from defunct retailers. It's in the basement of Omotesandō Hills, but you enter from a separate street entrance on Omote-sandō.

What's Nearby?

Takeshita-dōri Street

(竹下通り; Map p246; Jingūmae, Shibuya-ku; Ⓡ JR Yamanote line to Harajuku, Takeshita exit) This is Tokyo's famous fashion bazaar. It's an odd mixed bag: newer shops selling trendy, youthful styles alongside stores still invested in the trappings of decades of subcultures past (plaid and safety pins for the punks; colourful tutus for the *decora;* Victorian dresses for the Gothic Lolitas). Be warned: this pedestrian alley is a pilgrimage site for teens from all over Japan, which means it can be packed.

Ukiyo-e Ōta Memorial Museum of Art Museum

(浮世絵太田記念美術館; Map p246; 📞 03-3403-0880; www.ukiyoe-ota-muse.jp; 1-10-10 Jingūmae, Shibuya-ku; adult ¥700-1000, child free; 🕙 10.30am-5.30pm Tue-Sun; Ⓡ JR Yamanote line to Harajuku, Omote-sandō exit) This small museum (where you swap your shoes for slippers) is the best place in Tokyo to see *ukiyo-e*. Each month it presents a seasonal, thematic exhibition (with English curation notes), drawing from the truly impressive collection of Ōta Seizo, the former head of the Toho Life Insurance Company. Most exhibitions include a few works by masters such as Hokusai and Hiroshige. The museum closes the last few days of the month (between exhibitions).

Design Festa Gallery

(デザインフェスタ; Map p246; 📞 03-3479-1442; www.designfestagallery.com; 3-20-2 Jingūmae, Shibuya-ku; 🕙 11am-8pm; Ⓡ JR Yamanote line to Harajuku, Takeshita exit) **FREE** Design Festa has long been a champion of Tokyo's DIY art scene and its maze-like building is a Harajuku landmark. Inside there are dozens of small galleries rented by the day. More often than not, the artists themselves are hanging around, too.

★ **Local Knowledge**

Trends move fast in Harajuku. To keep up, follow @TokyoFashion on Instagram.

YULIA GRIGORYEVA/SHUTTERSTOCK ©

★ **Top Tip**

Combine a day of shopping with a tour of Omote-sandō's contemporary architecture (p50).

Walking Tour: Omote-sandō Architecture

Omote-sandō, a broad, tree-lined boulevard running through Harajuku, is known for its parade of upmarket boutiques designed by the who's who of (mostly) Japanese contemporary architects.

Start Tokyu Plaza
Distance 1.2km
Duration One hour

2 Andō Tadao's deceptively deep **Omotesandō Hills** (2003; 4-12-10 Jingūmae, Shibuya-ku) is a high-end shopping mall spiralling around a sunken central atrium.

1 Tokyu Plaza (2012; 4-30-3 Jingū-mae, Shibuya-ku), is a castle-like structure by up-and-coming architect Nakamura Hiroshi. There's a spacious roof garden on top.

3 The flagship boutique for **Dior** (2003; 5-9-11 Jingūmae, Shibuya-ku), designed by SANAA (composed of Sejima Kazuyo and Nishizawa Ryūe), has a filmy, white exterior that seems to hang like a dress.

4 Meant to evoke a stack of clothes trunks, Aoki Jun's design for **Louis Vuitton** (2002; 5-7-5 Jingūmae, Shibuya-ku) features offset panels of tinted glass behind sheets of metal mesh of varying patterns. Gallery **Espace Louis Vuitton Tokyo** is on the top floor.

HARAJUKU

START

Omote-sandō

Cat St

Omotesandō Hills

5 The criss-crossing strips of concrete on Itō Toyō's construction for **Tod's** (2004; 5-1-15 Jingūmae, Shibuya-ku) take their inspiration from the zelkova trees below.

7 Kengo Kuma's design for Taiwanese pineapple cake shop **Sunny-Hills** (2014; 3-10-20 Minami-Aoyama, Minato-ku) uses 3D-modelled latticework.

Take a Break...
Anniversaire Café (http://cafe.anniversaire.co.jp; 3-5-30 Kita-Aoyama, Minato-ku; ⊘11am-9pm Mon-Fri, 9am-9pm Sat & Sun) has an attractive patio for people watching.

KITA-AOYAMA

Aoyama-dori

Omote-sandō

Omote-sandō

⑤

⑦
FINISH

MINAMI-AOYAMA

⑥

6 Herzog and de Meuron designed this convex glass fish bowl for **Prada** (2003; 5-2-6 Minami-Aoyama, Minato-ku).

Classic Photo Close-up of the bubbly facade of the Prada building.

YASEMIN OLGUNOZ BERBER/SHUTTERSTOCK ©

Tokyo National Museum

This is the world's largest collection of Japanese art, home to gorgeous silk kimonos, earthy tea-ceremony pottery, evocative scroll paintings done in charcoal ink and haunting examples of samurai armour and swords.

Great For...

☑ Don't Miss

The gilded Buddhas of the Gallery of Hōryū-ji Treasures.

Established in 1872, The Tokyo National Museum is divided into several buildings. Visitors with only a couple of hours should hone in on the Honkan (Main Gallery) and the Gallery of Hōryū-ji Treasures. There are English explanations throughout the museum.

Honkan (Main Gallery)

The Honkan houses the Japanese art collection. Second floor galleries are arranged by era; first floor galleries are arranged by medium, offering a deeper dive into traditional arts such as lacquerware, metalwork and ceramics.

The building was designed by Watanabe Jin in what is known as the Imperial Style, which mixes modernist ideas and materials with native Japanese forms (like the sloping tiled roof). For a couple of weeks in spring

❶ Need to Know

東京国立博物館, Tokyo Kokuritsu Hakubut-sukan; Map p254; ☑03-3822-1111; www.tnm.jp; 13-9 Ueno-kōen, Taitō-ku; adult/child ¥620/free; ⊙9.30am-5pm Tue-Thu, to 9pm Fri & Sat, to 6pm Sun; ☒JR lines to Ueno, Ueno-kōen exit

✕ Take a Break

There are restaurants in the Gallery of Hōryū-ji Treasures and in the Tōyōkan.

★ Top Tip

Allow two hours to take in the highlights, a half-day to do the whole Honkan in depth, or a whole day to see everything.

and autumn, the garden, with five **vintage teahouses**, is opened to the public.

Gallery of Hōryū-ji Treasures

The stunning **Gallery of Hōryū-ji Treasures** (法隆寺宝物館; Map p254; ☑03-5777-8600) – oddly moody for a museum – displays masks, metalwork and sculptures from the Hōryū-ji (in Nara Prefecture, dating from 607 and one of Japan's earliest temples). Most impressive is the spot-lit first floor exhibition of 48 gilt Buddha statues, each only 30cm to 40cm tall and all slightly different. The spare, elegant building (1999) was designed by Taniguchi Yoshio.

Heiseikan

Accessed via a passage on the 1st floor of the Honkan, the **Heiseikan** (平成館; Map p254; adult/child & senior/student ¥620/free/410)

houses the **Japanese Archaeological Gallery**, full of pottery, talismans and articles of daily life from Japan's Palaeolithic and Neolithic periods. The second floor is used for temporary exhibitions; these can be fantastic, but note that they cost extra and often lack the English signage found throughout the rest of the museum.

Tōyōkan

The **Tōyōkan** (Gallery of Asian Art; Map p254; adult/child & senior/student ¥620/free/410) houses the museum's collection of Buddhist sculptures from around Asia, Chinese ceramics and more, offering a bigger picture of art in the region over the last few millennia. The three-storied building, also by Taniguchi Yoshio, has been renovated recently and showcases its holdings beautifully.

Kuroda Memorial Hall

Kuroda Seiki (1866–1924) is considered the father of modern Western-style painting in Japan. The **Kuroda Memorial Hall** (黒田記念室; Map p254; ☎03-5777-8600; www.tobunken.go.jp/kuroda/index_e.html; 13-9 Ueno-kōen, Taitō-ku; ☺9.30am-5pm Tue-Sun; ☒JR lines to Ueno, Ueno-kōen exit) **FREE**, a 1928-vintage annex to Tokyo National Museum, displays some of his key works. The most famous of his paintings, including *Reading* (1891) and *Lakeside* (1897), are in a room that only opens a few times a year; check the website for a schedule.

What's Nearby?

The Tokyo National Museum sits on the edge of **Ueno-kōen** (上野公園; Map p254; www.ueno-bunka.jp; Ueno-kōen, Taitō-ku; ☒JR lines to Ueno, Ueno-kōen or Shinobazu exit), a park with cultural facilities, shrines, temples and Tokyo's zoo. There's also a large pond here, with giant lotuses that bloom in summer.

Ueno Tōshō-gū   Shinto Shrine
(上野東照宮; Map p254; ☎03-3822-3455; www.uenotoshogu.com; 9-88 Ueno-kōen, Taitō-ku; adult/child ¥500/200; ☺9am-5.30pm Mar-Sep, to 4.30pm Oct-Feb; ☒JR lines to Ueno, Shinobazu exit) This shrine inside Ueno-kōen was built in honour of Tokugawa Ieyasu, the warlord who unified Japan. Resplendent in gold leaf and ornate details, it dates to 1651 (though it has had recent touch-ups). You can get a pretty good look from outside the gate, if you want to skip the admission fee.

Ueno Zoo   Zoo
(上野動物園, Ueno Dōbutsu-en; Map p254; ☎03-3828-5171; www.tokyo-zoo.net; 9-83 Ueno-kōen,

☑ Don't Miss

The Tokyo National Museum's Kuromon (Black Gate), transported from the Edo-era mansion of a feudal lord.

Asakura Museum of Sculpture, Taitō

PHILLIP MAGUIRE/SHUTTERSTOCK ©

Taitō-ku; adult/child ¥600/free; ⊘9.30am-5pm Tue-Sun; 🚉JR lines to Ueno, Ueno-kōen exit) Japan's oldest zoo, established in 1882, is home to animals from around the globe, but the biggest attractions are the giant pandas that arrived from China in 2011 – Rī Rī and Shin Shin. Following several disappointments, the two finally had a cub, Xiang Xiang, in 2017. There's also a whole area devoted to lemurs, which makes sense given Tokyoites' love of all things cute.

Ameya-yokochō   Market

(アメヤ横町; Map p254; www.ameyoko.net; 4 Ueno, Taitō-ku; ⊘10am-7pm, some shops close Wed; 🚉JR lines to Okachimachi, north exit) Step into this partially open-air market paralleling and beneath the JR line tracks, and ritzy, glitzy Tokyo feels like a distant memory. It got its start as a black market,

Meerkat, Ueno Zoo

KOREA PANDA/SHUTTERSTOCK ©

post-WWII, when American goods (which included *ameya* – candy and chocolates) were sold here. Today you can pick up everything from fresh seafood to vintage jeans and bargain sneakers.

Asakura Museum of Sculpture, Taitō   Museum

(朝倉彫塑館; Map p254; ☎03-3821-4549; www. taitocity.net/taito/asakura; 7-16-10 Yanaka, Taitō-ku; adult/child ¥500/250; ⊘9.30am-4.30pm Tue, Wed & Fri-Sun; 🚉JR Yamanote line to Nippori, north exit) Sculptor Asakura Fumio (artist name Chōso; 1883–1964) designed this atmospheric house himself. It combined his original Japanese home and garden with a large studio that incorporated vaulted ceilings, a 'sunrise room' and a rooftop garden with wonderful neighbourhood views. It's now a reverential museum with many of the artist's signature realist works, mostly of people and cats, on display.

SCAI the Bathhouse   Gallery

(スカイザバスハウス; Map p254; ☎03-3821-1144; www.scaithebathhouse.com; 6-1-23 Yanaka, Taitō-ku; ⊘noon-6pm Tue-Sat; ⑤Chiyoda line to Nezu, exit 1) FREE This 200-year-old bathhouse has for several decades been an avant-garde gallery space, showcasing Japanese and international artists in its austere vaulted space. Closed between exhibitions.

Yanaka Ginza   Area

(谷中銀座; Map p254; www.yanakaginza.com; 🚉JR Yamanote line to Nippori, north exit) Yanaka Ginza is pure, vintage mid-20th-century Tokyo, a pedestrian street lined with butcher shops, vegetable vendors and the like. Most Tokyo neighbourhoods once had stretches like these (until supermarkets took over). It's popular with Tokyoites from all over the city, who come to soak up the nostalgic atmosphere, plus the locals who shop here.

★ Top Tip

Spend the morning at the Tokyo National Museum and the afternoon exploring Ueno-kōen or nearby Yanaka (p88).

Tokyo National Museum

HISTORIC HIGHLIGHTS

It would be a challenge to take in everything the sprawling Tokyo National Museum has to offer in a day. Fortunately, the Honkan (Japanese Gallery) is designed to give visitors a crash course in Japanese art history from the Jōmon era (13,000–300 BC) to the Edo era (AD 1603–1868). The works on display here are rotated regularly, to protect fragile ones and to create seasonal exhibitions, so you're always guaranteed to see something new.

Buy your ticket from outside the main gate then head straight to the Honkan with its sloping tile roof. Stow your coat in a locker and take the central staircase up to the 2nd floor, where the exhibitions are arranged chronologically. Allow two hours for this tour of the highlights.

The first room on your right starts from the beginning with **ancient Japanese art** ❶. Pick up a free copy of the brochure *Highlights of Japanese Art* at the entrance to the first room on your right. The exhibition starts here with the **Dawn of Japanese Art**, covering the most ancient periods of Japan's history.

Continue to the **National Treasure Gallery** ❷. 'National Treasure' is the highest distinction awarded to a work of art in Japan. Keep an eye out for more National Treasures, labelled in red, on display in other rooms throughout the museum.

Moving on, stop to admire the **courtly art gallery** ❸, the **samurai armour and swords** ❹ and the ***ukiyo-e* and kimono** ❺.

Next, take the stairs down to the 1st floor, where each room is dedicated to a different decorative art, such as lacquerware or ceramics. Don't miss the excellent examples of **religious sculpture** ❻, and folk art and **Ainu and Ryūkyū cultural artefacts** ❼.

Finish your visit with a look inside the enchanting **Gallery of Hōryū-ji Treasures** ❽.

Ukiyo-e & Kimono (Room 10)
Chic silken kimono and lushly coloured *ukiyo-e* (woodblock prints) are two icons of the Edo-era (AD 1603–1868) *ukiyo* – the 'floating world', or world of fleeting beauty and pleasure.

TOKYO NATIONAL MUSEUM ©

Japanese Sculpture (Room 11)
Many of Japan's most famous sculptures, religious in nature, are locked away in temple reliquaries. This is a rare chance to see them up close.

MUSEUM GARDEN

Don't miss the garden if you visit in spring and autumn during the few weeks it's open to the public.

Heiseikan & Japanese Archaeology Gallery

Research & Information Centre

Hyōkeikan

Kuro-mon

Main Gate

Gallery of Hōryū-ji Treasures
Surround yourself with miniature gilt Buddhas from Hōryū-ji, one of Japan's oldest Buddhist temples, founded in 607. Don't miss the graceful Pitcher with Dragon Head, a National Treasure.

TOKYO NATIONAL MUSEUM ©. PHOTOS BY SATO AKIRA

Samurai Armour & Swords (Rooms 5 & 6)

Glistening swords, finely stitched armour and imposing helmets bring to life the samurai, those iconic warriors of Japan's medieval age.

Courtly Art (Room 3-2)

Literature works, calligraphy and narrative picture scrolls are displayed alongside decorative art objects, which allude to the life of elegance led by courtesans a thousand years ago.

④

⑤

①

②

③

Honkan (Japanese Gallery) 2nd Floor

⑦

⑥

Honkan (Japanese Gallery) 1st Floor

Museum Garden & Teahouses

Honkan (Japanese Gallery)

Tōyōkan (Gallery of Asian Art)

National Treasure Gallery (Room 2)

A single, superlative work from the museum's collection of 88 National Treasures (perhaps a painted screen, or a gilded, hand-drawn sutra) is displayed in a serene, contemplative setting.

GIFT SHOP

The museum gift shop, on the 1st floor of the Honkan, has an excellent collection of Japanese art books in English.

Dawn of Japanese Art (Room 1)

The rise of the imperial court and the introduction of Buddhism changed the Japanese aesthetic forever. These clay works from previous eras show what came before.

Ainu and Ryūkyū Collection (Room 16)

See artefacts from Japan's historical minorities – the indigenous Ainu of Hokkaidō and the former Ryūkyū Empire, now Okinawa.

Yoyogi-kōen (p41)

KANOKPOLTOKUMHERD/SHUTTERSTOCK ©

Cherry-Blossom Viewing

Come spring, thousands upon thousands of cherry trees around the city burst into white and pink flowers. Tokyoites gather in parks and along river banks for cherry-blossom-viewing gatherings called hanami.

Great For...

☑ **Don't Miss**

Yozakura – the cherry blossoms at night.

Hanami Parties

Hanami is a centuries-old tradition, a celebration of the fleeting beauty of life symbolised by the blossoms, which last only a week or two. It's the one time of year you'll see Tokyoites let their hair down *en masse* as a carnivalesque spirit envelope the city.

There are essentially two ways to take advantage of the season: to picnic in a park or to stroll along a path lined with *sakura* (cherry) trees. Picnics usually start early and the most gung-ho *hanami*-goers will turn up very early to secure a prime spot with a plastic ground sheet; however you can usually find a good sliver of ground whenever you turn up (unless you've got a large group). You can get a ground sheet, along with food and booze, at a convenience

Shinjuku-gyoen (新宿御苑; Map p253; ☎03-3350-0151; www.env.go.jp/garden/shinjukugyoen; 11 Naito-chō, Shinjuku-ku; adult/child ¥200/50; ⊗9am-4.30pm Tue-Sun; ⑤Marunouchi line to Shinjuku-gyoenmae, exit 1) is the best spot for families (or anyone seeking a more peaceful backdrop). The former imperial garden has a nicely manicured lawn, fixed opening hours, charges a small admission fee and – officially – doesn't allow alcohol, all of which encourages a less-debauched atmosphere.

Ueno-kōen (p54) is Tokyo's classic *hanami* spot. While some do go for spots under the trees here, this park is better for strolling as it doesn't have a lawn.

Another famous strolling spot is Naka-Meguro's canal, **Meguro-gawa** (目黒川; Map p246; ⑤Hibiya line to Naka-Meguro, main exit). Local restaurants set up street stalls offering more upmarket food and drink than you'll find anywhere else. This one can get very crowded; go earlier in the day on a weekday.

store. It's common for *hanami* to last well into the evening, as public parks in Tokyo have no curfew.

Well-known strolling spots usually have food and drink vendors in the evenings. This is the most popular time to visit, when the blossoms are typically illuminated by lanterns.

Top Spots

Grassy Yoyogi-kōen (p41) is a guaranteed good time. It's not the prettiest of parks but it has lots of *sakura* and sees the most spirited (read: boozy) bacchanals. **Inokashira-kōen** (井の頭公園; www.kensetsu.metro.tokyo.jp/seibuk/inokashira/index.html; 1-18-31 Gotenyama, Musashino-shi; ⓡJR Chūō-Sōbu line to Kichijōji, Kōen exit), which has a photogenic pond flanked with cherry trees, is also popular, especially with students.

Day Trip: Mt Fuji

Catching a glimpse of Mt Fuji (富士山; 3776m), Japan's highest and most famous peak, will take your breath away. Dawn from the summit? Pure magic (even when it's cloudy). Fuji-san is among Japan's most revered and timeless attractions. Hundreds of thousands of people climb it every year, continuing a centuries-old tradition of pilgrimages up the sacred volcano.

Great For...

Fuji Subaru
Line Fifth
Station

Fuji-Hakone-Izu
National Park

Taishikan

Fujisan
Hotel

Mt Fuji ◎

Subashiri
Fifth Station

Gotemba
Fifth Station

Fujinomiya
Fifth Station

Hōei-san
(2693m)

ⓘ Need to Know

The official climbing season runs from 1 July to 10 September.

★ Top Tip

Check summit weather conditions before planning a climb at www.snow-forecast.com/resorts/Mount-Fuji/6day/top.

Climbing Mt Fuji

There are four trails up Mt Fuji: Yoshida, Subashiri, Gotemba and Fujinomiya. The mountain is divided into 10 'stations' from base (first station) to summit (10th); however, the trails start at the fifth station, which is accessible by road.

The Yoshida Trail is far and away the most popular route up the mountain, because buses run directly from Tokyo to the trailhead at the **Fuji Subaru Line Fifth Station** (at 2300m; sometimes called the Kawaguchi-ko Fifth Station or just Mt Fuji Fifth Station). It also has the most huts (with food, water and toilets). For this hike, allow five to six hours to reach the top and about three hours to descend, plus 1½ hours for circling the crater at the top. When descending, make sure you don't go down the Subashiri Trail, which intersects with the Yoshida Trail at the 8th station.

Know Before You Climb

Make no mistake: Mt Fuji is a serious mountain and a reasonable level of fitness is required. It's high enough for altitude sickness, and on the summit it can go from sunny and warm to wet, windy and cold remarkably quickly. Even if conditions are fine, you can count on it being close to freezing in the morning, even in summer. Visibility can rapidly disappear.

At a minimum, bring clothing appropriate for cold and wet weather, including a hat and gloves. If you're climbing at night, bring a torch (flashlight) or headlamp, and spare batteries. Water and food are available from mountain huts, but at a significant

Hikers viewing the sunrise from the summit of Mt Fuji

markup (and you'll need cash); mountain huts also have toilets (¥200).

Descending the mountain is much harder on the knees than ascending; hiking poles will help. To avoid altitude sickness, be sure to take it slowly and take regular breaks. If you're suffering severe symptoms, you'll need to make an immediate descent.

Timing Your Climb

Most climbers aim to get to the top just before dawn, but not too much before dawn (because it will be cold and windy). One strategy, the most popular, is to start out around 9pm or 10pm and climb through the night. The other is to start in the afternoon, sleep for a bit in a mountain hut halfway up the mountain and then begin again in the early morning hours. This is the safer approach, as it gives you more time to acclimatise to the altitude.

It's a very busy mountain during the two-month climbing season. You won't be bounding up it so much as staring at the back of the person in front of you for hours. To avoid the worst of the crush head up on a weekday, or start earlier during the day. And definitely don't climb during the mid-August Obon holiday.

Authorities strongly caution against climbing outside the regular season, when the weather is highly unpredictable and first-aid stations on the mountain are closed. Once snow or ice is on the mountain, Fuji becomes a very serious and dangerous undertaking and should only be attempted by those with winter mountaineering equipment and plenty of experience. Do not climb alone; a guide will be invaluable.

Mountain Huts

Conditions in mountain huts are spartan: a blanket on the floor sandwiched between other climbers. Booking ahead is highly recommended; Fuji Mountain Guides (p64) can assist with reservations (for a ¥1000 fee). Let huts know if you need to cancel at the last minute; no-shows are still expected to pay.

Fujisan Hotel   Hut ¥

(富士山ホテル; ☑late Jun–mid-Sep 0555-24-6512, reservations 0555-22-0237; www.fujisan hotel.com; per person with/without 2 meals from ¥8350/5950; ☺) One of the largest and most popular rest huts open on Mt Fuji during the climbing season, the Fujisan Hotel is at the Eighth Station where the Yoshida and

> **☑ Don't Miss**
>
> Watching the sunrise from the summit is a profound, once-in-a-lifetime experience.

NONCHANON/SHUTTERSTOCK ©

> **✕ Take a Break**
>
> Mountain huts offer hikers simple hot meals in addition to a place to sleep. Most huts allow you to rest inside as long as you order something.

Subashiri Trails meet. There's usually some English-speaking staff here. Bookings are accepted from 1 April and are highly recommended. Credit cards accepted.

Taishikan   Hut ¥

(太子館; ☏0555-22-1947; www.mfi.or.jp/w3/home0/taisikan; per person incl 2 meals from ¥8500) One of several rest huts open during the climbing season on Mt Fuji, located at the Eighth Station of the Yoshida Trail. There is usually some English-speaking staff here, warm sleeping bags are provided, and vegetarian or halal meals are available if requested in advance. Reservations accepted from 1 April. Cash only.

Equipment Rental

Want to climb Mt Fuji, but don't want to invest in (or schlep) all the requisite gear? **Yamadōgu Rental** (やまどうぐレンタル屋; Map p253; ☏050-5865-1615; www.yamarent.com; 6th fl, 1-13-7 Nishi-Shinjuku, Shinjuku-ku; ⊗noon-7pm Mon-Sat Sep-May, noon-7pm Wed-Mon Jun, 6.30am-7pm every day Jul & Aug; ☒JR Yamanote line to Shinjuku, west exit) can set you up with individual items (shoes, poles, rain jacket etc) or a full kit including a backpack (from ¥10,500 for two days). Most of the gear is from Japanese outdoor brand Montbell. Reserve in advance online.

During the Fuji climbing season, they have a shop at the Yoshida trail 5th station where you can return the gear after climbing.

Tours

It's certainly not necessary to use a tour operator when climbing in season, though it can make arranging logistics from overseas easier. Another perk is that they may lead you to a route other than the Yoshida Trail, meaning less frustrating crowds.

Fuji Mountain Guides   Hiking

(☏042-445-0798; www.fujimountainguides.com; 2-day Mt Fuji tours per person ¥48,600) Aimed at foreign visitors, these excellent tours are run both in and out of season by highly experienced and very professional bilingual international guides. Transport to and from Tokyo, mountain guide, two meals and one night in a mountain hut is included; gear rental is available for extra.

Discover Japan Tours   Hiking

(www.discover-japan-tours.com; tours per person from ¥10,000) Reputable company running self-guided overnight treks to/from Shinjuku, timed for sunrise arrival, on summer Saturdays, with a stop at a public hot spring on the way back. Groups of up to eight can arrange a private tour (¥60,000) any day of the week, including outside the climbing season.

Fuji Five Lakes

Outside the climbing season, you can hunt for views of Mt Fuji in the Fuji Five Lake region, where placid lakes, formed by ancient eruptions, serve as natural reflecting pools. Kawaguchi-ko is the most popular

Shinkansen (bullet train) passing Mt Fuji

lake, with plenty of accommodation, eating and hiking options around it. The other lakes are Yamanaka-ko, Sai-ko, Shōji-ko and Motosu-ko.

Several hiking trails through the foothills, open year-round, offer rewarding vistas – and are far less of a slog than climbing the actual mountain. Ask for a map at the **Kawaguchi-ko Tourist Information Center** (☑0555-72-6700; ◔8.30am-5.30pm).

From roughly mid-April to early December (weather permitting), buses travel from Kawaguchi-ko to the Fuji Subaru Line Fifth Station (one way/return ¥1540/2100, one hour), so even if you can't climb you can still get up close to the hulking volcano.

Getting There & Around

During the climbing season, Keiō Dentetsu Bus (https://highway-buses.jp) runs direct buses (¥2700, 2½ hours; reservations necessary) from the **Shinjuku Bus Terminal** (バスタ新宿, Busta Shinjuku; Map p253; ☑03-6380-4794; www.shinjuku-busterminal.co.jp; 4th fl, 5-24-55 Sendagaya, Shibuya-ku; 🛜; 🚃JR Yamanote line to Shinjuku, new south exit) to Fuji Subaru Line Fifth Station, for the Yoshida Trail. The other trails are best accessed as part of a tour or with private transportation.

Year-round, buses run between Shinjuku and Kawaguchi-ko (¥1750, 1¾ hours).

★ **Local Knowledge**

There is a Japanese saying, 'He who climbs Mt Fuji once is a wise man; he who climbs it twice is a fool.'

ⓘ **Need to Know**

See the 'Official Web Site for Mt Fuji Climbing' (www.fujisan-climb.jp) for maps and detailed climbing info.

BLANSCAPE/SHUTTERSTOCK ©

SEAN PAVONE/SHUTTERSTOCK ©

Shibuya Crossing

This is the Tokyo you've dreamed about and seen in movies: the mind-boggling crowds, the glowing lights and the giant video screens beaming larger-than-life celebrities over the streets.

Rumoured to be the busiest intersection in the world (and definitely in Japan), Shibuya Crossing, also known as Shibuya Scramble, is like a giant beating heart, sending people in all directions with every pulsing light change. Hundreds of people – and at peak times upwards of 3000 people – cross at a time, coming from all directions at once yet still managing to dodge each other with a practised, nonchalant agility. Then, in the time that it takes for the light to go from red to green again, all corners have replenished their stock of people – like a video on loop. All told, it's been estimated that on busy days, 500,000 people use the crossing – as many as some of Tokyo's busiest train stations.

Mag's Park (Map p246; 1-23-10 Jinnan, Shibuya-ku; ☺11am-11pm; ℝJR Yamanote line to Shibuya, Hachikō exit), on the rooftop of the

Great For...

☑ **Don't Miss**

The crossing at night, all lit up.

Shibuya
Crossing ◎ Miyamasu-zaka

Shibuya Ⓢ

Jingū-dōri

❶ Need to Know

渋谷スクランブル交差点, Shibuya Scramble; Map p246; ℝ JR Yamanote line to Shibuya, Hachikō exit

✕ Take a Break

Get a meal or coffee at d47 Shokudō (p132).

★ Top Tip

There's a good view of the crossing from Shibuya train station, across from the mural, Myth of Tomorrow (p67).

Shibuya 109-2 department store, has the best views over the crossing.

What's Nearby?

Hachikō Statue
Statue

(ハチ公像; Map p246; Hachikō Plaza; ℝ JR Yamanote line to Shibuya, Hachikō exit) Meet Tokyo's most famous pooch, Hachikō. This Akita dog came to Shibuya Station every day to meet his master, a professor, returning from work. After the professor died in 1925, Hachikō continued to come to the station daily until his own death nearly 10 years later. The story became legendary and a small statue was erected in the dog's memory in front of Shibuya Station.

Shibuya Center-gai
Street

(渋谷センター街, Shibuya Sentā-gai; Map p246; ℝ JR Yamanote line to Shibuya, Hachikō exit) Shibuya's main drag is closed to cars and chock-a-block with fast-food joints and high-street fashion shops. At night, lit bright as day, with a dozen competing soundtracks (coming from who knows where), wares spilling onto the streets and strutting teens, it feels like a block party – or Tokyo's version of a classic Asian night market.

Myth of Tomorrow
Public Art

(明日の神話, Asu no Shinwa; Map p246; ℝ JR Yamanote line to Shibuya, Hachikō exit) Okamoto Tarō's mural, Myth of Tomorrow (1967), was commissioned by a Mexican luxury hotel but went missing two years later. It finally turned up in 2003 and, in 2008, the haunting 30m-long work, which depicts the atomic bomb exploding over Hiroshima, was installed inside Shibuya Station. It's on the 2nd floor, in the corridor leading to the Inokashira line.

A sumo wrestler prepares for a bout

Sumo at Ryōgoku Kokugikan

The purifying salt sails into the air; the two giants leap up and crash into each other; a flurry of slapping and heaving ensues: from the ancient rituals to the thrill of the quick bouts, sumo is a fascinating spectacle. Bashō (grand tournaments) are held in Tokyo three times a year, for 15 days each January, May and September, at Ryōgoku Kokugikan, the national sumo stadium.

Great For...

ℹ️ Need to Know

両国国技館, Ryōgoku Sumo Stadium; Map p254; ☏03-3623-5111; www.sumo.or.jp; 1-3-28 Yokoami, Sumida-ku; tickets ¥3800-11,700; 🚃JR Sōbu line to Ryōgoku, west exit

★ Top Tip

Rent a radio (¥100 fee, plus ¥2000 deposit) to listen to commentary in English.

Tournaments

Tournaments are all-day events: doors open at 8am for the early matches that take place between junior wrestlers. The stakes (and pageantry) begin in earnest in the afternoon, when the *makuuchi* (top-tier) wrestlers enter the ring followed by the *yokozuna* (the top of the top), accompanied by sword-bearing attendants. Many spectators skip the morning, arriving around 2pm or 3pm. The final, most exciting, bouts of the day (featuring the *yokozuna*) finish around 6pm. Tournament ticket holders are allowed to exit and re-enter the stadium once, through the south gate only.

Getting Tickets

Tickets can be bought online five weeks prior to the start of the tournament from the official ticketing site, Ticket Oosumo (http://sumo.pia.jp/en). Note that there is a ¥1000 handling fee per ticket. You can also buy tickets directly from the box office in front of the stadium, though they do sell out, especially on the first and last days of the tournament.

Around 200 general-admission tickets (the cheapest ticket available is ¥2100) are sold each day of the tournament on a first-come-first-served basis at the box office. You'll have to line up very early (say 6am) on the last couple of days of the tournament to snag one.

Sumo Basics

Sumo is a ritualistic form of wrestling that developed out of ancient Shintō rites for a good harvest. Two large and amply muscled men, their hair in a topknot and clothed only in *mawashi* (loin cloths) face off in a packed

The January *bashō* (grand sumo tournament)

earth *dōyo* (ring) over which hangs a roof resembling that of a shrine. Before bouts, which typically last only seconds, the *rikishi* (wrestlers) rinse their mouths with water and toss salt into the ring – both purification rituals. They also perform the *shiko* movement, where they squat, clap their hands and alternately raise each leg as high as it can go before stamping it down – a show of strength and agility.

Size is important in sumo, but woe betide any *rikishi* who relies solely on bulk as, more often than not, it's *kimari-te* (wrestling techniques) that win the day. There are 82 offi-cial *kimari-te* that a *rikishi* may legitimately employ, including *oshidashi* (pushing an opponent's arms underneath or in the chest to force him out of the ring); *uwatenage* (grabbing an opponent's *mawashi* from outside the opponent's arms and throwing him to the ground); and *yorikiri* (lifting an opponent out of the ring by his *mawashi*). Illegal moves include punching with a closed fist, boxing ears, choking, grabbing an opponent in the crotch area and hair-pulling.

What's Nearby?

Edo-Tokyo Museum   Museum
(江戸東京博物館; Map p254; ☎03-3626-9974; www.edo-tokyo-museum.or.jp; 1-4-1 Yokoami, Sumida-ku; adult/child ¥600/free; ◷9.30am-5.30pm, to 7.30pm Sat, closed Mon; 🚆JR Sōbu line to Ryōgoku, west exit) Tokyo's history museum documents the city's transformation from tidal flatlands to feudal capital to modern metropolis via detailed scale re-creations of townscapes, villas and tenement homes, plus artefacts such as *ukiyo-e* and old maps. Reopened in March 2018 after a renovation, the museum also has interactive displays, multilingual touch-screen panels and audio guides. Still, the best way to tour the museum is with one of the gracious English-speaking volunteer guides, who can really bring the history to life.

Japanese Sword Museum   Museum
(刀剣博物館; Map p254; ☎03-6284-1000; www.touken.or.jp; 1-12-9 Yokoami, Sumida-ku; adult/child ¥1000/free; ◷9.30am-5pm Tue-Sun; 🚆JR Sōbu line to Ryōgoku, west exit) For visitors with an interest in Japanese sword-making – a keen art that continues to this day – this museum features exhibitions from contemporary craftspeople. There's good English information on the different styles and components (and more English-language references for sale in the small gift shop).

> ### ✕ Take a Break
> The stadium's basement banquet hall serves *chanko-nabe* (the protein-rich stew eaten by the wrestlers) for ¥300. Or visit nearby Kappō Yoshiba (p147).

J. HENNING BUCHHOLZ/SHUTTERSTOCK ©

> ### ☑ Don't Miss
> Not in town during a tournament? See morning sumo practice at Arashio Stable (p198). Check website for details.

Sensō-ji

Sensō-ji is the capital's oldest temple, far older than Tokyo itself. According to legend, in AD 628, two fishermen brothers pulled out a golden image of Kannon (the Bodhisattva of compassion) from the nearby Sumida-gawa. Sensō-ji was built to enshrine it. Today the temple stands out for its evocation of an older Japan, rarely visible in Tokyo today.

Great For...

❶ Need to Know

浅草寺; Map p254; ☎03-3842-0181; www.
senso-ji.jp; 2-3-1 Asakusa, Taitō-ku; ⓧ24hr;
Ⓢ Ginza line to Asakusa, exit 1; **FREE**

★ **Top Tip**

Stop by the nearby **Asakusa Culture Tourist Information Center** (浅草文化観光センター; Map p254; ☎03-3842-5566; www.city.taito.lg.jp; 2-18-9 Kaminari-mon, Taitō-ku; ⏰9am-8pm; 📶; ⑤Ginza line to Asakusa, exit 2) for information on local events.

Kaminari-mon

The temple precinct begins at the majestic **Kaminari-mon** (雷門; Thunder Gate; Map p254), which means Thunder Gate. An enormous 670kg *chōchin* (lantern) hangs from the centre. On either side are a pair of ferocious protective deities: Fūjin, the god of wind, on the right; and Raijin, the god of thunder, on the left. Kaminari-mon has burnt down countless times over the centuries; the current gate dates to 1970.

Nakamise-dōri

Beyond Kaminari-mon is the shrine precinct's bustling shopping street, Nakamise-dōri. Along with the usual tourist swag you can find some true gems (artisan crafts, for example) and oddities (such as wigs done up in traditional hair-

styles). There are also numerous snack vendors serving up traditional treats like crunchy *sembei* (rice crackers) and *age-manju* (deep-fried *anko* – bean-paste – buns).

At the end of Nakamise-dōri is **Hōzō-mon** (宝蔵門; Map p254), another gate with fierce guardians. On the gate's back side are a pair of 2500kg, 4.5m-tall *waraji* (straw sandals) crafted by some 800 villagers in northern Yamagata Prefecture. These are meant to symbolise the Buddha's power, and it's believed that evil spirits will be scared off by the giant footwear.

Hondō (Main Hall)

The current Hondō, with its dramatic sloping roof, was constructed in 1958, replacing the one destroyed in WWII air raids. The style is similar to the previous one, though

Sanja Matsuri, Asakusa-jinja

the roof tiles are made of titanium. The Kannon image (a tiny 6cm) is cloistered away from view deep inside (and admittedly may not exist at all). Nonetheless, a steady stream of worshippers visits the temple to cast coins, pray and bow in a gesture of respect.

In front is a large cauldron with smoking incense. The smoke is said to bestow health and you'll see people wafting it over their bodies. Off the courtyard stands the 53m-high **Five-Storey Pagoda** (五重塔; Map p254), the 1973 reconstruction of a pagoda built by Tokugawa Iemitsu; it is the second-highest pagoda in Japan.

☑ Don't Miss

The minutes just before the sun sinks make for some of the best pictures of this photogenic sanctuary.

YUKIHIPO/SHUTTERSTOCK ©

Fortune Telling

One of the fun parts of a temple visit is drawing an *omikuji* (paper fortune). On either side of the approach to the Main Hall, there will be kiosks selling them. Drop a ¥100 coin into the slot, grab a silver canister and shake it. Then extract a stick and note its number (in kanji). Find the matching drawer and withdraw your *omikuji* (there's English on the back) and return the stick to the canister. Fortunes can be shockingly bad, but if you get 大凶 (*dai-kyō*, Great Curse), don't fear: just tie the paper on the nearby rack, ask the gods for better luck, and try again!

Asakusa-jinja

On the east side of the temple complex is **Asakusa-jinja** (浅草神社; Map p254; ☑03-3844-1575; www.asakusajinja.jp; ☺9am-4.30pm), built in honour of the brothers who discovered the Kannon statue that inspired the construction of Sensō-ji. The current building, painted a deep shade of red, dates to 1649 and is a rare example of early Edo architecture.

What's Nearby?

Asahi Super Dry Hall   Architecture
(フラムドール; Flamme d'Or; Map p254; 1-23-1 Azuma-bashi, Sumida-ku) Also known as Asahi Beer Hall, the headquarters of the brewery – designed by Philippe Starck and completed in 1989 – remains one of Tokyo's most distinctive buildings. The tower, with its golden glass facade and white top floors, is supposed to evoke a giant mug of beer, while the golden blob atop the lower jet-black building is the flame (locals, however, refer to it as the 'golden turd').

✖ Take a Break

End the day with a beer at Asahi Sky Room (p115).

Ghibli Museum, Mitaka

Ghibli Museum, Mitaka

Even those uninitiated in the magical world of master animator Miyazaki Hayao will find this museum dedicated to him and his works enchanting. Fans won't want to leave.

Master animator Miyazaki Hayao and his Studio Ghibli (pronounced 'jiburi') have been responsible for some of the best-loved films in Japan – and the world. Miyazaki designed this museum himself, and it's redolent of the dreamy, vaguely steampunk atmosphere that makes his animations so enchanting.

The building itself looks like an illustration from a European fairy tale. Inside, there is an imagined workshop filled with the kinds of books and artworks that inspired the creator, as well as vintage machines from animation's history.

This museum rewards curiosity and exploration; peer through a small window, for example, and you'll see little soot sprites (as seen in *Spirited Away;* 2001). A spiral staircase leads to a purposefully overgrown rooftop terrace with a 5m-tall statue of the

Great For...

☑ Don't Miss

The original animated shorts, which can only be seen here.

Robot Soldier from *Laputa* (Castle in the Sky; 1986)

COWARDLION/SHUTTERSTOCK © ROBOT SOLDIER © MUSEO D'ARTE GHIBLI

ℹ Need to Know

ジブリ美術館; www.ghibli-museum.jp; 1-1-83 Shimo-Renjaku, Mitaka-shi; adult ¥1000, child ¥100-700; ⏱10am-6pm Wed-Mon; 🚉JR Chūō-Sōbu line to Mitaka, south exit

✕ Take a Break

The museum has its own restaurant, but it's routinely packed. Head to Inokashira-kōen and Kichijōji for better options.

> **★ Top Tip**
>
> Shuttle buses (return/one way ¥320/210; every 20 minutes) depart for the museum from bus stop no 9 outside the south exit of Mitaka Station.

Robot Soldier from *Laputa* (*Castle in the Sky;* 1986). A highlight for children (sorry grown-ups!) is a giant, plush replica of the cat bus from the classic *My Neighbor Totoro* (1988) that kids can climb on.

Inside the museum, Saturn Theatre shows Ghibli short animations (you'll get a ticket for this when you enter). The film lineup changes regularly to keep fans coming back.

Getting Tickets

Tickets can be purchased up to four months in advance from overseas travel agents or up to one month in advance through the convenience store Lawson's online ticket portal. Both options are explained in detail on the website. For July and August visits especially, we recommend buying tickets as soon as you can

from an agent as they will definitely sell out early. Tickets are nontransferable; you may be asked to show an ID.

Inokashira-kōen

The Ghibli Museum is on the western edge of Inokashira-kōen, one of Tokyo's best parks. You can walk through the park to or from the museum in about 30 minutes, using Kichijōji Station (one stop before Mitaka on the JR Sōbu-Chūō line). Inokashira-kōen has a big pond flanked by woodsy strolling paths. Don't miss the shrine here to the goddess Benzaiten, one of Japan's eight lucky gods. There are a few cafes and restaurants in the park, too.

Universe of Water Particles on a Rock Where People Gather

teamLab Borderless

Opened in 2018, digital art collective teamLab created 60 installations for this museum that blurs the boundary between art and the viewer: many works are interactive. Not sure how? That's the point – approach the installations, move and touch them (or just stand still) and see how they react. There is no suggested route; teamLab Borderless is all about exploration.

Great For...

ℹ️ Need to Know

☎03-6406-3949; https://borderless. teamlab.art; 1-3-8 Aomi, Kōtō-ku; adult/child ¥3200/1000; ⏰10am-7pm Mon-Thu & Sun, to 9pm Fri & Sat, closed 2nd & 4th Tue; 👶; 🚃Yurikamome line to Aomi

★ **Top Tip**

Buy tickets in advance online, as they often sell out.

The Crystal World

Each room here feels like a discreet world – and wandering through the museum feels a bit like being inside a fantasy role-playing game. Inside the maze-like Crystal World, strands of shimmering light extend from floor to ceiling like disco stalagmites. Some of the installations (like this one) have mirrored floors; for this reason we recommend wearing trousers. Trainers are a good idea, too.

Forest of Lamps

Many of the artworks here are optimised for photography, none more so than the magical Forest of Lamps. Approach one of the Venetian glass lamps and watch it bloom into colour, setting off a chain reaction. Only a limited number of people are allowed in for a few minutes at a time. As this is among the most popular installations, you'll likely have to queue for it.

Athletics Forest

The collection of installations on the 2nd floor is designed with kids in mind – but grown-ups can join in, too. Jump up and down on a bouncy plain and see your energy transformed into expanding stars. Add colour to a drawing of an animal or insect and watch as it is born into an animated creature – then follow it on its course along the crags and divots of this playful indoor landscape.

There are no minimum age or height requirements to enter teamLab Borderless; however, keep in mind the museum is dark and often crowded. Prams must be parked at the entrance.

Weightless Forest of Resonating Life

En Teahouse

Stop for a cup of tea (¥500) at this digitally enhanced teahouse and see flowers come to life in your teacup; the petals blow away in the breeze when you've finished. And while you're here, don't miss the digital calligraphy installation of an *ensō,* a circle drawn in one stroke and a classic symbol of Zen Buddhism.

What's Nearby?

Unicorn Gundam   Statue

(ユニコーンガンダム; 1-1-10 Aomi, Kōtō-ku; 🚉Yurikamome line to Daiba, south exit) This is truly an only-in-Tokyo sight: a 19.7m-tall model of an RX-0 Unicorn Gundam from the iconic Mobile Suit Gundam anime franchise. It undergoes a transformation four times a day (at 11am, 1pm, 3pm and 5pm) into 'destroy mode'; light shows take place on the half-hour between 7pm and 9.30pm. The statue is in front of the Diver City shopping mall.

Odaiba Kaihin-kōen   Park

(お台場海浜公園, Odaiba Marine Park; www.tptc.co.jp; 1-4-1 Daiba, Minato-ku; ⊘24hr; 🚉Yurikamome line to Odaiba Kaihin-kōen) There are good views of Tokyo from this park's promenades and elevated walkways – especially at night when old-fashioned *yakatabune* (low-slung wooden pleasure boats), decorated with lanterns, traverse the bay. Note that swimming here is not permitted.

National Museum of Emerging Science & Innovation (Miraikan)   Museum

(未来館; www.miraikan.jst.go.jp; 2-3-6 Aomi, Kōtō-ku; adult/child ¥620/210; ⊘10am-5pm Wed-Mon; 🚉Yurikamome line to Telecom Center, north exit) *Miraikan* means 'hall of the future', and the hands-on exhibits here present the science and technology that will possibly shape the years to come. Don't miss the demonstrations of humanoid robot ASIMO (11am, 1pm, 2pm and 4pm) and the lifelike android Otonaroid (demonstration 11.30am; interactive experience 3pm to 5pm). The Gaia dome theatre/planetarium (adult/child ¥300/100) has an English audio option and is popular; book online one week in advance. A multilingual smartphone app turns your visit into a game.

☑ **Don't Miss**

Download the teamLab app ahead of time and look for more ways to interact with the installations.

TEAMLAB BORDERLESS, ODAIBA, TOKYO ©

✗ **Take a Break**

Stop for lunch at one of the restaurants in nearby Toyosu Market (p85) on your way here.

Onsen

Don't be shy! Many Japanese would argue that you couldn't possibly understand their culture without taking a dip in an onsen (natural hot-spring bath). The blissful relaxation that follows can turn a sceptic into a convert.

Don't let Tokyo's slick surface and countless diversions fool you; underneath the city it's pure, bubbling primordial pleasure. In the city, onsen can be found in elaborate day spas or humble public bathhouses (called *sentō*).

Bathing Basics

First of all, relax: really. All you need to know to avoid causing alarm is to wash yourself before getting into the bath. But yes, you do need to get naked. Baths and changing rooms are gender segregated, though some day spas have communal areas where guests wear bathing suits or pyjamas (for saunas).

Upon entering a spa or bathhouse, the first thing you'll encounter is a row of lockers for your shoes. At the front desk you'll either pay your admission up front (always

---

Great For...

☑ **Don't Miss**

A soak in a *rotemburo* (outdoor bath).

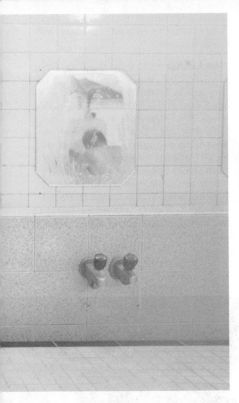

ⓘ Need to Know

Bathhouses can be identified by *noren* (half-length curtains over the doorway), printed with the hiragana for hot water, ゆ (yu), or sometimes the kanji, 湯.

✕ Take a Break

Beer is considered the ultimate after-bath indulgence; many bathhouses sell it.

★ Top Tip

Know your kanji: 女 means women and 男 means men.

That little towel performs a variety of functions: you can use it to wash (but make sure to give it a good rinse afterwards) or to cover yourself as you walk around. It is not supposed to touch the water though, so leave it on the side of the bath or – as the locals do – folded on top of your head.

In the baths, keep splashing to a minimum and your head above the water (and your heart above water if you're prone to dizziness). Before heading back to the changing room, wipe yourself down with the towel to avoid dripping on the floor.

the case at *sentō*) or be given a wristband (often the case at spas). The wristband can be used to open and close your locker in the changing room and also to charge any food, drinks or additional services to your tab, which you'll settle upon checking out. Some places may keep your shoe locker key at the front desk as a deposit.

Next, head to the correct changing room. Take everything off here, storing your clothes and belongings in the lockers or baskets provided. If there are no lockers, you can ask to leave valuables at the front desk.

Enter the bathing room with only a small towel. Park yourself on a stool in front of one of the taps and give yourself a thorough wash. Make sure you rinse off all the suds. When you're done, it's polite to rinse off the stool for the next person.

Day Spas

Day spas offer a huge variety of baths and saunas, often including *rotemburo* (outdoor baths) and *ganbanyoku* (heated stone saunas). They also usually offer massages, facials and body scrubs. It's entirely possible to spend the better part of a day in one. Those in central Tokyo are used to foreign visitors and usually have dos and don'ts posted in multiple languages. Towels and robes or pyjamas are provided and the washing and changing rooms have toiletries, disposable razors and combs, hair dryers and anything else you might need.

Ōedo Onsen Monogatari   Onsen

(大江戸温泉物語; ☏03-5500-1126; www.ooedoonsen.jp; 2-6-3 Aomi, Kōtō-ku; adult/child ¥2720/1058, surcharge Sat & Sun ¥220;

⊙11am-9am, last entry 7am; 🚃Yurikamome line to Telecom Center, south exit or Rinkai line to Tokyo Teleport, exit B with free shuttle bus) Come experience the truly Japanese phenomenon that is an amusement park centred on bathing. There are multiple tubs to choose from, filled with real hot-spring water (pumped from 1400m below Tokyo Bay), and a lantern-lit re-creation of an old Tokyo downtown area. Come after 6pm for a ¥540 discount. Visitors with tattoos will be denied admission.

There's a huge variety of baths here, including jet baths, pools of natural rock and, on the ladies' side, personal bucket-shaped baths made of cedar. Upon entering, visitors change their clothes for a choice of colourful *yukata* (light cotton kimonos) to wear while they stroll around the complex, which is a lantern-lit re-creation of an old Tokyo downtown area, with food stalls and carnival games.

Spa LaQua   Onsen

(スパ ラクーア; Map p254; ☎03-5800-9999; www.laqua.jp; 5th-9th fl, Tokyo Dome City, 1-1-1 Kasuga, Bunkyō-ku; weekday/weekend ¥2850/3174; ⊙11am-9am; Ⓢ Marunouchi line to Kōrakuen, exit 2) One of Tokyo's few true onsen, this chic spa complex, renovated in 2017, relies on natural hot-spring water from 1700m below ground. There are indoor and outdoor baths, saunas and a bunch of add-on options, such as *akasuri* (Korean-style whole-body exfoliation). It's a fascinating introduction to Japanese health and beauty rituals.

Ōedo Onsen Monogatari (p83)

Thermae-yu
Onsen

(テルマー湯; Map p253; ☑03-5285-1726; www.thermae-yu.jp; 1-1-2 Kabukichō, Shinjuku-ku; weekdays/weekends & holidays ¥2365/2690; ☺11am-9am; ☒JR Yamanote line to Shinjuku, east exit) The best (and most literal) example to date that red-light district Kabukichō is cleaning up its act: this sparkling-clean onsen (hot springs) complex. The tubs, which include several indoor and outdoor ones (sex-segregated), are filled with honest-to-goodness natural hot-spring water. There are several saunas, including a hot-stone sauna (*ganbanyoku*; ¥810 extra). Towels included. No tattoos allowed.

> ★ **Top Tip**
>
> See Tokyo Sentō (www.1010.or.jp/english) for info on local bathhouses.

Sentō

Sentō, mostly frequented by neighbourhood regulars, can be a little intimidating, but also a great local experience. Towels and toiletries (besides the communal bar of soap) aren't provided, though are available to purchase for a small fee.

Rokuryu Kōsen
Bathhouse

(六龍鉱泉; Map p254; ☑03-3821-3826; 3-4-20 Ikenohata, Taitō-ku; ¥460; ☺3.30-11pm Tue-Sun; ⑤Chiyoda line to Nezu, exit 2) Dating from 1931, this gem of a neighbourhood *sentō*, has a beautiful mural of the wooden arched bridge Kintai-kyo in Iwasaki on the bathhouse wall. The amber-hued water is packed with minerals that are reputed to be excellent for your skin, if you can stand the water temperature – a scalding-hot 45°C in the cooler of the two pools!

Jakotsu-yu
Bathhouse

(蛇骨湯; Map p254; ☑03-3841-8645; www.jakotsuyu.co.jp; 1-11-11 Asakusa, Taitō-ku; adult/child ¥460/180; ☺1pm-midnight Wed-Mon; ⑤Ginza line to Tawaramachi, exit 3) Unlike most *sentō*, the tubs here are filled with pure hot-spring water, naturally the colour of weak tea. Another treat is the lovely, lantern-lit, rock-framed *rotemburo* (outdoor bath). Jakotsu-yu is a welcoming place; it has English signage and doesn't have a policy against tattoos.

ANTHONY PLUMMER/LONELY PLANET ©

> ❶ **Need to Know**
>
> Day spas usually refuse entry to customers with tattoos because of the association of tattoos with the *yakuza* (Japanese mafia); *sentō* generally have no such restrictions.

豊洲市場
TOYOSU MARKET

Toyosu Market

In 2018 Tokyo's central wholesale market moved from its iconic Tsukiji location to this new facility in Toyosu. It's a structure dreamed up by bureaucrats; access is limited, but smoother than it was at Tsukiji.

The market is divided into three blocks (5, 6 and 7), all connected via promenades that also run directly to the train station, and is well signposted in English.

Tuna Auction

The highlight for many visitors is the tuna auction, where the *naka-oroshi* (intermediate wholesalers) gamble on bluefin tuna brought in from all over the world. The auction starts around 5am and finishes by 6.30am. A limited number of visitors can observe the auction up close from a mezzanine-level viewing platform that is only partially shielded by glass; for details see the market website. Otherwise anyone can watch it from the glassed-in corridors on the 2nd floor of block 7.

Great For...

☑ **Don't Miss**

Getting up early to see the tuna auction, followed by a decadent sushi breakfast at one of the restaurants in the market.

❶ Need to Know

豊洲市場, Toyosu Shijō; www.shijou.metro.
tokyo.jp; 6-chōme Toyosu, Kōtō-ku; ⊙5am-
5pm Mon-Sat, closed some Wed; 🚃Yurika-
mome line to Shijō-mae

★ Local Knowledge

Toyosu Market replaced the wholesale
market at Tsukiji. Before Tsukiji, Tokyo's
official market was in Nihombashi, on
the banks of the river.

★ Top Tip

See the market website for opening
days and the latest info on how to visit
the tuna auction.

Market Restaurants

Sushi Dai   Sushi ¥¥

(寿司大; 🕿03-6633-0042; 3rd fl, Bldg 6, Toyosu
Market, 6-5-1 Toyosu, Kōtō-ku; course meal
¥4500; ⊙5.30am-1pm, closed Sun & market holidays; ⊖🔟🚶; 🚃Yurikamome line to Shijō-mae)
There is no better-value sushi in Tokyo than
the *omakase* (chef's choice) course here.
The menu changes daily (and sometimes
hourly), but you're guaranteed to get 10
pieces of *nigiri* (hand-pressed) sushi made
from seafood picked up from the fish
market downstairs, prepared one at a time,
pre-seasoned to perfection (and with zero
boring fillers). Expect to queue.

Daiwa Sushi   Sushi ¥¥

(大和寿司; 🕿03-6633-0220; 1st fl, Bldg 5,
Toyosu Market, 6-3-1 Toyosu, Kōtō-ku; course meal
from ¥4320; ⊙5.30am-1pm, closed Sun & market

holidays; ⊖; 🚃Yurikamome line to Shijō-mae)
One of Tsukiji's most famous sushi restaurants has made the move to the new Toyosu
Market. The course meal includes seven
pieces of *nigiri* sushi and one roll – all made
with premium seafood. If you're still hungry
you can order more sushi à la carte (¥300
to ¥800 per piece). Go early (before 9am),
or there might be a queue.

Mosuke Dango   Sweets ¥

(茂助だんご; 🕿03-6633-0873; 2nd fl, Bldg 7,
Toyosu Market, 6-6-1 Toyosu, Kōtō-ku; per piece
from ¥170; ⊙5.30am-1pm, closed Sun & market
holidays; 🍴🔟; 🚃Yurikamome line to Shijō-mae)
The original Mosuke, a street vendor, began
making *dango* (soft rice-flour balls) in 1898,
back when the fish market was in Nihombashi. Now on its third market, Mosuke
Dango still serves its famous *shōyu dango*
(with soy-sauce glaze) and *tsubuan dango*
(made from chunky *azuki*-bean paste),
but with the addition of a cafe eat-in space
(*matcha* ¥500).

Walking Tour: Yanaka

Yanaka, long beloved by local artists, is a charming part of Tokyo. There are lots of temples and old wooden buildings, creating a sense that time stopped several decades ago.

Start Tokyo National Museum
Distance 3km
Duration Two hours

NISHI-NIPPORI

FINISH
7 Yanaka Ginza

Classic Photo Snap Yanaka Ginza from the Yūyake Dandan 'Sunset Stairs'.

7 The classic mid-20th-century shopping street, **Yanaka Ginza** (p55), has food vendors and craft stores.

2 See the works of long-time Yanaka resident and painter Allan West at his studio, **Art Sanctuary Allan West** (p165)

3 This ancient, thick-trunked **Himalayan cedar tree** is a local landmark.

4 At **Enju-ji** (1-7-36 Yanaka, Taitō-ku; http://nichika-do.jp; ☺10am-4pm; Ⓢ Chiyoda line to Nezu, exit 1) Nichika-sama, the 'god of strong legs', is enshrined; the temple is popular with runners.

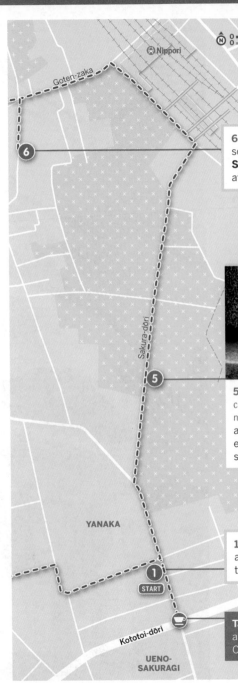

Nippori

Goten-zaka

0 200 m
0 0.1 miles

6 Once the home studio of a sculptor, the **Asakura Museum of Sculpture, Taitō** (p55) is now an attractive museum.

Sakura-dōri

5 Yanaka-reien (www.yanakaginza. com; JR Yamanote line to Nippori, north exit) is one of Tokyo's most atmospheric and prestigious cemeteries (also a favourite sunning spot of Yanaka's many stray cats).

YANAKA

1 SCAI the Bathhouse (p55) is a classic old public bathhouse turned contemporary art gallery.

START

Take a Break There's good coffee and a vintage vibe at Kayaba Coffee (p145).

Kototoi-dōri

UENO-SAKURAGI

Kabukiza Theatre

Dramatic, intensely visual kabuki is Japan's most recognised art form. Kabuki developed in the Edo period (1603–1868), and an afternoon at the theatre has been a favourite local pastime ever since. Descendants of the great actors of the day still appear on Tokyo stages, drawing devoted fans. Established in 1889 (and rebuilt in 2013), Kabukiza is Tokyo's dedicated kabuki theatre.

Great For...

❶ Need to Know

歌舞伎座; Map p250; ☎03-3545-6800; www.kabukiweb.net; 4-12-15 Ginza, Chūō-ku; tickets ¥4000-20,000, single-act tickets ¥800-2000; 🚇Hibiya line to Higashi-Ginza, exit 3

☑ **Don't Miss**

Captioning guides, which provide translations of the dialogue as well as points for understanding the significance of key scenes, are available for rent (full program/single act ¥1000/¥500; ID required as deposit).

Understand Kabuki

Kabuki actually got its start in Kyoto: around the year 1600, a charismatic shrine priestess and her entourage began publicly performing a new (and a bit bawdy) style of dance. People dubbed it 'kabuki', a slang expression that meant 'cool' or 'in vogue' at the time. It was also a gateway to prostitution, which eventually led the shogunate to ban the female performers. Adolescent men took their place, though that didn't solve the problem. Finally, in 1653, the authorities mandated that only adult men with shorn forelocks could perform kabuki, which gave rise to one of kabuki's most fascinating elements, the *onnagata* (actors who specialise in portraying women).

But it was in the urbane circles of Edo that kabuki evolved into what we know today. Those exaggerated moves? They're not-so-subtle references to the off-duty samurai or the dandyish merchant swaggering around the pleasure quarters – both characters lifted from everyday life. Kabuki deals in archetypes; the make-up signals whether a character is good or evil, noble or ruled by passion. But it is not simplistic: though it gets lost in translation (even for modern Japanese) many of the plays, and especially the confrontations, are meant to be funny.

More than by plot, however, kabuki is driven by its actors, who train for the profession from childhood. In its heyday, kabuki actors outshone even those swaggering samurai and merchants; they were the ultimate influencers. Sons (biological or adopted) follow their fathers into a *yago* (kabuki acting house); the leading families of modern kabuki (such as Bandō and Ichikawa) go back many generations.

Kabuki has been likened to a moving woodblock print, and when the actors pause in dramatic poses – called *mie* – the whole stage really does look fit to be framed. At such pivotal moments enthusiastic fans shout out the actor's *yago*.

The kabuki stage employs a number of devices, such as the *hanamichi* (the walkway that extends into the audience), which is used for dramatic entrances and exits. Naturally the best seats are those that line the *hanamichi*.

Performances

Twice-daily performances are held 25 days out of the month at Kabukiza, with a new lineup of acts each month. A full kabuki performance comprises three or four acts – usually from different plays – over an

Performance schedule

✕ **Take a Break**

The tea salon Jugetsudo (p139) offers a view of Kabukiza's roof garden.

afternoon or an evening (typically 11am to 3.30pm or 4.30pm to 9pm).

There are intervals of 15 to 30 minutes between acts; during the longest one, it is tradition to eat a *bentō* (boxed meal). Concession stands selling *bentō* (around ¥1000), snacks and drinks can be found inside the theatre or in the basement entrance connected to the subway. As the break isn't that long, it's best to buy something before the show. It's okay to eat at your seat during intermissions.

If four-plus hours sounds too long, 90 sitting and 60 standing *makumi* (single act tickets; ¥500 to ¥1500, depending on the play) are sold on the day for each act. You'll be at the back of the auditorium, but the views are still good.

Getting Tickets

Tickets go on sale from the 12th day of the preceding month and can be purchased online from the Kabukiza website. You'll need to have the same credit card with you to pick up tickets from the vending machines in front of the theatre and in the basement passage from the subway station. Single act ticket sales began an hour or two before each act; see the website for exact times (and other details). Some acts tend to be more popular than others, perhaps featuring a famous actor in a famous role, and may sell out quickly.

Tsurugaoka Hachiman-gū

KORKUSUNG/SHUTTERSTOCK ©

Day Trip: Kamakura

An ancient feudal capital and centre of Zen Buddhism, seaside Kamakura is packed with temples, and boasts the Daibutsu (Big Buddha) statue; it also has a laid-back, earthy vibe and great restaurants.

Great For...

☑ Don't Miss

See Kamakura's signature sight, the Daibutsu (p94). On a sunny day there's a great hike here (p96).

Sights

You can walk to most temples and shrines from Kamakura or Kita-Kamakura stations; coming from Tokyo, Kita-Kamakura is one stop before Kamakura. Sites in the west, such as the Daibutsu, can be reached via the Enoden Enoshima line from Kamakura Station to Hase (¥190).

Daibutsu   Monument

(大仏; ☎0467-22-0703; www.kotoku-in.jp; Kōtoku-in, 4-2-28 Hase; adult/child ¥200/150; ◷8am-5.30pm Apr-Sep, to 5pm Oct-Nov) Kamakura's most iconic sight, an 11.4m bronze statue of Amida Buddha (*Amitābha* in Sanskrit), is in Kōtoku-in, a Jōdo sect temple. Completed in 1252, it's said to have been inspired by Yoritomo's visit to Nara (where Japan's biggest Daibutsu holds court) after the Minamoto clan's

Daibutsu

M17/SHUTTERSTOCK ©

❶ Need to Know

Kamakura is about one by hour by train via the JR Yokosuka line from Tokyo Station or the Shōnan Shinjuku line from Shinjuku or Shibuya.

✕ Take a Break

Kamakura has a wide range of touristy restaurants and cafes, including plenty of options for vegetarians.

★ Top Tip

Visit the **Tourist Information Center** (鎌倉市観光総合案内所; ☎0467-22-3350; www.kamakura-info.jp; 1-1-1 Komachi; ☾9am-5pm), just outside the east exit of Kamakura Station. Staff usually speak English.

victory over the Taira clan. Once housed in a huge hall, today the statue sits in the open, the hall having been washed away by a tsunami in 1498.

Kenchō-ji　　　　Buddhist Temple

(建長寺; www.kenchoji.com; 8 Yamanouchi; adult/child ¥300/100; ☾8.30am-4.30pm) Established in 1253, Japan's oldest Zen monastery is still active today. The central Butsuden (Buddha Hall) was brought piece by piece from Tokyo in 1647. Its Jizō Bosatsu statue, unusual for a Zen temple, reflects the valley's ancient function as an execution ground – Jizō consoles lost souls. Other highlights include a bell cast in 1253 and a juniper grove, believed to have sprouted from seeds brought from China by Kenchō-ji's founder some seven centuries ago.

Tsurugaoka Hachiman-gū　　　Shinto Shrine

(鶴岡八幡宮; ☎0467-22-0315; www.tsurugaoka-hachimangu.jp; 2-1-31 Yukinoshita; ☾5am-8.30pm Apr-Sep, from 6am Oct-Mar) **FREE** Kamakura's most important shrine is, naturally, dedicated to Hachiman, the god of war. Minamoto no Yoritomo himself ordered its construction in 1191 and designed the pine-flanked central promenade that leads from the shrine to the coast. The sprawling grounds are ripe with historical symbolism: the Gempei Pond, bisected by bridges, is said to depict the rift between the Minamoto (Genji) and Taira (Heike) clans.

Hase-dera　　　　Buddhist Temple

(長谷寺; Hase Kannon; ☎0467-22-6300; www.hasedera.jp; 3-11-2 Hase; adult/child ¥300/100; ☾8am-5pm Mar-Sep, to 4.30pm Oct-Feb) The focal point of this Jōdo sect temple, one of the most popular in the Kantō region, is a 9m-high carved wooden *jūichimen* (11-faced) Kannon statue. Kannon (*avalokiteshvara* in Sanskrit) is the Bodhisattva of infinite compassion and, along with Jizō, is one of Japan's most popular Buddhist deities. The temple is about a 10-minute walk from the Daibutsu and dates back to AD 736, when the statue is said to have washed up on the shore near Kamakura.

Engaku-ji   Buddhist Temple
(円覚寺; ☑0467-22-0478; www.engakuji.or.jp; 409 Yamanouchi; adult/child ¥300/100; ⊙8am-4.30pm Mar-Nov, to 4pm Dec-Feb) Engaku-ji is one of Kamakura's five major Rinzai Zen temples. It was founded in 1282 for Zen monks to pray for soldiers who lost their lives defending Japan against Kublai Khan. All of the temple structures have been rebuilt over the centuries; the Shariden, a Song-style reliquary, is the oldest, last rebuilt in the 16th century. At the top of the long flight of stairs is the Engaku-ji bell, the largest bell in Kamakura, cast in 1301.

Activities

The **Daibutsu Hiking Course** is a 3km wooded trail connecting Kita-Kamakura with the Daibutsu (p94) in Hase (allow about 1½ hours). It passes several small, quiet temples and shrines.

The path begins at the steps just up the lane from pretty **Jōchi-ji** (浄智寺; 1402 Yamanouchi; adult/child ¥200/100; ⊙9am-4.30pm) in Kita-Kamakura. Near the shrine **Zeniarai-benten** (銭洗弁天; 2-25-16 Sasuke; ⊙8am-4.30pm) FREE a cavelike entrance leads to a clearing where visitors come to

Jizō statues (p95)

bathe their money in natural springs, with the hope of bringing financial success.

From here, continue down the paved road, turn right at the first intersection, walk along a path lined with cryptomeria and ascend through a succession of *torii* (shrine gates). You'll reach **Sasuke-inari-jinja** (佐助稲荷神社; 2-22-10 Sasuke; ⊘24hr) **FREE**, a hilltop enclave strewn with *kitsune*

(fox totems), before meeting up with the Daibutsu path once again. To hike in the opposite direction, follow the road beyond Daibutsu; the trail entrance is on the right, just before a tunnel.

Eating & Drinking

Matsubara-an   Soba ¥¥

(松原庵; ☑0467-61-3838; www.matsubara-an. com/shops/kamakura.php; 4-10-3 Yuiga-hama; mains ¥960-1850, set meals from ¥3200; ⊘11am-10pm; ◉) Dinner reservations are recommended for this upscale soba restaurant in a lovely old house. Try the *goma seiro soba* (al dente noodles served cold with sesame dipping sauce). Dine alfresco or indoors where you can watch noodles being handmade. From Yuiga-hama Station (Enoden Enoshima line) head towards the beach and then take the first right. Look for the blue sign.

Magokoro   Fusion ¥¥

(麻心; ☑0467-38-7355; www.magokoroworld.jp; 2nd fl, 2-8-11 Hase; meals ¥800-1400; ⊘11.30am-8pm Tue-Sun; 🛜📶◉) ✒ Boho beachfront spot mixing ocean views with an organic hemp-based menu, including vegetarian hemp taco rice, several vegan options, macrobiotic cakes and hemp beer (no, it doesn't get you high). From Hase Station, walk to the beach, then turn left on the coastal road.

Magnetico   Bar

(☑467-33-5992; 4-1-19 Yukinoshita; ⊘11.30am-3pm & 5.30-10pm Mon, Tue, Thu & Fri, 11.30am-11pm Sat & Sun; 🛜◉) Run by a couple of relaxed reggae dudes, this louche hang-out has Japanese craft beers on tap, island rhythms on the stereo and a menu of tacos, fried chicken and other comfort food. It's a five-minute walk east from the main entrance of Tsurugaoka Hachiman-gū, Kamakura's main shrine.

> ★ **Local Knowledge**
>
> In summer, head to Kamakura's beach, Yuigahama, where seasonal shacks set up on the sand sell food and drink.

Imperial Palace East Garden (p100)

COLOBUSYETI/GETTY IMAGES ©

Imperial Palace

Take a tour of the leafy grounds of the imperial family's residence, or just stroll along the ancient moat and climb an old castle keep in the garden.

In its heyday, Edo-jō was the largest fortress in the world. When the shogunate fell and the emperor moved to Tokyo, the castle became the imperial residence – Kōkyo. WWII air raids levelled most of the palace and the current ferro-concrete buildings were completed in the 1960s. The moats and imposing stone walls visible around the perimeter of the palace grounds belonged to the original castle.

Surrounding the palace is Kōkyo-gaien, a 115-hectare national garden, which includes public green spaces and cultural facilities; unlike the palace compound, it is open to the public with no restrictions.

Palace Tours

The only way to see the palace's inner compound is as part of an official tour organised by the Imperial Household

Great For...

☑ **Don't Miss**

The view of the palace bridges and watchtower from Kōkyo-gaien Plaza.

Statue of the samurai Kusunoki Masashige

AON_SKYNOTLMIT/SHUTTERSTOCK ©

Fukiage Imperial Gardens

Area not open to public.

Imperial Palace 🚇

Ōtemachi Ⓢ

Uchibori-dōri

Hibiya-dōri

Tokyo Ⓢ

Kōkyo-gaien Plaza

Sakuradamon Ⓢ

Ⓢ

Nijūbashimae Ⓢ

❶ Need to Know

皇居, Kōkyo; Map p250; ☎03-5223-8071; http://sankan.kunaicho.go.jp; 1 Chiyoda, Chiyoda-ku; ⊙tours usually 10am & 1.30pm Tue-Sat; ⑤Chiyoda line to Ōtemachi, exits C13b & C10; **FREE**

✕ Take a Break

Wind down the day with a cocktail at Peter: the Bar (p182), which is adjacent to Kōkyo-gaien Plaza.

★ Top Tip

The Imperial Palace East Garden is closed on Mondays and Fridays, so don't come on those days if that's the part you wish to see.

Agency. Tours (lasting around 1¼ hours) run at 10am and 1.30pm usually on Tuesday through to Saturday, but not on public holidays or afternoons from late July through to the end of August. They're also not held at all from 28 December to 4 January or when Imperial Court functions are scheduled.

Arrive no later than 10 minutes before the scheduled departure time at **Kikyō-mon** (桔梗門; Map p250; ⊙tour bookings 8.45am-noon & 1-5pm), the starting and ending point. You will need to show your passport.

Reservations are taken – via the website, phone or by post – up to one month in advance (and no later than four days in advance via the website). Alternatively, go to the office at Kikyō-mon from 8.30am (for the morning tour) or noon (for the

afternoon tour) – if there is space available you'll be able to register.

The tour will give you a glimpse of the outside of the Kyūden, the building that contains the throne room, Matsu-no-Ma (Pine Chamber), and a few other state-houses. Unfortunately, the tour doesn't enter any of the palace buildings.

You'll also have the opportunity for a close-up view of two watch towers, **Fujimi-yagura** and **Fushimi-yagura** (伏見櫓; Map p250; 1-1 Chiyoda, Chiyoda-ku; ⑤Hibiya line to Hibiya, exit B6), that date to the days of Edo-jō. Fushimi-yagura, constructed in 1559, actually predates Edo-jō; it was dismantled and reassembled from the grounds of Kyoto's long-destroyed Fushimi Castle by the third Tokugawa shogun.

Explanations on palace tours are given only in Japanese; download the free app (www.kunaicho.go.jp/e-event/app.html) for explanations in English, Chinese, Korean, French or Spanish.

Imperial Palace East Garden

Once part of the original castle compound, the **Imperial Palace East Garden** (東御苑; Kōkyo Higashi-gyoen; Map p250; ⏰9am-4pm Nov-Feb, to 4.30pm Mar–mid-Apr, Sep & Oct, to 5pm mid-Apr–Aug, closed Mon & Fri year-round) `FREE` is now a public garden. Here you can get up-close views of the massive stones used to build the castle walls, and even climb the ruins of one of the keeps, off the upper lawn. The large lawn is where the castle's Honmaru (main keep) was once located. Don't miss the Ninomaru Grove, a woodland area that is one of the prettiest parts of the garden, with a pond and the elegant teahouse, Suwa-no-chaya.

Entry is free, but the number of visitors at any one time is limited, so it never feels crowded. There are three gates: most people enter through Ōte-mon, the closest gate to Tokyo Station.

Free two-hour guided walking tours of the East Garden are offered on Wednesday, Saturday and Sunday; meet at the JNTO Tourist Information Center (p233) before 1pm.

Kōkyo-gaien Plaza

Kōkyo-gaien Plaza (皇居外苑広場, Kōkyo-gaien Hiroba; Map p250; www.env.go.jp/garden/kokyogaien; Ⓢ Hibiya line to Hibiya, exit B6) is the grassy expanse southeast of the palace compound, planted with roughly 2000, immaculately maintained Japanese black pine trees. It is the closest you can get to the actual palace without taking the palace tour. There is a famous view from here, of two of the palace bridges, stone **Megane-bashi** (眼鏡橋; Map p250; Ⓢ Hibiya line to Hibiya, exit B6) and iron **Nijū-bashi** (二重橋; Map p250;

[S]Hibiya line to Hibiya, exit B6), with Fushimi-yagura (p99) rising behind them. Megane-bashi – 'Eyeglass Bridge' – is so nicknamed because its support arches reflected in the water create the appearance of spectacles; both bridges date to the 1880s.

What's Nearby?

The National Museum of Modern Art (MOMAT) and Crafts Gallery are inside Kitanomaru-kōen, part of Kōkyo-gaien.

National Museum of Modern Art (MOMAT)   Museum
(国立近代美術館, Kokuritsu Kindai Bijutsukan; Map p250; ☎03-5777-8600; www.momat.go.jp;

GO LAIZOLA/GETTY IMAGES ©

☑ **Don't Miss**

MOMAT's 'Room with a View', which overlooks the Imperial Palace East Garden.

3-1 Kitanomaru-kōen, Chiyoda-ku; adult/child ¥500/free, 1st Sun of month free; ⊙10am-5pm Tue-Thu & Sun, to 8pm Fri & Sat; [S]Tōzai line to Takebashi, exit 1b) Regularly changing displays from the museum's superb collection of more than 12,000 works, by both local and international artists, are shown over floors 2 to 4; special exhibitions are mounted on the ground floor. All pieces date from the Meiji period onward and impart a sense of how modern Japan has developed through portraits, photography, contemporary sculptures and video works. The museum closes in between exhibitions, so first check the schedule online.

Crafts Gallery   Museum
(東京国立近代美術館　工芸館; Map p250; www.momat.go.jp; 1 Kitanomaru-kōen, Chiyoda-ku; adult/child ¥250/free, 1st Sun of month free; ⊙10am-5pm Tue-Sun; [S]Tōzai line to Takebashi, exit 1b) Housed in a vintage red-brick building, this annex of MOMAT stages excellent changing exhibitions of *mingei* (folk crafts): ceramics, lacquerware, bamboo, textiles, dolls and much more. Some exhibits feature works by contemporary artisans, including some by Japan's officially designated 'living national treasures'.

Intermediatheque   Museum
(インターメディアテク; Map p250; ☎03-5777-8600; www.intermediatheque.jp; 2nd & 3rd fl, JP Tower, 2-7-2 Marunouchi, Chiyoda-ku; ⊙11am-6pm, to 8pm Fri & Sat, usually closed Sun & Mon; [R]JR Yamanote line to Tokyo, Marunouchi exit) **FREE** Dedicated to interdisciplinary experimentation, Intermediatheque cherry-picks from the vast collection of the University of Tokyo (Tōdai) to craft a fascinating, contemporary museum experience. Go from viewing the best ornithological taxidermy collection in Japan to a giant pop art print or the beautifully encased skeleton of a dinosaur. A handsome Tōdai lecture hall is reconstituted as a forum for events.

★ **Local Knowledge**

The 5km loop around the Imperial Palace's moats is a popular jogging course.

TAKASHI IMAGES/SHUTTERSTOCK ©

Rikugi-en

Considered by many to be Tokyo's most elegant garden, Rikugi-en was originally completed in 1702 at the behest of a feudal lord. It's hidden away in the city's sleepy north; it's a rarely crowded, blissful and timeless retreat.

Rikugi-en is a classic example of an Edo-era strolling garden, one of only three such gardens that remain in Tokyo. Strolling gardens are designed as a series of sensory encounters that unfold along a meandering path, usually around a central body of water. The encounters are typically visual, but they can be auditory, too – rushing water, for example.

Famous Views

The garden has 88 viewpoints that evoke scenes from poetry and legend or recreate (in miniature) famous vistas found in Japan and China. An example of the former is the bridge, Togetsukyō, created from two huge stone slabs, that references a poem about a crane flying over a moonlit field. Another is the craggy rock in the garden's pond, called Hōrai-jima, which represents

Great For...

☑ **Don't Miss**

Sipping tea while overlooking the garden's pond.

ⓘ Need to Know

六義園; ☏03-3941-2222; http://teien.
tokyo-park.or.jp/en/rikugien; 6-16-3
Hon-Komagome, Bunkyō-ku; adult/child/
senior ¥300/free/150; ⊙9am-5pm; ⓢNam-
boku line to Komagome, exit 2

✕ Take a Break

There's a teahouse and a snack stand
inside the park.

★ Top Tip

Pair a trip to Rikugi-en with one to the
Tokyo National Museum (p52); it's five
stops away on the JR Yamanote line.

the Taoist 'Isle of Immortals'. The hill,
Fujishiro-tōge, is named after a real one in
Wakayama Prefecture; climb to the top for
panoramic views over the garden.

Stone markers around the garden make
note of some other scenic viewpoints (even
the most erudite Japanese visitor wouldn't
get them all); some are signposted with
English explanations as well. Free, hour-
long guided tours in English are offered at
11am and 2pm on the 1st and 3rd Sunday of
the month.

Teahouses

Rikugi-en also has two vintage wooden
teahouses: Tsutsuji-chaya dates to the Meiji
period and is perfectly primed for viewing
the maples in autumn. Takimi-chaya is
perched on the edge of the stream where
you can enjoy the view of a mini waterfall

over rocks and giant koi (carp) swimming
in the water.

Fukiage-chaya is not an antique but
is attractive all the same – and it actually serves tea. Here you can sip *matcha*
(powdered green tea; ¥510) and enjoy a
seasonal *wagashi* (sweet) alfresco on the
edge of the pond.

Seasonal Blooms

The garden is most famous for its maple
leaves, which turn bright red around late
November and early December. During this
time, the park stays open until 9pm and
the trees are illuminated after sunset. In
early spring you can catch plum blossoms,
followed by the flowering of the magnificent
weeping cherry tree near the entrance. In
winter, see the pruned pine trees strung
with ropes to protect their branches from
snowfall.

National Art Center Tokyo (p107), designed by Kisho Kurokawa

Roppongi Art Triangle

The area nicknamed 'Roppongi Art Triangle' is anchored by three of Tokyo's leading art museums: Mori Art Museum, Suntory Museum of Art and the National Art Center Tokyo. Smaller art spaces and ambitious building projects exist in their midst.

Great For...

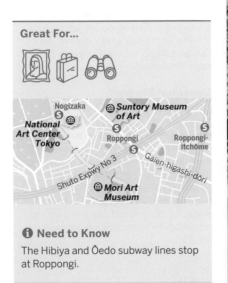

Nogizaka

Suntory Museum of Art

National Art Center Tokyo

Roppongi

Roppongi-itchōme

Gaien-higashi-dōri

Shuto Expwy No 3

Mori Art Museum

ℹ Need to Know

The Hibiya and Ōedo subway lines stop at Roppongi.

★ **Top Tip**

Save your ticket stub from any of the three major museums to get discounted admission at the other two.

Mori Art Museum

Mori Art Museum (森美術館; Map p252; www.mori.art.museum; 52nd fl, Mori Tower, Roppongi Hills, 6-10-1 Roppongi, Minato-ku; adult/child ¥1800/600; ☺10am-10pm Wed-Mon, to 5pm Tue, inside Sky Deck 10am-11pm; ⑤Hibiya line to Roppongi, exit 1) is Tokyo's leading space for contemporary art. It has no permanent exhibition; instead, large-scale, original shows introduce major local and global artists and movements. Past exhibitions have focused on the works of Chinese artist and dissident Ai Weiwei and native son Murakami Takashi. Unlike most museums, Mori Art Museum is open late – until 10pm daily except Tuesday.

The museum, which sits atop the 52nd and 53rd floors of Mori Tower, is part of the postmodern mega mall, Roppongi Hills.

Scattered around the mall are several pieces of public art, including one of Louise Bourgeois' giant Maman spider sculptures.

Suntory Museum of Art

The **Suntory Museum of Art** (サントリー美術館; Map p252; ☎03-3479-8600; www.suntory.com/sma; 4th fl, Tokyo Midtown, 9-7-4 Akasaka, Minato-ku; admission varies, child free; ☺10am-6pm Sun-Wed, to 8pm Fri & Sat; ⑤Ōedo line to Roppongi, exit 8) stages shows on both traditional Japanese arts – often involving a deep dive into a particular medium or era – and contemporary design. On a few Thursday afternoons a month it hosts tea ceremony demonstrations. The museum, designed by architect Kuma Kengō, is inside shopping and dining complex Tokyo Midtown (p160).

Port of Reflections (2014) by Leandro Erlich, Mori Art Museum

National Art Center Tokyo

Like the other two museums, **National Art Center Tokyo** (国立新美術館; Map p252; ☑03-5777-8600; www.nact.jp; 7-22-1 Roppongi, Minato-ku; admission varies; ◷10am-6pm Wed, Thu & Sun-Mon, to 8pm Fri & Sat; Ⓢ Chiyoda line to Nogizaka, exit 6) has no permanent collection. But it does have the country's largest exhibition space for visiting shows, which have included titans such as Renoir and Modigliani.

Apart from exhibitions, a visit here is recommended to admire the building's awesome undulating glass facade, the work of architect Kurokawa Kishō. There's

☑ Don't Miss

Admission to the Mori Art Museum is shared with the observatory Tokyo City View (p114).

COURTESY MORI ART MUSEUM, TOKYO ©

also a great gift shop, Souvenir from Tokyo (p159).

21_21 Design Sight

An exhibition and discussion space dedicated to all forms of design, **21_21 Design Sight** (21_21デザインサイト; Map p252; ☑03-3475-2121; www.2121designsight.jp; Tokyo Midtown, 9-7-6 Akasaka, Minato-ku; adult/child ¥1100/free; ◷11am-7pm Wed-Mon; Ⓢ Ōedo line to Roppongi, exit 8) acts as a beacon for local art enthusiasts, whether they be designers themselves or simply onlookers. The striking concrete and glass building, bursting out of the ground at sharp angles, was designed by Pritzker Prize–winning architect Tadao Ando.

Complex 665

Complex 665 (Map p252; 6-5-24 Roppongi, Minato-ku; ◷11am-7pm Tue-Sat; Ⓢ Hibiya line to Roppongi, exit 1) is the shared location of three leading commercial art galleries: Taka Ishii (www.takaishiigallery.com), ShugoArts (http://shugoarts.com) and Tomio Koyama Gallery (www.tomiokoyamagallery.com). The free shows cover a broad spectrum of Japanese contemporary works and are generally worth a look. Note that the galleries are closed in between exhibitions.

Design Hub

Also inside Tokyo Midtown, **Design Hub** (Map p252; ☑03-6743-3776; www.designhub.jp; 5th fl, Midtown Tower, 9-7-1 Akasaka, Minato-ku; ◷11am-8pm; Ⓢ Ōedo line to Roppongi, exit 8) FREE hosts interesting exhibitions on various themes usually involving graphic design. Some exhibitions tackle social issues, while others facilitate dialogue between disciplines.

✕ Take a Break

Bricolage Bread & Co (p137) is great for brunch or a light meal.

TODD FONG PHOTOGRAPHY/GETTY IMAGES ©

Tsukiji Market

The central wholesale market may no longer be here, but the warren of stalls that made up the former 'outer market' remain, retaining some of the atmosphere of old Tsukiji.

This lively and colourful market is a one-stop shop for everything you need to prepare and serve a great Japanese meal. It grew up organically around Tsukiji's famed seafood and produce wholesale market, as a place for chefs to pick up anything else they might need, be it laver for wrapped sushi rolls or dried fish for making stock.

Market Food

Tsukiji Market is also a fantastic place to eat, with great street food and several small restaurants specialising in seafood.

Yamachō   Japanese ¥

(山長; Map p250; 03-3248-6002; 4-16-1 Tsukiji, Chūō-ku; omelette slices ¥100; ⊙6am-3.30pm) Don't miss the delicious oblongs of sunshine-yellow egg on sticks sold at this venerable purveyor of *tamago-yaki*

Great For...

☑ **Don't Miss**

A highlight of visiting the market is the food vendors, hawking freshly shucked oysters, deep-fried fish cakes and more.

CURIOSO/SHUTTERSTOCK ©

Tsukiji

Tsukijishijō

Shin-Ōhashi-dōri

Harumi-dōri

Tsukiji Market

❶ Need to Know

場外市場, Jōgai Shijō; Map p250; www.tsukiji.
or.jp; 6-chōme Tsukiji, Chūō-ku; ⊙mostly 5am-
2pm; ⑤Hibiya line to Tsukiji, exit 1

✗ Take a Break

Grab a latte from nearby Turret Coffee
(p139).

★ Top Tip

Most shops close by 2pm; some are
closed on Sundays and Wednesdays.

¥1500; ⊙7am-3pm Mon, Tue, Thu-Sat; 🍴) Specialising in fish roe, this sparkling clean stall
has a few counter seats and also does take-
away rice bowls and noodle dishes covered
with generous amounts of *ikura* (salmon
roe) or *mentaiko* (cod roe). The rice bowls
are served with a delicious clear fish soup
and condiments that you pour over the rice
to make the dish *ochazuke*.

What's Nearby?

Hama-rikyū Onshi-teien   Gardens
(浜離宮恩賜庭園, Detached Palace Garden;
Map p250; ☑03-3541-0200; www.tokyo-park.
or.jp/teien; 1-1 Hama-rikyū-teien, Chūō-ku; adult/
child ¥300/free; ⊙9am-5pm; ⑤Ōedo line to
Shiodome, exit A1) This beautiful garden, one
of Tokyo's finest, is all that remains of a
shogunate palace that was also an outer
fort for Edo Castle. The main features are a
large duck pond with an island that's home
to a functioning tea pavilion, Nakajima no
Ochaya (p139), as well as three other teahouses and wonderfully manicured trees
(black pine, Japanese apricot, hydrangeas
etc), some hundreds of years old.

(Japanese rolled-egg omelettes). They
come in a variety of flavours and you can
watch them being expertly made as you
line up to buy.

Kimagure-ya   Sandwiches ¥
(気まぐれ屋; Map p250; 6-21-6 Tsukiji, Chūō-ku;
sandwiches ¥140-200; ⊙5am-10am Mon-Sat)
Locals adore the *ebi-katsu sando* (deep-
fried prawn sandwiches) made by genial
Matsubara-san out of a stall in his grand-
father's old barber shop – and so will you.
He also serves one of the cheapest coffees
(¥140) you'll find in Tokyo. The earlier you
get here the better, as the sandwiches sell
out fast.

Tadokoro Shokuhin   Japanese ¥
(田所食品; Map p250; ☑03-3541-7754; 4-9-11
Tsukiji, Chūō-ku; noodles ¥700, rice bowls from

Akihabara Pop Culture

Akihabara – or 'Akiba', as it's known to locals – is the centre of Tokyo's otaku (geek) subculture. But you don't have to obsess about manga or anime to enjoy this quirky neighbourhood: with its neon-bright electronics stores, retro arcades, cosplay cafes – and the chance to drive go-karts through the streets – it's equal parts sensory overload, cultural mind-bender and just plain fun.

Great For...

ℹ️ Need to Know

The JR Yamanote and Sōbu lines stop at Akihabara; Electric Town exit is the most convenient. The Hibiya subway line also stops at Akihabara.

★ **Top Tip**

Stop in at **Akiba Info** (Map p254; ☏080-3413-4800; www.akiba-information.jp; 2nd fl, Akihabara UDX Bldg, 4-14-1 Soto-Kanda, Chiyoda-ku; ⏰11am-5.30pm Tue-Sun; 📶; 🚃JR Yamanote line to Akihabara, Electric Town exit) for an English-language map of the neighbourhood.

MariCAR
Scenic Drive

(マリカー; Map p254; ☏080-8899-8899; https://maricar.com; 4-12-9 Soto-Kanda, Chiyoda-ku; 1/2/3hr tours ¥5000/7500/10,000; ◷10am-8pm; ⓢGinza line to Suehirochō, exit 1) Experience Tokyo as if in a real-life video game on these fun go-karting tours around the city where you can dress up in brightly coloured onesies. You must, however, have a valid International Driving Permit (or a Japanese driving licence). The two-hour course will get you out to Tokyo Skytree and down to Ginza.

Before you start there's a short tutorial on how to drive the go-karts, then you're on the road with trucks and buses, so absolutely speak up if you're not comfortable.

Mandarake Complex
Manga, Anime

(まんだらけコンプレックス; Map p254; ☏03-3252-7007; www.mandarake.co.jp; 3-11-12 Soto-Kanda, Chiyoda-ku; ◷noon-8pm; ⓡJR Yamanote line to Akihabara, Electric Town exit) When *otaku* (geeks) dream of heaven, it probably looks a lot like this giant go-to store for manga and anime. Eight storeys are piled high with comic books, action figures, *cosplay* accessories and cel art just for starters. The 1st floor has cases of some (very expensive) vintage toys.

@Home Cafe
Cafe

(@ほぉ〜むカフェ; Map p254; ☏03-3255-2808; www.cafe-athome.com; 4th-7th fl, 1-11-4 Soto-Kanda, Chiyoda-ku; ◷11am-10pm Mon-Fri, from 10am Sat & Sun; 🄿; ⓡJR Yamanote line to Akihabara, Electric Town exit) 'Maid cafes' with *kawaii* (cute) waitresses, dressed as saucy French or prim Victorian maids, are a stock-in-trade of Akiba. @Home is one that's suitable if you have kids in tow. You'll be welcomed as *go-shujinsama* (master) or *o-jōsama* (miss) the minute you enter. Admission is ¥700 for one hour plus one drink order (from ¥570).

Yodobashi-Akiba
Electronics

(ヨドバシカメラ Akiba; Map p254; ☏03-5209 1010; www.yodobashi-akiba.com; 1-1 Kanda Hanaoka-chō, Chiyoda-ku; ◷9.30am-10pm; ⓡJR Yamanote line to Akihabara, Shōwa-tōriguchi exit) This is the monster branch of Yodobashi Camera where many locals shop. It has eight floors of electronics, state-of-the-art camera and audio equipment, and household appliances, but also toys, cosmetics and even food at competitive prices. Ask about export models and VAT-free purchases.

Super Potato Retro-kan
Arcade

(スーパーポテトレトロ館; Map p254; ☏03-5289 9933; www.superpotato.com; 1-11-2 Soto-

☑ Don't Miss
Tokyo's latest craze: go-karting. Make sure to book ahead and have an international driving licence.

✕ Take a Break
Walk over the Kanda-gawa for tasty noodles at Kanda Yabu Soba (p143).

kanda, Chiyoda-ku; ⊘11am-8pm Mon-Fri, from 10am Sat & Sun; 및JR Yamanote line to Akihabara, Electric Town exit) Are you a gamer keen to sample retro computer games? On the 5th floor of this store specialising in used video games, there's a retro video arcade where you can get some old-fashioned consoles at a bargain ¥100 per game.

What's Nearby?

Kanda Myōjin   Shinto Shrine

(神田明神, Kanda Shrine; Map p254; ☑03-3254-0753; www.kandamyoujin.or.jp; 2-16-2 Soto-kanda, Chiyoda-ku; 및JR Chūō or Sōbu lines to Ochanomizu, Hijiri-bashi exit) **FREE** Tracing its history back to AD 730, this splendid Shintō shrine boasts vermilion-lacquered halls surrounding a stately courtyard. Its present location dates from 1616 and the *kami* (gods) enshrined here are said to bring luck

in business and in finding a spouse. There are also plenty of anime characters, since this is Akiba's local shrine.

3331 Arts Chiyoda   Gallery

(Map p254; ☑03-6803-2441; www.3331.jp; 6-11-14 Soto-Kanda, Chiyoda-ku; ⊘ground fl 10am-9pm, exhibition space noon-7pm Wed-Mon; ♿; 및Ginza line to Suehirochō, exit 4) **FREE** A major exhibition space, smaller art galleries and creative studios now occupy this former high school, which has evolved into a forward-thinking arts hub for Akiba. It's a fascinating place to explore. On the ground floor, there's a good cafe and a shop selling cute design items, as well as a play area for kids stocked with recycled toys.

---

❶ Need to Know

Read up on anime, manga and more on p217.

VASSAMON ANANSUKKASEM/SHUTTERSTOCK ©

View over Sumida

City Views

There's nothing quite like seeing the city from a couple of hundred metres in the air. By night, Tokyo appears truly beautiful, as if the sky were inverted and the stars glittered below you.

Great For...

☑ Don't Miss

On a clear day look west for a chance to spot Mt Fuji.

Tokyo Metropolitan Government Building — Observatory

(東京都庁, Tokyo Tochō; Map p253; www.metro.tokyo.jp/english/offices; 2-8-1 Nishi-Shinjuku, Shinjuku-ku; ☉observatories 9.30am-11pm; ⑤Ōedo line to Tochōmae, exit A4) **FREE** Tokyo's city hall – a landmark building designed by Tange Kenzō – has observatories (202m) atop both the south and north towers of Building 1 (the views are virtually the same). On a clear day (morning is best), you may catch a glimpse of Mt Fuji beyond the urban sprawl to the west; after dark, it's illuminated buildings all the way to the horizon. Direct-access elevators are on the ground floor; last entry is at 10.30pm.

Tokyo City View — Viewpoint

(東京シティビュー; Map p252; ☎03-6406-6652; www.roppongihills.com; 52nd fl, Mori

Tokyo Metropolitan Government Building

COWARDLION/SHUTTERSTOCK ©

Nishi-Shinjuku, Shinjuku-ku; ⊙5pm-midnight Sun-Wed, to 1am Thu-Sat; 🛈; 🚇Ōedo line to Tochōmae, exit A4) Head to the Park Hyatt's 52nd floor to swoon over the sweeping nightscape from the floor-to-ceiling windows at this bar of *Lost in Translation* fame. There's a cover charge of ¥2500 if you visit or stay past 8pm (7pm Sunday); go earlier and watch the sky fade to black. Cocktails start at ¥2160. Note: dress code enforced and 15% service charge levied.

Asahi Sky Room   Bar

(アサヒスカイルーム; Map p254; ☎03-5608-5277; www.asahibeer.co.jp/area/search/shop.psp.html/90218704.htm; 22nd fl, Asahi Super Dry Bldg, 1-23-1 Azuma-bashi, Sumida-ku; ⊙10am-10pm; 🛈; 🚇Ginza line to Asakusa, exit 4) Spend the day at the religious sites and end it at the Asahi altar, on the 22nd floor of the golden-tinged Asahi Super Dry Building. The venue itself isn't noteworthy, but the views over Sumida-gawa are spectacular, especially at sunset.

Tower, Roppongi Hills, 6-10-1 Roppongi, Minato-ku; adult/child ¥1800/600; ⊙10am-11pm Mon-Thu & Sun, to 1am Fri & Sat; 🚇Hibiya line to Roppongi, exit 1) From this 250m-high vantage point, on the 52nd floor of Mori Tower, you can see 360-degree views of the seemingly never-ending city. Admission is included in the entry price for Mori Art Museum (p106), though you will pay the same fee to visit after the museum is closed. Weather permitting, you can also go out to the external rooftop **Sky Deck** (additional adult/child ¥500/300; 11am to 8pm) for al fresco views.

Drinks with a View

New York Bar   Bar

(ニューヨークバー; Map p253; ☎03-5323-3458; http://restaurants.tokyo.park.hyatt.co.jp/en/nyb.html; 52nd fl, Park Hyatt Tokyo, 3-7-1-2

Karaoke

Karaoke isn't just about singing: it's an excuse to let loose, a bonding ritual, a reason to keep the party going past the last train and a way to kill time until the first one starts in the morning.

Karaoke Basics

In Japan, karaoke (カラオケ; pronounced kah-rah-oh-kay) is usually sung in a private room among friends (though some bars have karaoke as well). Admission is typically charged per person per half-hour, with a minimum charge of one hour.

First up, go to the front desk to sign up for a room. Most places offer a variety of packaged deals that include a set number of singing hours with or without unlimited drinks; these can be good value. You can also just go in for the minimum one hour and decide later on if you wish to continue (be warned though: you probably will).

Most places in busy areas of Tokyo have at least one staff member who can communicate in basic English. You'll be able to choose from a wide range of English-language songs and the touch screen devices used to search

Great For...

☑ **Don't Miss**

Finding your signature song and letting your inner diva shine.

DAI/GETTY IMAGES ©

❶ Need to Know

Karaoke parlours can be found near any major train station – and especially in nightlife districts such as Shinjuku, Shibuya and Roppongi.

✕ Take a Break

Food and drinks can be ordered by the phone in the room and are brought to the door.

★ Top Tip

Karaoke rates fluctuate by day and time; the cheapest time to go is on a weekday afternoon.

¥150/410; ⏱11am-5am; 🖥📱; 🚃JR Yamanote line to Shibuya, Hachikō exit) This is Shibuya's most popular karaoke spot for two reasons: it doesn't have the same dated look as the generic chains and you get the first hour free (though, technically, you need to buy one drink; from ¥465). Staff speak some English and the English song list is extensive. It's on the 8th floor of the building with the Marui department store.

Pasela Resorts Karaoke

(パセラリゾーツ; Map p252; 📞0120-911-086; www.pasela.co.jp/shop/roppongi/karaoke; 5-16-3 Roppongi, Minato-ku; per hr per person Sun-Thu ¥1100, Fri & Sat ¥1300; ⏱noon-6am Sun-Thu, to 7am Fri & Sat; 📱; ⓈHibiya line to Roppongi, exit 3) With decor that is a cut above the other yodelling parlours, Pasela offers six floors of karaoke rooms (including swanky VIP suites), an extensive selection of Western songs, and wine, champagne and sweets on the menu. The two-hour *nomi-hōdai* (all-you-can-drink) package (per person ¥3700, ¥4200 on Friday; room rental included) is a good deal.

for songs by artist or title will have an English function too.

Each room has a telephone connected to the front desk; staff will ring when you have about 10 minutes remaining, giving you the chance to extend your singing session. They'll also ring to tell you when time is up, at which point head to the front desk to settle your bill.

Karaoke Parlours

Major chains to look for include: Karaoke-kan (カラオケ館), Pasela (パセラ), Big Echo (ビッグエコー) and Uta Hiroba (歌広場). They're brightly lit and easy to spot.

Karaoke Rainbow Karaoke

(Map p246; 📞03-6455-3240; www.karaoke-rainbow.com; 8th fl, Shibuya Modi, 1-21-3 Shibuya, Shibuya-ku; per 30min before/after 7pm

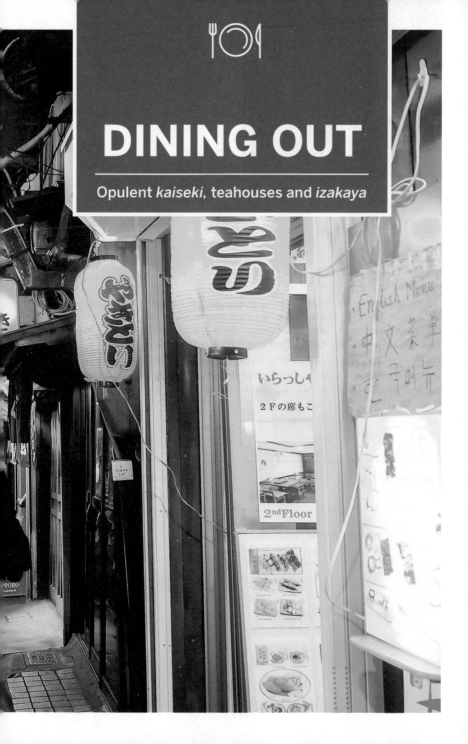

DINING OUT

Opulent *kaiseki*, teahouses and *izakaya*

Dining Out

As visitors to Tokyo quickly discover, the people here are absolutely obsessed with food. The city has a vibrant and cosmopolitan dining scene and a strong culture of eating out – popular restaurants are packed most nights of the week. Best of all, you can eat very well on any budget.

Dining highlights include getting sushi breakfast at the fish market, visiting a classic izakaya (Japanese pub-eatery), eating yakitori (grilled chicken skewers) at a stall in a yokochō (alleyway) and going for late-night ramen.

In This Section

Price Ranges & Tipping

The following price ranges represent the cost of a meal for one person.

¥ less than ¥2000

¥¥ ¥2000–¥5000

¥¥¥ more than ¥5000

Tipping is not customary, though most high-end restaurants will add a 10% service charge to the bill.

Previous page: Restaurants on Omoide-yokochō (p124)

Map areas

Ueno & Yanaka
Classic Japanese restaurants with heaps of atmosphere (p144)

Asakusa & Ryōgoku
Unpretentious Japanese fare, old-school charm and modest prices (p146)

Shinjuku & Ikebukuro
High-end restaurants, under-the-tracks dives and everything in-between (p124)

Kōenji & Kichijōji
Nothing fancy, but lots of local faves doing Japanese standards (p126)

Kanda & Akihabara
Historic eateries and comfort food (p143)

Harajuku & Aoyama
Fashionable lunch spots and cafes (p126)

Marunouchi & Nihombashi
Great for lunch and traditional Japanese cuisine (p140)

Roppongi & Around
Splurge-worthy restaurants and lots of international cuisine (p136)

Ginza & Tsukiji
Street vendors in Tsukiji; teahouses & fine dining in Ginza (p138)

Shibuya & Shimo-Kitazawa
Trendy *izakaya*, bistros and coffee shops (p130)

Ebisu & Meguro
Cosmopolitan and hip, with excellent options for all budgets (p135)

Tokyo Bay

Useful Phrases

I'd like to reserve a table for (two).
(2人)の予約を
お願いします。
(fu·ta·ri) no yo·ya·ku o
o·ne·gai shi·mas

That was delicious!
おいしかった。
oy·shi·kat·ta

Please bring the bill.
お勘定をください。
o·kan·jō o ku·da·sai

Must Trys

Ramen Egg noodles in a richly flavoured broth, topped with grilled pork and more. For the best places to try ramen, see p42.

Sushi Raw fish on vinegar-seasoned rice.

Tempura Seafood and vegetables deep-fried in a fluffy, light batter.

Tonkatsu Tender pork cutlets battered and deep-fried, served with a side of grated cabbage.

Yakitori Chicken skewers (and veggies, too) grilled on hot coals.

The Best...

Experience Tokyo's best restaurants and cuisines

Brunch

Bricolage Bread & Co (p137) Chic space with excellent coffee and tartines.

Iki Espresso (p147) Get your avocado toast fix in up-and-coming Kiyosumi.

Rose Bakery (p139) Organic salads and delicious cakes.

Izakaya

Narukiyo (p134) Cult-fave spot on the fringes of Shibuya.

Shinsuke (p146) Century-old local institution adored by sake aficionados.

Kanae (p125) Classic *izakaya* dishes, beautifully presented.

Donjaca (p125) Vintage mid-20th-century vibe and homestyle food.

Historic Restaurants

Sasa-no-Yuki (p145) Making tofu from scratch every morning since 1691.

Kizushi (p143) Sushi in the style of a century ago.

Hantei (p145) Deep-fried skewers in a 100-year-old heritage house.

Budget Options

Commune 2nd (p128) Hip outdoor space serving all kinds of dishes.

Misojyu (p146) Trendy new spot for miso soup and creative *onigiri* (rice balls).

Delifucious (p135) Fish burgers from a former sushi chef.

Vegetarian & Vegan

Ain Soph (p139) Pretty vegan spreads and a chic cafe vibe; more branches around the city.

Mominoki House (p129) Long-running macrobiotic restaurant with many vegan options.

Nagi Shokudō (p132) Hip (and hidden) vegan hang-out.

Japanese Classics

Kanda Yabu Soba (p143) Specialising in soba since 1880.

Maisen (p126) Long-time favourite for *tonkatsu* (deep-fried pork cutlets), in a former bathhouse.

Bird Land (p140) Upscale *yakitori* (grilled chicken skewers) from free-range heirloom birds.

Nihonbashi Tamai (p143) *Anago* (saltwater conger eel) served grilled in a lacquered box.

☆ Lonely Planet's Top Choices

Inua (p144) Tokyo's hottest table, from Noma alum Thomas Frebel, with all the foraging and farm-to-table goodness you'd expect.

Kyūbey (p140) Rarefied Ginza sushi at its finest.

Tempura Kondō (p140) Works of batter-fried art from master chef and tempura-whisperer Kondō Fumio.

Mensho (p44) Leading light of the nouveau-ramen movement.

Tonki (p135) Iconic *tonkatsu* (deep-fried pork cutlet) restaurant, beloved by generations of Tokyoites.

Sweets

Ouca (p135) Ice cream in all kinds of Japanese speciality flavours.

Himitsu-dō (p144) Popular spot for summer favourite *kakigōri* (shaved ice).

Nezu-no-Taiyaki (p144) Queue with locals for fish-shaped bean-paste cakes.

⊗ Shinjuku & Ikebukuro

Ohitotsuzen Tanbo
Japanese ¥

(おひつ膳田んぼ; Map p253; ☎03-3320-0727; www.tanbo.co.jp; 1-41-9 Yoyogi, Shibuya-ku; meals ¥1550-2350; ⊙11am-10pm; 🚇JR Yamanote line to Yoyogi, west exit) 🍜 The speciality here is the least glamorous part of the meal – the rice, which comes from an organic farm the restaurant manages in Niigata Prefecture. It's served as *ochazuke,* a classic comfort food of rice topped with meat or fish over which hot tea is poured. English instructions explain how to eat it.

Gochisō Tonjiru
Japanese ¥

(ごちそうとん汁; Map p253; ☎03-6883-9181; 1-33-2 Yoyogi, Shibuya-ku; meals from ¥840; ⊙11.30am-midnight; 🚇JR Yamanote line to Yoyogi, west exit) *Tonjiru,* a home-cooking classic, is a hearty miso soup packed with root veggies (such as burdock root, *daikon/*radish, potato and carrot) and chunks of pork. At this neighbourhood hang-out, styled more like a bar than a restaurant, the pork comes in the form of melting-off-the-bone barbecued spare ribs. Choose between a Kyoto-style light miso or a Tokyo-style dark miso.

Omoide-yokochō
Yakitori ¥

(思い出横丁; Map p253; Nishi-Shinjuku 1-chōme, Shinjuku-ku; skewers from ¥150; ⊙varies by shop; 🚇JR Yamanote line to Shinjuku, west exit) Literally 'Memory Lane' (and less politely known as Shonben-yokochō, or 'Piss Alley'), Omoide-yokochō started as a postwar black market and somehow managed to stick around. Today, it's one of Tokyo's most recognisable sights. There are dozens of small restaurants, mostly serving *yakitori* (chicken, and other meats or vegetables, grilled on skewers), packed into the alley here; several have English menus.

Yong Xiang Sheng Jian Guan
Chinese ¥

(永祥生煎館; 1st fl, Sun City Hotel, 1-29-2 Nishi-Ikebukuro, Toshima-ku; 4 dumplings for ¥400; ⊙11.30am-10pm; 🚇JR Yamanote line to Ikebukuro, west exit) This tiny shop in Ikebukuro's Chinatown deals in Shanghai street food, namely *shēngjiān* (pan-fried pork buns;

Sushi restaurant

called *yaki-shōronpo* in Japan). Warning: they're as hot as they are delicious. Also on the menu: wontan soup (¥480; ワンタンスープ) and spare ribs (¥480; スペアリブ). There's just a small counter for eating.

Berg
Cafe ¥

(ベルグ; Map p253; www.berg.jp; basement fl, Lumine Est, 3-38-1 Shinjuku, Shinjuku-ku; morning set ¥410; ⏰7am-11pm; 🚃JR Yamanote line to Shinjuku, east exit) Wedged inside the fashion-forward Lumine Est department store (itself inside the frenetic Shinjuku Station), Berg stands still. The cramped, cult-status coffee shop still charges just ¥216 for a cup (and ¥324 for a beer). The highly recommended 'morning set' (*mōningu setto*), served until noon, includes coffee, hard-boiled egg, potato salad and toast. The front is covered in picture menus.

Kanae
Izakaya ¥¥

(鼎; Map p253; 📞050-3467-1376; basement fl, 3-12-12 Shinjuku, Shinjuku-ku; cover charge ¥540; dishes ¥660-1980; ⏰5pm-midnight Mon-Sat, 4.30-11pm Sun; 🚃JR Yamanote line to Shinjuku, east exit) Kanae is a perfect example of one of Shinjuku-sanchōme's excellent and all but undiscoverable *izakaya*: delicious sashimi, seasonal dishes and simple staples (the potato salad is famous) in the basement of an unremarkable building (there's a white sign with a sake barrel out front). Seating is at the counter or at a handful of tables; reservations recommended.

Donjaca
Izakaya ¥¥

(呑者家; Map p253; 📞03-3341-2497; 3-9-10 Shinjuku, Shinjuku-ku; cover charge ¥300, dishes ¥350-900; ⏰5pm-7am; 🚇Marunouchi line to Shinjuku-sanchōme, exit C6) Donjaca, in business since 1979, has many telltale signs of a classic Shōwa-era (1926–89) *izakaya*: red vinyl stools, lantern lighting and hand-written menus covering the wall. The food is equal parts classic (grilled fish and fried chicken) and inventive: a house speciality is *nattō gyōza* (dumplings stuffed with fermented soybeans). Excellent sake, too.

🍽 Tokyo's Food Alleys

Tokyo has not (yet!) completely erased all traces of an older city, the one of narrow alleyways and wooden buildings. Some of these alleys shelter small restaurants and bars; spending an evening in one is a must-do local experience. They're often called *yokochō*, which means 'side town'.

Shinjuku's Omoide-yokochō (p124) is the most famous one. Ebisu-yokochō (p135) is trendy refashioning of a retro market. Kōenji Gādo-shita (p126) is a collection of spots under the elevated JR tracks. Hoppy-dōri (p146) is a strip of casual *izakaya* with outdoor seating.

Omoide-yokochō
URAIWONS/SHUTTERSTOCK ©

Kozue
Japanese ¥¥¥

(梢; Map p253; 📞03-5323-3460; www.hyatt.com; 40th fl, Park Hyatt Tokyo, 3-7-1-2 Nishi-Shinjuku, Shinjuku-ku; lunch set menu ¥2480-10,800, dinner set menu ¥14,040-24,850; ⏰11.30am-2.30pm & 5.30-9.30pm; 🚇Ōedo line to Tochōmae, exit A4) It's hard to beat Kozue's combination of exquisite seasonal Japanese cuisine, artisan crockery and distractingly good views over Shinjuku. As the kimono-clad staff speak English and the restaurant caters well to dietary restrictions and personal preferences, this is a good splurge spot for diners who don't want to give up complete control. Reservations essential for dinner and recommended for lunch; 15% service charge.

Sampling Japanese Tea

Here *o-cha* (お茶; tea) means green tea and broadly speaking there are two kinds: *ryokucha* (steeped with leaves) and *matcha*, which is made by whisking dried and milled leaves with water until a cappuccino level of frothiness is achieved. As *matcha* is quite bitter, it is served with *wagashi* (traditional sweets made from sugar, rice flour and bean paste).

The complementary tea served in a standard Japanese restaurant is usually *bancha*, ordinary-grade green tea, with a brownish colour. (In summer, you might get cold *mugicha*, roasted barley tea, instead.) After dinner, restaurants often serve *hōjicha* (ほうじ茶), roasted green tea, which is weaker and less caffeinated.

To sample the more rarefied stuff – like *gyokuro* (玉露), the highest grade of loose-leaf green tea, shaded from the sun and picked early in the season – visit one of Tokyo's excellent teahouses. Department store basement food halls are good places to shop for loose tea.

⊗ Kōenji & Kichijōji

Kōenji Gādo-shita   Street Food ¥

(高円寺ガード下; Kōenji, Suginami-ku; ⏰5pm-late; 🚃JR Sōbu line to Kōenji, north exit) This is Kōenji's signature *nomiyagai* (eating and drinking strip), a collection of shabby (and cheap!) *yakitori* (chicken, and other meats or vegetables, grilled on skewers) stalls, spruced-up wine bars and more underneath the overhead JR tracks. Since most places are supertiny and the rail lines provide cover, there is often outside seating on folding tables or overturned beer carts.

Tensuke   Tempura ¥¥

(天すけ; 📞03-3223-8505; 3-22-7 Kōenji-kita, Suginami-ku; lunch from ¥1000, dinner ¥1350-4600; ⏰noon-2pm & 6-10pm Tue-Sun; 🚃JR Sōbu line to Kōenji, north exit) A legitimate candidate for eighth wonder of the modern world is Tensuke's *tamago* (egg) tempura, which comes out batter-crisp on the outside and runny in the middle. It's served on rice with seafood and vegetable tempura as part of the *tamago tempura teishoku* (玉子天ぷら定食; ¥1600) or *tamago ranchi* (玉子ランチ; ¥1300; lunchtime only). There's a blue-and-orange sign out front.

Steak House Satou   Steak ¥¥

(ステーキハウス さとう; 📞0422-21-6464; www.shop-satou.com; 1-1-8 Kichijōji Honchō, Mitaka-shi; lunch set ¥1800-10,000; dinner set ¥2600-10,000; ⏰11am-2.30pm & 5-8pm Mon-Fri, 11am-2.30pm & 4.30-8.30pm Sat & Sun; 🚃JR Chūō-Sōbu line to Kichijōji, north exit) This is a classic Japanese-style steak house, where the meat is cooked at the counter on a *teppan* (iron hotplate), diced, then paired with rice, miso soup and pickles. The beef is high-grade *wagyū* (beef from Japanese black cattle) and priced very reasonably. We recommend ordering the chef's choice (lunch/dinner ¥4000/7000).

⊗ Harajuku & Aoyama

Maisen   Tonkatsu ¥

(まい泉; Map p246; 📞0120-428-485; www.mai-sen.com; 4-8-5 Jingūmae, Shibuya-ku; lunch/dinner from ¥990/1580; ⏰11am-10.45pm; 🚻; 🚇Ginza line to Omote-sandō, exit A2) Maisen is famous both for its *tonkatsu* (breaded, deep-fried pork cutlets) and its setting (an old public bathhouse). There are different grades of pork on the menu, including prized *kurobuta* (black pig), but even the cheapest

☆ Best Tokyo Sweets

Ouca (p135)

Higashiya Man (p129)

Himitsu-dō (p144)

Suzukien (p147)

Clockwise from top: *wagashi* (traditional sweets); cooking *dorayaki* (pancake filled with sweet adzuki paste); rabbit-themed desserts

Omoide-yokochō (p124)

is melt-in-your-mouth divine; the very reasonable lunch set is served until 4pm.

Sakurai Japanese Tea Experience
Teahouse ¥

(櫻井焙茶研究所; Map p246; ☎03-6451-1539; www.sakurai-tea.jp; 5th fl, Spiral Bldg, 5-6-23 Minami-Aoyama, Minato-ku; tea from ¥1400, course from ¥4800; ☺11am-11pm; ⑤Ginza line to Omote-sandō, exit B1) Tea master (and former bartender) Sakurai Shinya's contemporary take on the tea ceremony is a must for anyone hoping to be better acquainted with Japan's signature brew. The course includes several varieties – you might be surprised how different tea can taste – paired with small bites, including some beautiful traditional sweets. Come in the evening for tea cocktails. Reservations recommended.

Commune 2nd
Market ¥

(Map p246; www.commune2nd.com; 3-13 Minami-Aoyama, Minato-ku; meals ¥1000-1500; ☺11am-10pm; ⑤Ginza line to Omote-sandō, exit A4) Commune 2nd is a collection of vendors offering inexpensive curries, hot dogs, beer and more. Purchase what you want from any of the stalls, then grab a seat at one of the shared picnic tables – this is one of Tokyo's rare alfresco dining spots. It's very popular, especially on a warm Friday or Saturday night.

Aoyama Kawakami-an
Soba ¥

(青山川上庵; Map p246; ☎03-5411-7171; 3-14-1 Minami-Aoyama, Minato-ku; soba ¥920-1750; ☺11.30am-4am; ⑤Ginza line to Omote-sandō, exit A5) This Aoyama outpost of famed Karuizawa soba shop serves handmade, 100% buckwheat noodles all day and (nearly) all night. Go for broke with the (truly) jumbo tempura prawns or add on sides of Nagano specialities like *kurakake mame* (a kind of soy bean) and pickles made of *nozawana* (a kind of mustard leaf).

Gomaya Kuki
Ice Cream ¥

(ごまや くき; Map p246; http://gomayakuki. jp; 4-6-9 Jingūmae, Shibuya-ku; 2 scoops ¥500; ☺11am-7pm; ☒JR Yamanote line to Harajuku, Omote-sandō exit) *Goma* (sesame) ice cream is a must-try and this speciality shop is the place to try it. There are two varieties, made from high-grade *kurogoma* (黒ごま; black sesame) or *shirogoma* (白ごま; white sesame) from Mie Prefecture. To really taste the sesame, double down and get it *chōtokunō* (super extra strong). Literally thousands of seeds go into one scoop.

Harajuku Gyōza-rō
Dumplings ¥

(原宿餃子楼; Map p246; 6-4-2 Jingūmae, Shibuya-ku; 6 gyōza ¥290; ⏰11.30am-4.30am Mon-Sat, to 10pm Sun; 🚃JR Yamanote line to Harajuku, Omote-sandō exit) *Gyōza* (dumplings) are the only thing on the menu here, but you won't hear any complaints from the regulars who queue up to get their fix. Have them *sui* (boiled) or *yaki* (pan-fried), with or without *niniku* (garlic) or *nira* (chives) – they're all delicious. Expect to wait on weekends or at lunchtime, but the line moves quickly.

Aoyama Flower
Market Teahouse
Teahouse ¥

(Map p246; ☎03-3400-0887; www.afm-teahouse.com; 5-1-2 Minami-Aoyama, Minato-ku; ⏰11am-8pm Mon-Sat, to 7pm Sun; 🚇Ginza line to Omote-sandō, exit A5) Secreted in the back of a flower shop is this fairy-tale teahouse with flower beds running under the glass-top tables and more overhead, plus cut blooms in vases on every available surface. Tea comes by the pot and starts at ¥750; there are pretty sweets and salad spreads on the menu too. Reservations aren't accepted so you may have to queue.

Koffee Mameya
Coffee ¥

(コーヒーマメヤ; Map p246; www.koffee-mameya.com; 4-15-3 Jingūmae, Shibuya-ku; coffee ¥350-1100; ⏰10am-6pm; 🚇Ginza line to Omote-sandō, exit A2) At any given time, Koffee Mameya has 15 to 20 different beans on rotation from indie roasters around Japan (and some from overseas). Get a cup brewed on the spot or purchase beans for home use; English-speaking baristas can help you narrow down the selection. There's no seating, but you can loiter at the counter.

Higashiya Man
Sweets ¥

(ひがしや まん; Map p246; ☎03-5414-3881; www.higashiya.com/shop/man; 3-17-14 Minami-Aoyama, Minato-ku; sweets from ¥200;

⏰11am-7pm, to 8pm Jul & Aug; 🚇Ginza line to Omote-sandō, exit A4) *Manjū* (まんじゅう) – that's where the shop's name comes from; it's not just for men! – are hot buns stuffed with sweetened red-bean paste. They're steamed fresh at this take-away counter, a popular pit stop for Aoyama shoppers. Inside the tiny shop there's a greater selection of traditional Japanese sweets, many packaged beautifully for gifts.

Agaru Sagaru
Nishi-iru Higashi-iru
Japanese ¥¥

(上下西東; Map p246; ☎03-3403-6968; basement fl, 3-25-8 Jingūmae, Shibuya-ku; small plates ¥500-900, dinner course ¥3500-5000; ⏰5.30-11.30pm Tue-Sun; 🚃JR Yamanote line to Harajuku, Takeshita exit) This chill little restaurant serves Kyoto-style food (deceptively simple, with the ingredients – always seasonal – taking centre stage) without pretense. The five-dish course (¥3500) – presented in succession and prettily plated – is perfect for when you want to indulge, but not too much. (The seven-dish course requires advance reservations.) Also, it looks like a cave.

Mominoki House
Japanese ¥¥

(もみの木ハウス; Map p246; www.mominoki-house.net; 2-18-5 Jingūmae, Shibuya-ku; lunch course ¥980-1480, dinner course ¥4500; ⏰11am-3pm & 5-10pm Mon-Sat, to 9pm Sun; 🚃; 🚃JR Yamanote line to Harajuku, Takeshita exit) 🌿 This pioneering macrobiotic restaurant has been running since 1976, long enough to see many a Harajuku trend come and go (and to see some famous visitors, like Sir Paul McCartney). Chef Yamada's menu is heavily vegan, but also includes free-range chicken and *Ezo shika* (Hokkaidō venison). Inside, the restaurant looks like a grown-up tree fort and features several cosy, semiprivate booths.

Eatrip
Bistro ¥¥¥

(Map p246; ☎03-3409-4002; www.restaurant-eatrip.com; 6-31-10 Jingūmae, Shibuya-ku; course ¥5400-8640; ⏰6pm-midnight Tue-Sat, 11.30am-3pm Sat, 11.30am-5pm Sun; 🚃JR Yamanote line to Harajuku, Omote-sandō exit) 🌿 Eatrip is one

Kissaten: Independent Coffee Shops

Kissaten (喫茶店) – or '*kissa*' for short – is the old word for coffee shop, the one used before chains like Starbucks arrived in Japan and changed the game. Today the word is used to describe independently run coffee shops that either date from the early or mid-20th century – when Japan's coffee first wave hit – or at least look like they do. In addition to pour-over or siphon-brewed coffee (you'll get no espresso drinks here), most *kissa* serve a 'morning set' (モーニング セット; *mōningu setto*), until around 11am. It includes thick, buttery toast and a hard-boiled egg for little more than the original price of a cup of coffee. Iconic Tokyo *kissa* include Berg (p125), Sabōru (p143) and Kayaba Coffee (p145).

of the big players in Tokyo's farm-to-table organic movement. Working with domestic food producers, it serves up neo-bistro-style dishes that reflect head chef Shiraishi Takayuki's global travels. Sample dish: *mahata* (grouper; from Mie Prefecture) sautéed with harissa (made in-house), squid ink and *daikon* (radish). Course menu only; reserve ahead.

Yanmo   Seafood ¥¥¥

(やんも; Map p246; ☎03-5466-0636; www. yanmo.co.jp/aoyama/index.html; basement fl, T Place Bldg, 5-5-25 Minami-Aoyama, Minato-ku; lunch/dinner set menu from ¥1200/7560; ⏰11.30am-2pm & 5.30-10.30pm Mon-Sat; ⓢGinza line to Omote-sandō, exit A5) Freshly caught seafood from the nearby Izu Peninsula is the speciality at this upscale, yet unpretentious, restaurant. The dinner courses, which include fish served as sashimi, steamed and grilled, are reasonably priced for what you get; reservations essential. The weekday grilled-fish lunch set (¥1200 to ¥1500; chosen from one of several seasonal options) is a bargain; there's usually a queue.

⊗ Shibuya & Shimo-Kitazawa

Camelback   Sandwiches ¥

(キャメルバック; Map p246; www.camelback. tokyo; 42-2 Kamiyama-chō, Shibuya-ku; sandwiches ¥450-900; ⏰8am-5pm Tue-Sun; 🖊; ⓢChiyoda line to Yoyogi-kōen, exit 2) The speciality here is the omelette sandwich – the kind of thick, fluffy rolled omelette you get at sushi shops – served on soft bread with just a hint of spicy mustard. It's only available as a set, with a drink (from ¥450). The coffee is good, too. Seating is on a bench outside.

Fuglen Tokyo   Cafe ¥

(Map p246; www.fuglen.no; 1-16-11 Tomigaya, Shibuya-ku; ⏰8am-10pm Mon & Tue, to 1am Wed & Thu, to 2am Fri, 9am-2am Sat, 9am-midnight Sun; 🛜; ⓢChiyoda line to Yoyogi-kōen, exit 2) This Tokyo outpost of a long-running Oslo coffee shop serves light-roast coffee by day (from ¥360) and some of the city's most creative cocktails (from ¥1250) by night (Wednesday to Sunday). It's Tomigaya's principal gathering spot, with indoor and outdoor seating. Fuglen often hosts events with special food and drink or music; check the website.

Gyūkatsu Motomura   Tonkatsu ¥

(牛かつ もと村; Map p246; ☎03-3797-3735; www.gyukatsu-motomura.com; basement fl, 3-18-10 Shibuya, Shibuya-ku; set meal from ¥1300; ⏰10am-10pm; 🚆JR Yamanote line to Shibuya, east exit) You know *tonkatsu*, the deep-fried breaded pork cutlet that is a Japanese staple; meet *gyūkatsu*, the deep-fried breaded beef cutlet and currently much-hyped dish. At Motomura, diners get a small individual grill to cook the meat to their liking. Set meals include cabbage, rice and soup. It's just off Meiji-dōri, at the southern end of Shibuya Stream.

Bear Pond Espresso   Cafe ¥

(☎03-5454-2486; www.bear-pond.com; 2-36-12 Kitazawa, Setagaya-ku; drinks ¥400-690; ⏰11am-5.30pm Wed-Mon; 🚆Odakyū or Keiō Inokashira line to Shimo-Kitazawa, north exit) Bear Pond's thick syrupy 'angel stain' espresso (¥690) is considered holy grail by many. The owner only pulls a limited number before noon; lattes etc are served all day. Service is sometimes testy – don't take it personally.

Sagatani Soba ¥

(嵯峨谷; Map p246; 2-25-7 Dōgenzaka, Shibuya-ku; noodles from ¥320; ⊙24hr; 頁JR Yamanote line to Shibuya, Hachikō exit) Proving that Tokyo is only expensive for those who don't know better, this all-night joint serves up bamboo steamers of delicious noodles for just ¥320. You won't regret 'splurging' on the *goma-dare soba* (ごまだれそば; buckwheat noodles with sesame dipping sauce) for ¥450. Look for the stone mill in the window and order from the vending machine.

Shirube Izakaya ¥

(汁べゑ; ☑03-3413-3785; 2-18-2 Kitazawa, Setagaya-ku; dishes ¥620-1080; ⊙5.30pm-midnight; 頁Odakyū or Keiō Inokashira line to Shimo-Kitazawa, southwest exit) It's easy to see why everyone loves this *izakaya*: the young chefs put on a dramatic show in the open kitchen and the creative takes on classics, while not exactly gourmet, are totally satisfying, especially the house speciality, *aburi*

saba (blowtorch grilled mackerel). The two-hour all-you-can-drink course (¥4000), which comes with seven dishes, is great value. There is a ¥400 cover; reservations recommended.

Little Nap Coffee Stand Coffee ¥

(リトルナップコーヒースタンド; Map p246; www.littlenap.jp; 5-65-4 Yoyogi, Shibuya-ku; ⊙9am-7pm Tue-Sun; ⑤Chiyoda line to Yoyogi-kōen, exit 3) Near Yoyogi-kōen's often overlooked west gate is this small coffee shop, popular with local dog walkers and joggers. Which isn't to say that convenience is the only appeal here: the lattes and single-origin pour-overs (¥450; from beans roasted at Little Nap's roaster up the street) are excellent.

Uoriki Seafood ¥

(魚力; Map p246; ☑03-3476-6709; www.uoriki6709.com; 40-4 Kamiyama-chō, Shibuya-ku; meals from ¥1050; ⊙11am-4pm & 5.30-8.30pm Mon-Sat; ⑤Chiyoda line to Yoyogi-kōen, exit 2) Uoriki is a fishmonger's run by the same family since 1905 (when Shibuya was practically still a village). There's a restaurant hidden in the back that serves inexpensive

Omoide-yokochō (p124)

yakizakana teishōku (set meals of grilled fish, rice and miso soup); the house speciality is *saba-miso* (mackerel simmered in miso).

Nata de Cristiano   Pastries ¥

(ナタ・デ・クリスチアノ; Map p246; ☑03-6804-9723; www.cristianos.jp/nata; 1-14-16 Tomigaya, Shibuya-ku; pastries ¥200-220; ⊘10am-7.30pm; ✍; ⑤Chiyoda line to Yoyogi-kōen, exit 2) This counter shop sells seriously good *pastéis de nata* (Portuguese egg tarts) along with savoury snacks like *bifanas* (seasoned pork sandwiches) – more evidence that you really can get everything in Tokyo. Take 'em to eat in nearby Yoyogi-kōen (p41), along with a bottle of Portuguese wine (from ¥800) – staff will open it for you and provide tiny plastic cups.

d47 Shokudō   Japanese ¥

(d47食堂; Map p246; www.hikarie8.com; 8th fl, Shibuya Hikarie, 2-21-1 Shibuya, Shibuya-ku; meals ¥1550-1780; ⊘11.30am-2.30pm & 6-10.30pm; ⓇJR Yamanote line to Shibuya, east exit) There are 47 prefectures in Japan and d47 serves a changing line-up of *teishoku* (set meals) that evoke the specialities of each, from the fermented tofu of Okinawa to the stuffed squid of Hokkaidō. A larger menu of small plates is available in the evening.

Nagi Shokudō   Vegan ¥

(なぎ食堂; Map p246; ☑03-3461-3280; http://nagishokudo.com; 15-10 Uguisudani-chō, Shibuya-ku; meal from ¥1080; ⊘noon-4pm daily, 6-11pm Mon-Sat; ☎✍; ⓇJR Yamanote line to Shibuya, west exit) A vegan haven in fast-food-laced Shibuya, Nagi serves up dishes like falafel and coconut curry. The most popular thing on the menu is a set meal with three small dishes, miso soup and rice. It's a low-key, homely place with mismatched furniture, catty-corner from a post office and hidden behind a concrete wall; look for the red sign.

Katsu Midori   Sushi ¥¥

(活美登利; Map p246; ☑03-5728-4282; www.katumidori.co.jp; 8th fl, Seibu Bldg A, 21-1 Udagawa-chō, Shibuya-ku; ⊘11am-11pm; ♨; ⓇJR Yamanote line to Shibuya, Hachikō exit) There's nearly always a queue at this very popular *kaiten-sushi* (conveyor-belt sushi

restaurant) inside Seibu department store, but it moves quickly. The menu is huge, including lots of nonseafood items; especially tasty is the sushi served *'aburi'* style – lightly seared with a blowtorch.

Ahiru Store   Bistro ¥¥

(アヒルストア; Map p246; ☑03-5454-2146; 1-19-4 Tomigaya, Shibuya-ku; dishes ¥900-2800; ⊘6pm-midnight Mon-Fri, 3-9pm Sat; ⑤Chiyoda line to Yoyogi-kōen, exit 2) This tiny counter bistro dishing up homemade sausages, fresh-baked bread and bio wines (¥1000 to ¥1200 per glass) has a huge local following. Reservations are accepted only for the first seating at 6pm on weekdays; otherwise join the queue (late, or during the middle of the week, is the best time to score a spot).

Kaikaya   Seafood ¥¥

(開花屋; Map p246; ☑03-3770-0878; www.kaikaya.com; 23-7 Maruyama-chō, Shibuya-ku; lunch from ¥850, dishes ¥850-2300, set course from ¥3500; ⊘11.30am-2pm & 5.30-10.30pm Mon-Fri, 5.30-10.30pm Sat & Sun; ⓇJR Yamanote line to Shibuya, Hachikō exit) Traveller favourite Kaikaya serves seafood, much of which is caught in nearby Sagami Bay, in a variety of styles. The whole casual set-up is a homage to the sea, with surfboards on the wall. The courses are a good deal; for à la carte orders, there's a ¥400 cover charge. Staff speak good English; reservations recommended.

Maru Bengara   Japanese ¥¥

(圓 弁柄; Map p246; ☑03-6427-7700; www.maru-mayfont.jp; 3rd fl, Shibuya Stream, 3-21-3 Shibuya, Shibuya-ku; lunch set ¥1240-3760, dinner course from ¥6480, à la carte dishes ¥920-3565; ⊘11am-3pm & 5-11pm; ⑤Ginza, Hanzōmon & Fukutoshin lines to Shibuya, exit 16b, ⓇJR Yamanote line to Shibuya, new south exit) Maru is a meal made easy: at lunch the restaurant does really good grilled fish *teishoku* (set meals); in the evenings, courses with sashimi, seasonal sides and vegetables, a main of meat or fish and a choice of Japanese-style desserts. It's part of the new Shibuya Stream complex, so you can get here right from the subway.

Best for Coffee
Cafe de l'Ambre (p138)
Bear Pond Espresso (p130)
Fuglen Tokyo (p130)
Onibus Coffee (p135)
Little Nap Coffee Stand (p131)

Top: Little Nap Coffee Stand (p131); Bottom left: Barista at Onibus Coffee (p135)

Out   Italian ¥¥

(アウト; Map p246; www.out.restaurant; Vort
Aoyama 103; 2-7-14 Shibuya, Shibuya-ku; pasta
¥2900; pasta & wine set ¥4000; ⊘6pm-2am
Tue-Sun; ◢; ℝJR Yamanote line to Shibuya, east
exit) Out serves only one dish – *tagliolini al
tartufo* (egg noodles with truffles) – take
it or leave it (we'll take it). The noodles are
made from scratch in-house with flour
imported from Italy; the truffles (rotated by
season) are shaved on top of the pasta at
the table; and the house wine is a boutique
Australian red (also rotated).

Matsukiya   Hotpot ¥¥¥

(松木家; Map p246; ✆03-3461-2651; 6-8
Maruyama-chō, Shibuya-ku; meals from ¥5400;
⊘5-11pm Mon-Sat; ℝJR Yamanote line to
Shibuya, Hachikō exit) There are only two
things on the menu at Matsukiya, established in 1890: *sukiyaki* (thinly sliced beef
cooked in sake, soy and vinegar broth, and
dipped in raw egg) and *shabu-shabu* (thin
slices of beef or pork swished in hot broth
and dipped in a citrusy soy or sesame
sauce). The beef is top-grade *wagyū* from

Ōmi. Meals include veggies and noodles
cooked in the broths.

Narukiyo   Izakaya ¥¥¥

(なるきよ; Map p246; ✆03-5485-2223; 2-7-14
Shibuya, Shibuya-ku; dishes ¥700-4800; ⊘6pm-
12.30am; ℝJR Yamanote line to Shibuya, east
exit) Cult favourite *izakaya*, Narukiyo serves
seasonal Japanese cuisine with creative
panache. The menu, which changes daily, is
handwritten on a scroll and totally unde-
cipherable; say the magic word, *omakase*
(chef's choice; set a price cap, say ¥5000 or
¥7000 per person), and trust that you're in
good hands. Reservations recommended.

Pignon   Bistro ¥¥¥

(ピニョン; Map p246; ✆03-3468-2331; www.
pignontokyo.jp; 16-3 Kamiyama-chō, Shibuya-ku;
dishes ¥1700-4200; ⊘6.30-10.30pm Mon-Sat;
ℝJR Yamanote line to Shibuya, Hachikō exit)
Pignon is a perfect example of where
Tokyo's dining scene is going: it's ostensibly
a bistro, sources its ingredients directly
from producers and has a menu influenced
by chef Yoshikawa Rimpei's global travels.
In other words, it's laying down local roots,

Korokke (croquettes)

riffing on the classics and chomping on the bit to break free from convention.

Ebisu & Meguro

Tonki
Tonkatsu ¥

(とんき; 📞03-3491-9928; 1-2-1 Shimo-Meguro, Meguro-ku; meals ¥1800; 🕐4-10.45pm Wed-Mon, closed 3rd Mon of the month; 🚉JR Yamanote line to Meguro, west exit) Tonki is a Tokyo *tonkatsu* (crumbed pork cutlet) legend, deep-frying with an unchanged recipe for nearly 80 years. The seats at the counter – where you can watch the perfectly choreographed chefs – are the most coveted, though there is usually a queue. There are tables upstairs.

Delifucious
Burgers ¥

(Map p246; 📞03-6874-0412; www.delifucious. com; 1-9-13 Higashiyama, Meguro-ku; burgers from ¥1000; 🕐noon-9pm Thu-Tue; 🚇Hibiya line to Naka-Meguro, main exit) What happens when a former Ginza sushi chef turns his attention to – of all things – hamburgers? You get fish burgers and *anago* (seafaring eel) hot dogs prepared with the same attention to ingredients, preparation and presentation that you'd expect from a high-end sushi counter (but at a far more acceptable price).

Ouca
Ice Cream ¥

(櫻花; Map p246; www.ice-ouca.com; 1-6-6 Ebisu, Shibuya-ku; ice cream from ¥400; 🕐11am-11.30pm Mar-Oct, noon-11pm Nov-Feb; 🚉JR Yamanote line to Ebisu, east exit) Green tea isn't the only flavour Japan has contributed to the ice-cream playbook; other delicious innovations available (seasonally) at this famous Ebisu ice-cream stand include *kuro-goma* (black sesame), *kinako kurosato* (roasted soybean flour and black sugar) and *beni imo* (purple sweet potato).

Onibus Coffee
Coffee ¥

(オニバスコーヒー; Map p246; 📞03-6412-8683; www.onibuscoffee.com; 2-14-1 Kami-Meguro, Meguro-ku; 🕐9am-6pm; 🚇Hibiya line to Naka-Meguro, south exit) Local hotspot Onibus Coffee perfectly nails two of Tokyo's current obsessions: third-wave coffee and

restored heritage buildings. The beans here are roasted in-house and the cafe is set in a lightly renovated former tofu shop.

Udon Yamachō
Udon ¥

(うどん山長; Map p246; 1-1-5 Ebisu, Shibuya-ku; udon ¥680-1180; 🕐11.30am-3.30pm & 5-11.30pm; 🚉JR Yamanote line to Ebisu, east exit) Go for bowls of Kansai-style udon (thick white wheat noodles) at this rustic-chic noodle joint alongside the Shibuya-gawa. In the evening you can order additional sides (such as seasonal veg tempura) and sake. The shop, with white curtains over the door, is next to a park with a slide shaped like an octopus (you'll see what we mean!).

Rangmang Shokudō
Shokudo ¥

(らんまん食堂; Map p246; 📞03-5489-4129; www.rangmang.com; 1-4-1 Ebisu-nishi, Shibuya-ku; dishes ¥460-660; 🕐11.30am-2.30pm & 6pm-midnight Mon-Fri, noon-2.30pm & 5-9.30pm Sat; 🚉JR Yamanote line to Ebisu) Fried chicken – which in Japan is lightly coated in a very fine starch – is having a moment and Rangmang Shokudō has a lot to do with that. Each order comes with four or five large bites, so you can eat light or go all out and sample several flavours. Staff recommend starting out with the classic *shio* (salt).

Ebisu-yokochō
Street Food ¥

(恵比寿横町; Map p246; www.ebisu-yokocho. com; 1-7-4 Ebisu, Shibuya-ku; dishes ¥500-1500; 🕐5pm-late; 🚉JR Yamanote line to Ebisu, east exit) Locals love this retro arcade chock-a-block with food stalls dishing up everything from humble *yaki-soba* (fried buckwheat noodles) to decadent *hotate-yaki* (grilled scallops). Seating is on stools; some of the tables are made from repurposed beer crates. It's loud and lively pretty much every night of the week; go early to get a table. Hours and prices vary by shop.

Yakiniku Champion
Barbecue ¥¥

(焼肉チャンピオン; Map p246; 📞03-5768-6922; www.yakiniku-champion.com; 1-2-8 Ebisu, Shibuya-ku; dishes ¥780-3300, course from ¥5600; 🕐5pm-midnight; 🚉JR Yamanote line to Ebisu, west exit) Champion is one of Tokyo's best spots for *yakiniku* – literally 'grilled

🍽 Department-Store Food Halls

The below-ground floors of Tokyo's department stores hold fantastic food halls called *depachika* (literally 'department-store basement'). There are usually a few eat-in shops as well as many takeaway counters – often outposts of famous restaurants and producers. **Food Show** (フードショー; Map p246; basement fl, 2-24-1 Shibuya, Shibuya-ku; ⊙10am-9pm; ✍; 🚇JR Yamanote line to Shibuya, Hachikō exit), Tokyu Department Store's food hall beneath Shibuya Station, is great.

Also check out the lower levels of Isetan (p154) and Mitsukoshi (p162).

Mitsukoshi
MATT MUNRO/LONELY PLANET ©

meat' and the Japanese term for Korean barbecue. The menu runs the gamut from sweetbreads to the choicest cuts of grade A5 *wagyū;* there's a diagram of the cuts as well as descriptions. It's very popular; reservations recommended.

Ippo   Izakaya ¥¥

(一歩; Map p246; ☎03-3445-8418; www.sakana bar-ippo.com; 2nd fl, 1-22-10 Ebisu, Shibuya-ku; cover charge ¥500, dishes ¥450-1700; ⊙6pm-3am; 🚇JR Yamanote line to Ebisu, east exit) This mellow little *izakaya* specialises in simple pleasures: fish and sake (there's an English sign out front that says just that). The friendly chefs speak some English and can help you decide what to have grilled, steamed, simmered or fried; if you can't

decide, the ¥2500 set menu is great value. The entrance is up the wooden stairs.

Higashi-Yama   Japanese ¥¥¥

(ヒガシヤマ; Map p246; ☎03-5720-1300; www. higashiyama-tokyo.jp; 1-21-25 Higashiyama, Meguro-ku; lunch/dinner from ¥1650/4950; ⊙11.30am-3pm Tue-Sat, 6pm-1am Mon-Sat; 🚇Hibiya line to Naka-Meguro, main exit) Higashi-Yama serves beautiful modern Japanese cuisine; the interior, a rustic take on minimalism, is stunning too. The restaurant is all but hidden, on a side street with little signage; see the website for a map. Tasting courses make ordering easy; the 'chef's recommendation' course (¥9020) is a worthwhile splurge. Advance bookings preferred.

😣 Roppongi & Around

Honmura-An   Soba ¥

(本むら庵; Map p252; ☎03-5772-6657; www. honmuraantokyo.com; 7-14-18 Roppongi, Minato-ku; noodles from ¥900, set meals lunch/dinner ¥1600/7400; ⊙noon-2.30pm & 5.30-10pm Tue-Sun, closed 1st & 3rd Tue of month; 🕾; 🚇Hibiya line to Roppongi, exit 4) This fabled soba shop, once located in Manhattan, now serves its handmade buckwheat noodles at this rustically contemporary noodle shop on a Roppongi side street. The noodles' delicate flavour is best appreciated when served on a bamboo mat, with tempura or with dainty slices of *kamo* (duck).

Sougo   Japanese ¥

(宗胡; Map p252; ☎03-5414-1133; www.sougo. tokyo; 3rd fl, Roppongi Green Bldg, 6-1-8 Roppongi, Minato-ku; set meals lunch/dinner from ¥1500/6500; ⊙11.30am-3pm & 6-11pm Mon-Sat; ✍; 🚇Hibiya line to Roppongi, exit 3) Sit at the long counter beside the open kitchen or in booths and watch the expert chefs prepare delicious and beautifully presented *shōjin-ryōri* (mainly vegetarian cuisine as served at Buddhist temples – some dishes use *dashi* stock, which contains fish). Lunch is a bargain. Reserve at least one day in advance for a vegan meal (lunch/dinner ¥7000/10,000).

Akasaka Ichiryu Bekkan   Korean ¥

(赤坂一龍 別館; ☑03-3582-7008; 2-13-17 Akasaka, Minato-ku; seolleongtang ¥1620; ◷24hr; ⑤Chiyoda line to Akasaka, exit 2) While it won't win any awards for its decor, this three-decades old, round-the-clock joint is beloved for its heart-warming rendition of the Korean beef-noodle soup *seolle-ongtang*. It's served with a full range of traditional Korean side dishes, including spicy kimchi. Look for a steaming bowl of noodles on the street outside.

Bricolage Bread & Co   Cafe ¥¥

(Map p252; ☑03-6804-3350; www.bricolage bread.com; 6-15-1 Roppongi, Minato-ku; mains ¥900-1600; ◷9am-7.30pm Tue-Sun; ⑤Hibiya line to Roppongi, exit 1) A collaboration between coffee shop Fuglen, Michelin-starred restaurant L'effervescence and Osaka-based bakery Le Sucré Coeur, this appealing spot is decorated like a chic country farmhouse, with an enormous flower display on its central table. Enjoy single-origin Aeropress coffee along with sweet and savoury *tartines* (open-faced sandwiches) on slices of delicious sourdough bread. The perfect spot for breakfast or lunch.

Jōmon   Izakaya ¥¥

(ジョウモン; Map p252; ☑03-3405-2585; www. teyandei.com; 5-9-17 Roppongi, Minato-ku; skewers ¥250-500, dishes from ¥580; ◷5.30-11.45pm Sun-Thu, until 5am Fri & Sat; ☑; ⑤Hibiya line to Roppongi, exit 3) This cosy kitchen has bar seating, rows of ornate *shōchū* (liquor) jugs lining the wall and hundreds of freshly prepared skewers splayed in front of the patrons – don't miss the heavenly *zabuton* beef stick. Jōmon is almost directly across from the Family Mart – look for the name in Japanese on the door. Cover charge ¥300 per person.

Kikunoi   Kaiseki ¥¥¥

(菊乃井; Map p252; ☑03-3568-6055; www. kikunoi.jp; 6-13-8 Akasaka, Minato-ku; lunch/dinner course from ¥11,900/16,000; ◷noon-12.30pm Tue-Sat, 5-7.30pm Mon-Sat; ⑤Chiyoda line to Akasaka, exit 7) Exquisitely prepared

Kikunoi

Izakaya, Ueno

seasonal dishes are as beautiful as they are delicious at this Tokyo outpost of one of Kyoto's most acclaimed *kaiseki* (Japanese haute cuisine) restaurants. Kikunoi's third-generation chef, Murata Yoshihiro, has written a book on *kaiseki* (translated into English) that the staff helpfully use to explain the dishes you are served.

Tofuya-Ukai   Kaiseki ¥¥¥

(とうふ屋うかい; Map p252; ✆03-3436-1028; www.ukai.co.jp/english/shiba; 4-4-13 Shiba-kōen, Minato-ku; set meals lunch/dinner from ¥5940/10,800; ⏰11.45am-3pm & 5-7.30pm Mon-Fri, 11am-7.30pm Sat & Sun; 🖉; Ⓢ Ōedo line to Akabanebashi, exit 8) One of Tokyo's most gracious restaurants is located in a former sake brewery (moved from northern Japan), with an exquisite traditional garden in the shadow of Tokyo Tower. Seasonal preparations of tofu and accompanying dishes are served in the refined *kaiseki* (Japanese haute cuisine) style. Make reservations well in advance. Vegetarians should advise staff when they book, and last orders for weekday lunch are by 3pm, for dinner 7.30pm.

✸ Ginza & Tsukiji

Cafe de l'Ambre   Cafe ¥

(カフェ・ド・ランブル; Map p250; ✆03-3571-1551; www.cafedelambre.com; 8-10-15 Ginza, Chūō-ku; ⏰noon-10pm Mon-Sat, to 7pm Sun; ®Ginza line to Ginza, exit A4) The sign over the door here reads 'Coffee Only' but, oh, what a selection (coffee from ¥700). Sekiguchi Ichiro started the business in 1948 sourcing and roasting aged beans from all over the world – he ran the place until close to his death at 103 in 2018. It's dark, retro and classic Ginza.

Cha Ginza   Teahouse ¥

(茶・銀座; Map p250; ✆03-3571-1211; www.uogashi-meicha.co.jp; 5-5-6 Ginza, Chūō-ku; ⏰teahouse noon-5pm Tue-Sat, shop 11am-6pm Tue-Sat; Ⓢ Ginza line to Ginza, exit B3) Take a pause for afternoon tea (¥700 to ¥1400) at this slick contemporary tea salon. The menu is seasonal, but will likely include a cup of perfectly prepared *matcha* (powdered green tea) and a small sweet or two, or a choice of *sencha* (premium green tea). The ground-floor shop sells top-quality teas from various growing regions in Japan.

Jugetsudo   Teahouse ¥

(寿月堂; Map p250; ☎03-6278-7626; www. maruyamanori.com; 5th fl, Kabuki-za Tower, 4-12-15 Ginza, Chūō-ku; ☺10am-7pm; ⑤Hibiya line to Higashi-Ginza, exit 3) This venerable tea seller's main branch is closer to Tsukiji, but this classy outlet in the Kabuki-za Tower has a Kengo Kuma–designed cafe where you can sample the various Japanese green teas, including *matcha;* sets, which include *wagashi* (Japanese sweets), cost ¥1100 to ¥2200. Enter on Shōwa-dōri.

Turret Coffee   Cafe ¥

(Map p250; http://ja-jp.facebook.com/turret coffee; 2-12-6 Tsukiji, Chūō-ku; ☺7am-6pm Mon-Sat, from noon Sun; ⑤Hibiya line to Tsukiji, exit 2) Kawasaki Kiyoshi set up his plucky indie coffee shop next to Starbucks. It takes its name from the three-wheeled delivery trucks that beetle around the fish market – there's one on the premises. Ideal for an early-morning espresso en route to or from the outer market area. Drinks cost ¥360 to ¥560.

Rose Bakery   Bakery ¥

(Map p250; ☎03-5537-5038; http://rosebakery. jp; 7th fl, Ginza Komatsu West, 6-9-5 Ginza, Chūō-ku; baked goods from ¥420, meals from ¥1100; ☺11am-9pm Mon-Fri, from 9am Sat & Sun; ☑; ⑤Ginza line to Ginza, exit A2) This chic branch of the top-class organic bakery chain is on the 7th floor of the same building as Dover Street Market Ginza (p161). Come here for great cakes, healthy salads, quiche and sandwiches.

Monja Kondō   Japanese ¥

(もんじゃ近どう; Map p250; ☎03-3533-4555; 3-12-10 Tsukishima, Chūō-ku; monjayaki ¥700-1500; ☺5-10pm Mon-Fri, from noon Sat & Sun; ⑤Ōedo line to Tsukishima, exit 8) *Monjayaki* is a Tokyo speciality, a batter, veg, seafood and meat fry-up with a loose, scrambled-egg-like texture. This place dating back to 1950 is said to be Tsukishima's oldest purveyor of the dish. There are some 90 different

toppings you can add to the basic mix, and the staff will help you to make it at your own table grill.

Nakajima no Ochaya   Teahouse ¥

(中島の御茶屋; Map p250; 1-1 Hama-rikyū Onshi-teien, Chūō-ku; tea ¥510 or ¥720; ☺9am-4.30pm; ⑧Ōedo line to Shiodome, exit A1) This beautiful teahouse from 1704 (and rebuilt in 1983) stands elegantly on an island in the central pond at Hama-rikyū Onshi-teien (p109), reached via a long cedar bridge. It's an ideal spot for a cup of *matcha* (powdered green tea) and a sweet while contemplating the very faraway 21st century beyond the garden walls.

Ain Soph   Vegan ¥¥

(Map p250; ☎03-6228-4241; www.ain-soph. jp; 4-12-1 Ginza, Chūō-ku; mains from ¥1680, bentō boxes & set menus lunch/dinner from ¥2480/3250; ☺11.30am-10pm Wed-Mon; ⑤Asakusa or Hibiya line to Higashi-Ginza, exit A7) Truly vegan restaurants are few and far between in Tokyo and ones that make so much effort over their food as Ain Soph are even rarer. Thank heavens then for this stylish place (bookings are essential for dinner) that serves delicious *bentō* box meals, vegan-cheese fondue, smoothies and fluffy American-style pancakes.

Apollo   Greek ¥¥

(Map p250; ☎03-6264-5220; www.theapollo.jp; 11th fl, Tōkyū Plaza Ginza, 5-2-1 Ginza, Chūō-ku; mains ¥1680-5980; ☺11am-11pm; ⑤Ginza line to Ginza, exits C2 & C3) Ginza's glittering lights are the dazzling backdrop to this ace import from Sydney with its delicious take on modern Greek cuisine. The Mediterranean flavours come through strongly in dishes such as grilled octopus and fennel salad, taramasalata, and lamb shoulder with lemon and Greek yoghurt. Portions are large and meant for sharing.

Ginza Sato Yosuke   Noodles ¥¥

(銀座 佐藤養助; Map p250; ☎03-6215-6211; www.sato-yoske.co.jp/en/shop/ginza; 6-4-17 Ginza, Chūō-ku; noodles from ¥1300; ☺11.30am-3pm & 5-10pm; ⑤Marunouchi line to Ginza, exit C2) A speciality of Akita

Prefecture, *inaniwa* wheat noodles have been made by seven generations of the Sato family. As you'll be able to tell from the glossy, silky-textured results, they've pretty much got it down to perfection. Sample the noodles in a hot chicken broth or cold dipping sauces such as sesame and miso or green curry.

Trattoria Tsukiji Paradiso!
Italian ¥¥

(トラットリア・築地パラディーゾ; Map p250; ☑03-3545-5550; www.tsukiji-paradiso. com; 6-27-3 Tsukiji, Chūō-ku; mains ¥1500-3600; ⊙11am-2pm & 6-10pm Thu-Tue; ⑤Hibiya line to Tsukiji, exit 2) Paradise for food lovers, indeed. This charming, aqua-painted trattoria serves seafood pasta dishes that will make you want to lick the plate clean. Its signature linguine is packed with shellfish in a scrumptious tomato, chilli and garlic sauce. Lunch (from ¥980) is a bargain, but you'll need to queue; book for dinner. The menu is in Japanese and Italian.

Sushikuni
Japanese ¥¥

(鮨國; Map p250; ☑03-3545-8234; 4-14-15 Tsukiji, Chūō-ku; seafood rice bowls from ¥3000; ⊙10am-3pm & 5-9pm Thu-Tue; ⑤Hibiya line to Tsukiji, exit 1) *Kaisen-don* (bowls of rice topped with a variety of raw fish) is a common dish at Tsukiji's many seafood restaurants. The toppings of rich, creamy *uni* (sea urchin roe) and salty *ikura* (salmon roe) are generous here and straight from the market.

Kyūbey
Sushi ¥¥¥

(久兵衛; Map p250; ☑03-3571-6523; www. kyubey.jp; 8-7-6 Ginza, Chūō-ku; set meals lunch/ dinner from ¥4400/11,000; ⊙11.30am-2pm & 5-10pm Mon-Sat; ⑤Ginza line to Shimbashi, exit 3) Since 1935, Kyūbey's quality and presentation have won it a moneyed and celebrity clientele. Despite the cachet, this is a relaxed restaurant. The friendly owner, Imada-san, speaks excellent English as do some of his team of talented chefs, who will make and serve your sushi, piece by piece. The ¥8000 lunchtime *omakase* (chef's choice) is great value.

Tempura Kondō
Tempura ¥¥¥

(てんぷら近藤; Map p250; ☑03-5568-0923; 9th fl, Sakaguchi Bldg, 5-5-13 Ginza, Chūō-ku; lunch/ dinner course from ¥6500/11,000; ⊙noon-3pm & 5-10pm Mon-Sat; ⑤Ginza line to Ginza, exit B5) Nobody in Tokyo does tempura vegetables like chef Kondō Fumio. The carrots are julienned to a fine floss; the corn is pert and juicy; and the sweet potato is comfort food at its finest. Courses include seafood, too. Lunch at noon or 1.30pm; last dinner booking at 8pm. Reserve ahead.

Bird Land
Yakitori ¥¥¥

(バードランド; Map p250; ☑03-5250-1081; www.ginza-birdland.sakura.ne.jp; 4-2-15 Ginza, Chūō-ku; dishes ¥500-2000, set meals from ¥6300; ⊙5-9.30pm Tue-Sat; ⑤Ginza line to Ginza, exit C6) This is as suave as it gets for gourmet grilled chicken. Chefs in whites behind a U-shaped counter dispense *yakitori* in all shapes, sizes, colours and organs – don't pass up the dainty serves of liver pâté or the tiny cup of chicken soup. Pair it with wine from the extensive list. Enter beneath Suit Company. Reservations recommended.

⊗ Marunouchi & Nihombashi

Chashitsu Kaboku
Teahouse ¥

(茶室 嘉木; Map p250; ☑03-6212-0202; www. ippodo-tea.co.jp; 3-1-1 Marunouchi, Chiyoda-ku; tea set ¥1080-2600; ⊙11am-7pm; Ⓡ JR Yamanote line to Yurakuchō, Tokyo International Forum exit) Run by famed Kyoto tea producer Ippōdō – which celebrated 300 years of business in 2017 – this teahouse is a fantastic place to experience the myriad pleasures of *ocha* (green tea). It's also one of the few places that serves *koicha* (thick tea), which is even thicker than ordinary *matcha* (powdered green tea). Sets are accompanied by a pretty, seasonal *wagashi*.

Dhaba India
South Indian ¥

(ダバ インディア; Map p250; ☑03-3272-7160; www.dhabaindia.com; 2-7-9 Yaesu, Chūō-ku; lunch/mains from ¥850/1370; ⊙11.15am-3pm &

Fuglen Tokyo (p130)

5-11pm Mon-Fri, noon-3pm & 5-10pm Sat & Sun; ⑤Ginza line to Kyōbashi, exit 5) Indian meals in Tokyo don't come much better than those served at this long-established restaurant with deep-indigo plaster walls. The food is very authentic, particularly the curries served with basmati rice, naan or crispy *dosa* (giant lentil-flour pancakes). Set lunches are spectacularly good value.

Nihonbashi Dashi Bar Hanare Japanese ¥

(日本橋だし場はなれ; Map p250; ☑03-5205-8704; www.ninben.co.jp/hanare; 1st fl, Coredo Muromachi 2, 2-3-1 Nihombashi-Muromachi, Chūō-ku; set meals ¥1025-1950, dishes ¥650-1300; ⏱11am-2pm & 5-11pm; ⑤Ginza line to Mitsukoshimae, exit A6) This casual restaurant from long-time producer (300-plus years!) of *katsuo-bushi* (dried bonito flakes), Ninben, naturally serves dishes that make use of the umami-rich ingredient. Set meals, with dishes such as hearty miso soups and *dashi takikokomi gohan* (rice steamed in stock), are good value, and healthy to boot.

Taimeiken Japanese ¥

(たいめいけん; Map p250; ☑03-3271-2463; www.taimeiken.co.jp; 1-12-10 Nihombashi, Chūō-ku; mains ¥750-2650; ⏱11am-8.30pm Mon-Sat, to 8pm Sun; ⑤Ginza line to Nihombashi, exit C5) This classic restaurant, open since 1931, specialises in *yōshoku* – Western cuisine adapted to the Japanese palate. Its signature dish is *omuraisu* (an omelette stuffed with ketchup-flavoured fried rice), to which you can add a side of borscht and coleslaw for the very retro price of ¥50 each. The *tampopo omuraisu* was created for Itami Jūzō's cult movie.

Nemuro Hanamaru Sushi ¥

(根室花まる; Map p250; ☑03-6269-9026; www.sushi-hanamaru.com; 4th fl, KITTE, 2-7-2 Marunouchi, Chiyoda-ku; sushi per plate ¥140-540; ⏱11am-10pm, until 9pm Sun; ⏺JR lines to Tokyo, Marunouchi south exit) The port of Nemuro in northern Hokkaidō is where this popular sushi operation first started. At this branch, on the 4th floor of the KITTE mall, it's a self-serve *kaiten-sushi* where the vinegared rice bites are delivered by

Tokyo on a Plate

The most common kind of sushi is called *nigiri-zushi* (hand-pressed sushi).

Other kinds of sush include *maki-zushi* (rolled sushi).

The pickled ginger (called gari) served with sushi is to cleanse your palate between pieces.

It's totally fine to eat *nigiri-zushi* and *maki-zishi* by hand.

Sushi is commonly dipped lightly in soy sauce.

Sushi is usually served with a touch of wasabi.

PROSTOCK-STUDIO/SHUTTERSTOCK ©

Japanese Sushi

Sushi Essentials

Most sushi restaurants offer set meals – say 10 or 12 pieces of sushi – of varying price (between ¥1500 and ¥5000, depending on the ingredients rather than portion size). These are always the most economical way to go. High-end places serve *omakase* (chef's choice) courses, which consist of a procession of some maybe 20 dishes and cost a minimum of ¥10,000 per person for dinner. On the other end of the spectrum are cheap *kaiten-zushi*, where ready-made plates of sushi are sent around the restaurant on a conveyor belt. The best thing about these restaurants is that you don't have to worry about ordering: just grab whatever looks good as it goes by.

Right: Nigiri-zushi
STRAY TOKI/SHUTTERSTOCK ©

☆ Top Five for Sushi

Sushi Dai (p87) The most famous spot for sushi breakfast inside Toyosu Market.

Kyūbey (p140) The high-end *omakase* experience.

Kizushi (p143) Historic restaurant serving classic Tokyo-style sushi.

Nemuro Hanamaru (p141) One of the city's best kaiten-sushi (conveyor-belt sushi restaurants).

Daiwa Sushi (p87) Great value sets, also fresh from Toyosu Market.

rotating conveyor belt. The line here can often be very long but it's worth the wait for the quality and price.

Nihonbashi Tamai
Japanese ¥¥

(玉ゐ 本店; Map p250; ☑03-3272-3227; www.anago-tamai.com; 2-9-9 Nihonbashi, Chūō-ku; mains from ¥1450; ☺11am-2.30pm & 5-9.30pm Mon-Fri, 11.30am-3.30pm & 4.30-9pm Sat & Sun; ⑤Ginza line to Nihombashi, exit C4) This Nihonbashi stalwart specialises in *anago* (seafaring eel), which is cheaper and not endangered like its freshwater cousin *unagi*. The eels are prepared to perfection here, laid out in lacquerware boxes (a style known as *hakomeshi*) and served either grilled or boiled – you can sample both cooking styles by asking for half and half.

Kizushi
Sushi ¥¥¥

(喜寿司; Map p250; ☑03-3666-1682; 2-7-13 Nihonbashi-Ningyōchō, Chūō-ku; course from ¥3500-10,000; ☺11.45am-2.30pm Mon-Sat, 5-9.30pm Mon-Fri, to 9pm Sat; ⑤Hibiya line to Ningyōchō, exit A3) While sushi has moved in the direction of faster and fresher, Kizushi, in business since 1923, is keeping it old school. Third-generation chef Yui Ryuichi uses traditional techniques, such as marinating the fish in salt or vinegar, from back when sushi was more about preservation than instant gratification. The shop is in a lovely old timber-frame house.

Tamahide
Japanese ¥¥¥

(玉ひで; Map p250; ☑03-3668-7651; www.tamahide.co.jp; 1-17-1 Nihonbashi-Ningyōchō, Chūō-ku; lunch from ¥1500, dinner set course from ¥6800; ☺11.30am-1.30pm & 5-10pm Mon-Sat; ⑤Hibiya line to Ningyōchō, exit A1) For generations, locals and visitors have been lining up outside this restaurant – in business since 1760 – to try its signature dish *oyakodon*, a sweet-savoury mix of chicken, soy broth and lightly cooked egg, served over a bowl of rice. It also has dishes using minced chicken or duck that are all delicious and filling. Pay before you sit down at lunch.

❖ Kanda & Akihabara

Kanda Yabu Soba
Soba ¥

(神田やぶそば; Map p254; ☑03-3251-0287; www.yabusoba.net; 2-10 Kanda-Awajichō, Chiyoda-ku; noodles ¥670-1910; ☺11.30am-8.30pm Thu-Tue; ⑤Marunouchi line to Awajichō, exit A3) Totally rebuilt following a fire in 2013, this is one of Tokyo's most venerable buckwheat noodle shops, in business since 1880. Come here for classic handmade noodles and accompaniments such as shrimp tempura *(ten-seiro soba)* or slices of duck *(kamo-nanban soba)*.

Kagawa Ippuku
Udon ¥

(香川 一福 神田店; Map p250; ☑03-557-3644; www.udon-ippuku-kanda.com; 1st fl, Tokyo Royal Plaza,1-18-11 Uchikanda, Chiyoda-ku; udon ¥430-820; ☺11am-8pm Mon-Sat, also closed 1st Mon of month; ☐Yamanote line to Kanda, west exit) Proof you don't need to shell out a small fortune to eat well in Tokyo is this humble restaurant specialising in *Sanuki-udon*, wheat noodles from Kagawa in Shikoku. Pay at the vending machine; you'll be handed an English menu to help with the options, which include the amount of noodles you wish and the toppings. The curry noodles are excellent.

Saboru
Cafe ¥

(さぼうる; Map p254; ☑03-3291-8404; 1-11 Kanda-Jimbōchō, Chiyoda-ku; coffee from ¥450; ☺9.30am-11pm Mon-Sat; ⑤Hanzōmon line to Jimbōchō, exit A7) Saboru checks the boxes of a classic mid-20th-century *kissaten*: dim lighting, low tables, lots of dark wood and strong *burendo kōhī* ('blend' coffee). And then it adds a few of its own pluses: totem poles, a Robinson Crusoe vibe and copious potted plants. Come before 11am for the good-value morning set (coffee, hard-boiled egg and two rolls for ¥500).

Isegen
Japanese ¥¥

(いせ源; Map p254; ☑03-3251-1229; www.isegen.com; 1-11-1 Kanda-Sudachō, Chiyoda-ku; lunch/dinner from ¥1000/3500; ☺11.30am-2pm & 5-9pm, closed Sat & Sun Apr-Oct;

⑤Marunouchi line to Awajichō, exit A3) This illustrious fish restaurant, in business since the 1830s, operates out of a handsome 1930 wooden building. The speciality is *ankō-nabe* (monkfish stew; ¥3500 per person, minimum order for two only in the evening), served in a splendid communal tatami room. Get a side of *kimo-zashi* (monkfish liver; ¥1500) – a prized delicacy – served pâté-style.

Kado
Japanese ¥¥

(カド; ☏03-3268-2410; http://kagurazaka-kado. com; 1-32 Akagi-Motomachi, Shinjuku-ku; set menus ¥3000-5000; ⊙restaurant 5-11pm Tue-Fri, bar from 4pm Tue-Fri & 2pm Sat & Sun; Ⓡ Tōzai line to Kagurazaka, exit 1) Set in an old wooden house with a white lantern out the front, Kado specialises in *katei-ryōri* (home-cooking). Dinner is a set course of seasonal dishes (such as grilled quail or fresh tofu). Bookings are required for the full selection of courses, but you can try turning up on the night and if there's space, you'll be able to eat.

Inua
Gastronomy ¥¥¥

(☏03-6683-7570; https://inua.jp; 2 -13-12 Fujimi, Chiyoda-ku; set menu ¥29,000; ⊙5-8.45pm Tue-Sat; Ⓡ JR Sobu line to Iidabashi, west exit) Helmed by Noma alumnus Thomas Frebel and a crack team of young chefs and front-of-house staff, Inua was Tokyo's most feted restaurant opening of 2018. With its focus on sourcing amazing local produce – be it prized enoki mushrooms from Hokkaidō, wild pepper from Okinawa or bee larva from Nagano – the 15-course set menu is a gourmet delight.

⊗ Ueno & Yanaka

Innsyoutei
Japanese ¥

(韻松亭; Map p254; ☏03-3821-8126; www.inn syoutei.jp; 4-59 Ueno-kōen, Taitō-ku; lunch/dinner from ¥1680/5500; ⊙restaurant 11am-3pm & 5-9.30pm, tearoom 3-5pm; Ⓡ JR lines to Ueno, Ueno-kōen exit) In a gorgeous wooden building dating to 1875, Innsyoutei (pronounced 'inshotei' and meaning 'rhyme of the pine cottage') has long been a favourite spot for fancy *kaiseki*-style meals while visiting

Ueno-kōen (p54). Without a booking (essential for dinner) you'll have a long wait but it's worth it. Lunchtime *bentō* (boxed meals) offer beautifully presented morsels and are great value.

Tayori
Japanese ¥

(Map p254; ☏03-5834-7026; www.tayori-osozai. jp; 3-12-4 Yanaka, Taitō-ku; set meals ¥1000; ⊙11.30am-8pm Wed-Mon; 🛜; Ⓡ Yamanote line to Nippori, Yanaka exit) Tucked down an alley off Yanaka Ginza (p55) is this design-savvy deli and cafe that subscribes to the farm-to-table ethos by telling customers all about its ingredients' provenance. The set meals are excellent value and the cool, artisan atmosphere makes it a prime spot to revive while you explore the area.

Kamachiku
Udon ¥

(釜竹; Map p254; ☏03-5815-4675; www.kama chiku.com; 2-14-18 Nezu, Bunkyō-ku; noodles from ¥850, small dishes ¥350-950; ⊙11.30am-2pm Tue-Sun, 5.30-9pm Tue-Sat; ⑤Chiyoda line to Nezu, exit 1) Freshly made udon are the speciality at this popular restaurant, in a beautifully restored brick warehouse from 1910 that's incorporated into a building designed by Kuma Kengo. In addition to noodles, the menu includes a good selection of sake and lots of small dishes (such as grilled fish, veggies and a delicious Japanese-style omelette).

Himitsu-dō
Sweets ¥

(ひみつ堂; Map p254; ☏03-3824-4132; http:// himitsudo.com; 3-11-18 Yanaka, Taitō-ku; ⊙10am-6pm, closed Mon Jun-Jul & Sep, closed Mon & Tue Oct-May; 🍴; Ⓡ JR Yamanote line to Nippori, north exit) Summer in Japan is synonymous with *kakigōri*, shaved ice topped with colorful syrups and sweetened condensed milk. So popular is Himitsu-dō, however, that a queue can form even in the dead of winter. One of the secrets to its success is natural ice harvested from frozen-over waters in Tochigi Prefecture; another is its rotating selection of over 100 flavours.

Nezu-no-Taiyaki
Sweets ¥

(根津のたいやき; Map p254; ☏03-3823-6277; https://twitter.com/taiyaki_nezu; 1-23-9-104

Nezu, Bunkyō-ku; tai-yaki ¥170; ☺10.30am
until sold out, closed irregularly; ; SChiyoda
line to Nezu, exit 1) This street stall, beloved
of locals for half a century, sells just one
thing: *tai-yaki* – hot, sweet, bean-jam buns
shaped like *tai* (sea bream), a fish considered to be lucky. Come early before they
sell out (always by 2pm and sometimes by
noon).

Kayaba Coffee Cafe ¥
(カヤバ珈琲; Map p254; ☎03-3823-3545;
http://kayaba-coffee.com; 6-1-29 Yanaka, Taitō-
ku; coffee ¥450; ☺8am-9pm Mon-Sat, to 6pm
Sun; SChiyoda line to Nezu, exit 1) This vintage
1930s coffee shop (the building is actually
from the '20s) in Yanaka is a hang-out for
local students and artists. Come early for
the 'morning set' (coffee and a sandwich
for ¥800; served 8am to 11am). In the
evenings, Kayaba morphs into a bar.

Hantei Japanese ¥¥
(はん亭; Map p254; ☎03-3287-9000; www.
hantei.co.jp; 2-12-15 Nezu, Bunkyō-ku; lunch/
dinner from ¥3200/3000; ☺noon-3pm & 5-10pm
Tue-Sun; SChiyoda line to Nezu, exit 2) Housed
in a beautifully maintained, century-old traditional wooden building, Hantei is a local
landmark. Delectable skewers of seasonal
kushiage (fried meat, fish and vegetables)
are served with small, refreshing side dishes. Lunch includes eight or 12 sticks and
dinner starts with six, after which you can
order additional rounds (three/six skewers
¥800/1600).

Ueno-Sakuragi
Nanohana Japanese ¥¥
(上野桜木 菜の花; Map p254; ☎03-3827-3511;
1-10-26 Ueno-Sakuragi, Taitō-ku; lunch/dinner
¥1580/5400; ☺11am-2pm & 5.30-9.30pm Tue-
Sat, 11am-4pm Sun; SChiyoda line to Nezu, exit
1) The family who run this charming little
restaurant source many of their organic
ingredients, including the rice, pickles and
vegetables for side dishes, from the chef's
mother who lives on Sado-ga-shima. The
house speciality is *ochazuke* – rice mixed
with cuts of raw fish, other toppings and a
clear broth.

🍽 Street Food

Street-food stands, called *yatai* (屋台),
don't have the same ubiquitous presence
in Tokyo as they do in other Asian cities.
However, you can find them in markets, including Tsukiji Market (p108) or
Ameya-yokochō (p55); heavily touristed
areas, such as Asakusa and Ueno-
kōen (p54); and always at festivals. Typical *yatai* food includes *okonomiyaki* (お好
み焼き; savoury pancakes), *yaki-soba* (焼
きそば; stir-fried noodles) and *tai-yaki* (
たい焼き; fish-shaped cakes stuffed with
bean paste).

Food trucks are popular with the
downtown office crowd, gathering daily
at lunchtime around Marunouchi's **Tokyo
International Forum** (東京国際フォーラ
ム; Map p250; ☎03-5221-9000; www.t-i-fo-
rum.co.jp; 3-5-1 Marunouchi, Chiyoda-ku;
☺7am-11.30pm; JR Yamanote line to Yūrakuchō, central exit) FREE. They also make
the weekend rounds of farmers markets,
like Farmer's Market @UNU (p146).

SAVVAPANF PHOTO/SHUTTERSTOCK ©

Sasa-no-Yuki Tofu ¥¥
(笹乃雪; Map p254; ☎03-3873-1145; www.
sasanoyuki.com; 2-15-10 Negishi, Taitō-ku;
dishes ¥400-700, lunch/dinner course from
¥2400/5600; ☺11.30am-8.30pm Tue-Sun; ;
JR Yamanote line to Uguisudani, north exit)
Sasa-no-Yuki opened its doors in the Edo
period and continues to serve its signature
dishes with tofu made fresh every morning
using water from the shop's own well.
Some treats to expect: *ankake-dofu* (tofu in
a thick, sweet sauce) and *goma-dofu* (sesame tofu). Vegetarians should not assume

Farmers Markets

On weekends farmers markets take place around the city and are a good place to get fresh fruit and bread, plus packaged goods (such as miso and pickles) to take home. There are usually food trucks as well. The biggest is the **Farmer's Market @UNU** (Map p246; www.farmersmarkets.jp; 5-53-7 Jingūmae, Shibuya-ku; ⏰10am-4pm Sat & Sun; ⑤Ginza line to Omote-sandō, exit B2) 🍴, held every weekend in Aoyama.

Check out the blog **Japan Farmers Markets** (www.japanfarmersmarkets. com) to see what else is happening and where.

everything is purely veggie – ask before ordering. There is bamboo out the front.

Shinsuke   Izakaya ¥¥

(シンスケ; Map p254; ☎03-3832-0469; 3-31-5 Yushima, Bunkyō-ku; dishes ¥500-2500, cover charge ¥300; ⏰5-9.30pm Mon-Fri, to 9pm Sat; ⑤Chiyoda line to Yushima, exit 3) In business since 1925, Shinsuke has honed the concept of an ideal *izakaya* to perfection: long cedar counter, 'master' in *happi* (traditional short coat) and *hachimaki* (traditional headband), and smooth-as-silk *daiginjō* (premium-grade sake). The menu, updated monthly, includes house specialities (such as *kitsune raclette* – deep-fried tofu stuffed with raclette cheese) and seasonal dishes; note portions are small. Reservations recommended.

⊗ Asakusa & Ryōgoku

Misojyu   Japanese ¥

(Map p254; ☎03-5830-3101; www.misojyu.jp; 1-7-5 Asakusa, Taitō-ku; miso soup ¥780, set menu from ¥1280; ⏰8.30am-7pm Tue-Sun; 🚆Tsukuba Express to Asakusa, exit 4) The Japanese meal staples of rice, in the form of *onigiri* (rice balls), and miso soup, are given a stylish update at Misojyu. All ingredients are

organic and recipes range from traditional to contemporary, such as miso soup with beef and tomato-and-brown-rice *onigiri* covered in tea leaves. A limited breakfast menu is served until 11am.

Dandelion Chocolate   Cafe ¥

(Map p254; ☎03-5833-7270; http://dandelion chocolate.jp; 4-14-6 Kuramae, Taitō-ku; ⏰10am-8pm; 🛜; ⑤Asakusa line to Kuramae, exit A3) Perhaps the most compelling reason to have Kuramae on your to-visit list is this superior cafe specialising in bean-to-bar small-batch chocolate, made on the premises. The stylish, barnlike setting and delicious drink and food offerings are impossible to resist. There's also a pleasant community park opposite should you prefer to take away.

Onigiri Yadoroku   Japanese ¥

(おにぎり 浅草 宿六; Map p254; ☎03-3874-1615; www.onigiriyadoroku.com; 3-9-10 Asakusa, Taitō-ku; set lunch 2/3 onigiri from ¥690/930, onigiri ¥280-690; ⏰11.30am-5pm Mon-Sat, 6pm-2am Thu-Tue; 🚆Tsukuba Express to Asakusa, exit 1) *Onigiri* (rice balls), wrapped in crispy sheets of *nori* (seaweed), are a great Japanese culinary invention. Try them freshly made at Tokyo's oldest *onigiri* shop, which feels more like a classy sushi counter. The set lunches are a great deal; at night there's a large range of flavours to choose from, along with alcohol.

Kintame   Japanese ¥

(近為; ☎03-3641-4561; www.kintame.co.jp; 1-14-5 Tomioka, Kōtō-ku; meals from ¥1390; ⏰11am-5.30pm Tue-Sun; ⑤Ōedo line to Monzen-Nakachō, exit 1) This branch of the famous Kyoto-based pickle shop provides tastings of its traditional preserves done in a variety of ways, including with salt, vinegar miso and soy sauce. At a communal table you can also try its filling and good-value meals of fish marinated in sake lees (the deposits produced during the alcohol's fermentation).

Hoppy-dōri   Izakaya ¥

(ホッピー通り; Map p254; 2-5 Asakusa, Taitō-ku; dishes ¥500-700; ⏰noon until late, varies by shop; ⓇTsukuba Express to Asakusa, exit 4) Along either side of the street popularly known as Hoppy-dōri – 'hoppy' is a cheap malt beverage – are rows of *izakaya* with outdoor seating on rickety stools and plastic tarps for awnings. Don't let that put you off – this is one of Asakusa's most atmospheric eating and drinking strips.

Sometarō   Okonomiyaki ¥
(染太郎; Map p254; ☑03-3844-9502; 2-2-2 Nishi-Asakusa, Taitō-ku; mains from ¥700; ◷noon-10pm; ⓈGinza line to Tawaramachi, exit 3) Sometarō is a fun and funky place to try *okonomiyaki* (savoury Japanese-style pancakes filled with meat, seafood and vegetables that you cook yourself). This historic, vine-covered house is a friendly spot where the menu includes a how-to guide for novice cooks. Tatami seating; cash only.

Suzukien   Ice Cream ¥
(壽々喜園; Map p254; ☑03-3873-0311; http://tocha.co.jp; 3-4-3 Asakusa, Taitō-ku; ice cream from ¥370; ◷10am-5pm, closed 3rd Wed of the month; ⓇTsukuba Express to Asakusa, exit 1) Suzukien boasts of having the most *matcha*-ful *matcha* ice cream around, and the deep moss-green Premium No 7 does not disappoint. In addition to the seven levels of *matcha,* you can try ice cream in *hōjicha* (roasted green tea), *genmaicha* (brown rice tea) and *kōcha* (black tea) flavours.

Daikokuya   Tempura ¥
(大黒家; Map p254; ☑03-3844-1111; www.tempura.co.jp; 1-38-10 Asakusa, Taitō-ku; meals ¥1550-2100; ◷11am-8.30pm Sun-Fri, to 9pm Sat; ⓈGinza line to Asakusa, exit 1) This is the place to get old-fashioned tempura fried in pure sesame oil, an Asakusa speciality. It's in a white building with a tile roof. If there's a queue (and there often is), you can try your luck at the annex one block over – it also serves set-course meals.

Kappō Yoshiba   Japanese ¥¥
(割烹吉葉; Map p254; ☑03-3623-4480; www.kapou-yoshiba.jp; 2-14-5 Yokoami, Sumida-ku; dishes ¥650-7800; ◷11.30am-2pm & 5-10pm

Mon-Sat; ⓈŌedo line to Ryōgoku, exit 1) The former Miyagino sumo stable is the location for this one-of-a-kind restaurant that has preserved the *dōyō* (practice ring) as its centrepiece. Playing up to its sumo roots, you can order the protein-packed stew *chanko-nabe* (for two people from ¥5200), but Yoshiba's real strength is its sushi, freshly prepared in jumbo portions.

Otafuku   Japanese ¥¥
(大多福; Map p254; ☑03-3871-2521; www.otafuku.ne.jp; 3rd fl, 1-2-6 Hanakawado, Taitō-ku; oden ¥100-500; ◷11.30am-2pm & 5-11pm Tue-Fri, 4-11pm Sat, until 9pm Sun; ⓇGinza line to Asakusa, exit 5) In business for over a century, Otafuku specialises in *oden,* a classic Japanese hotpot dish of vegetables and seafood simmered in a soy sauce and *dashi* (fish stock) broth. You can dine cheaply on radishes and kelp, or splash out on scallops and tuna or a full-course menu for ¥5400. It's above the Daily Yamazaki convenience store.

Iki Espresso   Cafe ¥¥
(☑03-6659-4654; www.ikiespresso.com; 2-2-12 Tokiwa, Kōtō-ku; mains ¥1200-1350; ◷8am-7pm; ☎; ⓈŌedo line to Kiyosumi-shirakawa, exit A1) A blast of Antipodean sunshine in the midst of Tokyo, Iki is a relaxed all-day Aussie cafe complete with avo on toast, ricotta hotcakes and long blacks rather than Americanos. The shopfront opens to the street and although by local standards it has plenty of seating, you may have to wait – particularly at weekends.

Asakusa Imahan   Japanese ¥¥¥
(浅草今半; Map p254; ☑03-3841-1114; www.asakusaimahan.co.jp; 3-1-12 Nishi-Asakusa, Taitō-ku; lunch/dinner from ¥2000/8000; ◷11.30am-9.30pm; ⓇTsukuba Express to Asakusa, exit 4) For a meal to remember, swing by this famous beef restaurant, in business since 1895. Choose between courses of sukiyaki and *shabu-shabu*; prices rise according to the grade of meat. For diners on a budget, Imahan sells 20 servings of a *gyudon* (rice topped with beef; ¥1500) per day.

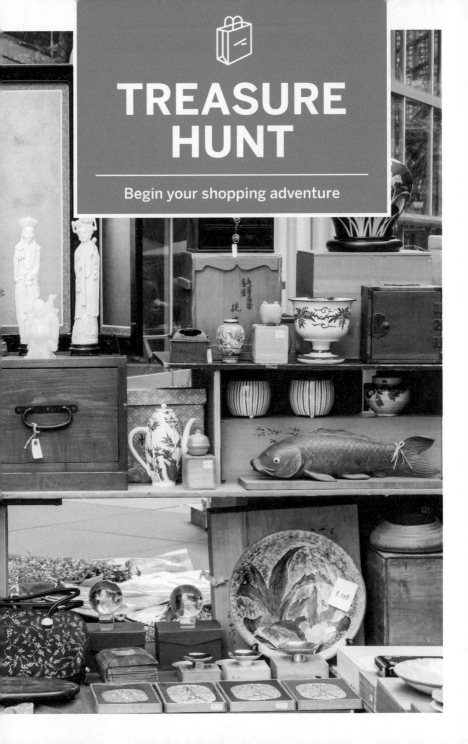

TREASURE HUNT

Begin your shopping adventure

Treasure Hunt

Since the Edo era, when courtesans set the day's trends in towering geta (traditional wooden sandals), Tokyoites have lusted after both the novel and the outstanding. The city remains the trendsetter for the rest of Japan and its residents shop — economy be damned — with an infectious enthusiasm. Join them in the hunt for the cutest fashions, the latest gadgets or the perfect teacup.

Shopping highlights include the grand department stores of Ginza and Nihombashi; the fashionable boutiques in Harajuku and Ebisu; and the traditional craft shops in Ueno and Asakusa.

Useful Phrases

I'd like to buy ... …をください。
... o ku·da·sai

How much is it? おいくらですか？
o·i·ku·ra des ka

Can I try it on? 試着できますか？
shi·cha·ku de·ki·mas ka

Can I look at it? それを見てもいいですか？
so·re o mi·te mo ī des ka

Previous page: Ōedo Antique Market (p166)
STEVE VIDLER/ALAMY STOCK PHOTO ©

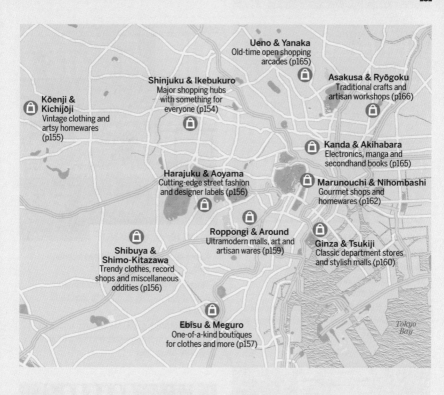

Ueno & Yanaka
Old-time open shopping arcades (p165)

Shinjuku & Ikebukuro
Major shopping hubs with something for everyone (p154)

Asakusa & Ryōgoku
Traditional crafts and artisan workshops (p166)

Kōenji & Kichijōji
Vintage clothing and artsy homewares (p155)

Kanda & Akihabara
Electronics, manga and secondhand books (p165)

Harajuku & Aoyama
Cutting-edge street fashion and designer labels (p156)

Marunouchi & Nihombashi
Gourmet shops and homewares (p162)

Roppongi & Around
Ultramodern malls, art and artisan wares (p159)

Ginza & Tsukiji
Classic department stores and stylish malls (p160)

Shibuya & Shimo-Kitazawa
Trendy clothes, record shops and miscellaneous oddities (p156)

Ebīsu & Meguro
One-of-a-kind boutiques for clothes and more (p157)

Tokyo Bay

Opening Hours

Department stores 10am to 8pm daily

Electronics stores 10am to 10pm daily

Boutiques noon to 8pm, closed irregularly

Sales Seasons

Major sales happen, sadly, just twice a year in Japan: at the beginning of January (after the New Year's holiday) and again at the beginning of July. Duration varies per shop, though one of several weeks (with progressive discounts, starting from 30% off) is common.

The Best...

Experience Tokyo's best shopping

Design

d47 design travel store (p156) Showcase for regional Japanese product design.

Good Design Store Tokyo by Nohara (p163) Goods that have earned Japan's official 'Good Design' stamp of approval.

Souvenir from Tokyo (p159) Curated collection of covetable items from local designers.

Home & Kitchen

Kama-asa (p166) Hand-forged kitchen knives.

Yanaka Matsunoya (p165) Handmade household staples, such as brooms and baskets.

Muji (pictured; p163) Minimalist, utilitarian and utterly indispensable homewares at reasonable prices.

Arts & Crafts

Takumi (p161) One-stop shop for earthy traditional crafts from all over Japan.

Itōya (pictured; p160) Ginza institution for stationery and art supplies.

Bengara (p167) Natural-dyed *noren* (door curtain) and other traditional textile items.

Food & Drink

Akomeya (p160) Beautifully packaged, traditional artisanal foodstuffs.

Toraya (p159) Centuries-old purveyor of sweets to the Imperial household.

Chabara (pictured; p165) Miso, soy sauce and more from top regional producers.

Fashion

Kapital (p157) Denim woven on vintage looms and lush textiles.

House @Mikiri Hassin (p47) Hidden spot for under-the-radar local brands.

Babaghuri (pictured; p166) Earthy looks made from recycled or renewable materials.

Pop Culture

Mandarake Complex (p112) Home sweet home for anime and manga fans.

KiddyLand (pictured; p48) Toy emporium stocked with all your favourites from Sanrio and Studio Ghibli.

Pokémon Center Mega Tokyo (p155) The gang's all here.

Books & Music

Daikanyama T-Site (pictured; p158) Designer digs for art and travel tomes.

Kinokuniya (p155) The city's best selection of books on Japan in English.

Union Record Shinjuku (p154) Crates and crates of vinyl, with lots of local stuff.

☆Lonely Planet's Top Choices

Tokyu Hands (p156) Fascinating emporium of miscellaneous oddities.

Okuno Building (p160) Dozens of tiny galleries and boutiques inside a vintage 1930s Ginza apartment building.

Beams Japan (p154) Floors of cool Japanese labels, original artwork and contemporary crafts.

Japan Traditional Crafts Aoyama Square (p159) Collection of high-end Japanese artisan work.

Isetan (p154) Fashion-forward department store with a great basement food floor.

🔒 Shinjuku & Ikebukuro

Beams Japan   Fashion & Accessories
(ビームス・ジャパン; Map p253; www.beams.
co.jp; 3-32-6 Shinjuku, Shinjuku-ku; ⏰11am-
8pm; 🚉JR Yamanote line to Shinjuku, east exit)
Beams, a national chain of trendsetting
boutiques, is a Japanese cultural institution and this multistorey Shinjuku branch
has a particular audience in mind: you,
the traveller. It's full of the latest Japanese
streetwear labels, traditional fashions with
cool modern twists, artisan crafts, pop art
and more – all contenders for that perfect
only-in-Tokyo souvenir. Set your budget
before you enter.

Isetan   Department Store
(伊勢丹; Map p253; 📞03-3352-1111; www.isetan.
co.jp; 3-14-1 Shinjuku, Shinjuku-ku; ⏰10.30am-
8pm; 🚇Marunouchi line to Shinjuku-sanchōme,
exit B3, B4 or B5) Isetan is our favourite Tokyo
department store for several reasons:
the up-and-coming Japanese fashion
designers (check the 2nd-floor Tokyo
Closet and 3rd-floor Re-Style boutiques
in the main building, and the 2nd floor of
the men's building); the homewares from
contemporary artisans (5th floor); and the
quite literally mouth-watering *depachika*
(basement food floor).

Union Record Shinjuku   Music
(ユニオンレコード新宿; Map p253; 3-34-1
Shinjuku, Shinjuku-ku; ⏰11am-9pm Mon-Sat, to
8pm Sun; 🚉JR Yamanote line to Shinjuku, east
exit) Music chain Disc Union is doubling
down on its commitment to analogue with
the opening of this new record shop, with
crates full of new and used, international
and Japanese artists.

Animate Ikebukuro   Manga & Anime
(アニメイト池袋本店; 📞03-3988-1351;
www.animate.co.jp; 1-20-7 Higashi-Ikebukuro,
Toshima-ku; ⏰10am-9pm; 🚉JR Yamanote line
to Ikebukuro, east exit) Akihabara might get
the most attention but Ikebukuro is a major
player in the anime-manga-gamer universe.
Case in point: Animate's Ikebukuro store is
the largest of its kind in Japan. It also gets
extra kudos from girl geeks (who are known
to prefer Ikebukuro to Akiba), thanks to

Shop in Yanaka Ginza (p55)

several floors devoted to their favourite series.

Books Kinokuniya Tokyo Books

(紀伊國屋書店; Map p253; ☎03-5361-3316; www.kinokuniya.co.jp/c/store/Books-Kinokuniya-Tokyo; 6th fl, Takashimaya Times Sq Minami-kan, 5-24-2 Sendagaya, Shibuya-ku; ◷10am-8.30pm; ☒JR Yamanote line to Shinjuku, south exit) A long-time lifeline for Tokyo expats, Kinokuniya stocks a broad selection of foreign-language books and magazines. Particularly of note is its fantastic collection of books on Japan in English and Japanese literature in translation; we love the notes handwritten by the staff with their recommendations.

Pokémon Center
Mega Tokyo Toys

(ポケモンセンターメガトウキョー; ☎03-5927-9290; www.pokemon.co.jp/gp/ pokecen/english/megatokyo_access.html; 2nd fl, Sunshine City, 3-1-2 Higashi-Ikebukuro, Toshima-ku; ◷10am-8pm; ⑤Yūrakuchō line to Higashi-Ikebukuro, exit 2) Japan's largest official Pokémon shop sells every piece of the series' merchandise with goods geared towards kids and grown-ups alike. Around the store are several statues, like the one of Pikachu riding on the back of a Mega Charizard Y, that you'll want to pose with.

🔒 Kōenji & Kichijōji

Mandarake Complex Anime, Manga

(まんだらけ; www.mandarake.co.jp; Nakano Broadway, 5-52-15 Nakano, Nakano-ku; ◷noon-8pm; ☒JR Chūō-Sōbu line to Nakano, north exit) This is the original Mandarake, the go-to store for all things manga (Japanese comics) and anime (Japanese animation). Once a small, secondhand comic-book store, Mandarake now has some 25 shops just inside the Nakano Broadway shopping centre. Each specialises in something different, be it books, cel art or figurines.

Sokkyō Vintage

(即興; www.sokkyou.net; 102 Nakanishi Apt Bldg, 3-59-14 Kōenji-minami, Suginami-ku;

Vintage Shops

For good secondhand and vintage shopping, head to Harajuku (the backstreets, not the main drags), Shimo-Kitazawa (north side) or Kōenji (everywhere around the station). You'll find merchandise to be expensive but of excellent quality.

◷1-9pm, holidays irregular; ☒JR Sōbu line to Kōenji, south exit) As far as vintage shops go, Sokkyō is more like a gallery of cool. The stock is impeccably edited down to a look that is both dreamy and modern. That said, we may have sent you on an impossible mission: the shop is in an ordinary timber-framed stucco house down an alley and marked only with a small 'open' sign.

Outbound Homewares

(アウトバウンド; http://outbound.to; 2-7-4-101 Kichijōji-honchō, Musashino-shi; ◷11am-7pm Wed-Mon; ☒JR Chūō-Sōbu line to Kichijōji, north exit) Outbound stocks beautiful homewares and objets d'art for your bohemian dream house. Works are earthy, made by contemporary artisans and displayed in gallery-like exhibitions.

PukuPuku Antiques

(ぷくぷく; http://pukupukukichi.blogspot. jp; 2-26-2 Kichijōji-honchō, Musashino-shi; ◷11.30am-7.30pm; ☒JR Chūō-Sōbu line to Kichijōji, north exit) The shelves of this small antiques shop are stacked with ceramics from the early Shōwa (昭和; 1926–89) period, through Taishō (大正; 1912–26) and Meiji

Variety Stores

Zakka-ten are shops that sell miscellaneous goods – an always evolving assortment of beauty products, clever kitchen gadgets and other odd but attractive sundries in cute packaging – all intended to add a little colour, ease or joy to daily life. They are excellent for souvenir hunting. Tokyu Hands (p156), which has several branches, is the classic example.

JANE RIX/SHUTTERSTOCK ©

(明治; 1868–1912) and all the way back to old Edo (江戸; 1603–1868) – stickers indicate the period. Pieces are fairly priced, with hundred-year-old saucers going for as little as a few hundred yen.

ⓐ Harajuku & Aoyama

See p46 for shopping in Harajuku.

ⓐ Shibuya & Shimo-Kitazawa

Tokyu Hands   Department Store

(東急ハンズ; Map p246; http://shibuya.tokyu-hands.co.jp; 12-18 Udagawa-chō, Shibuya-ku; ⊙10am-9pm; ⨁JR Yamanote line to Shibuya, Hachikō exit) This DIY and *zakka* (miscellaneous things) store has eight fascinating floors of everything you didn't know you needed – reflexology slippers, bee-venom face masks and cartoon-character-shaped rice-ball moulds, for example. Most stuff is inexpensive, making it perfect for souvenir

and gift hunting. Warning: you could lose hours in here.

d47 design travel store   Design

(Map p246; ☑03-6427-2301; 8th fl, Shibuya Hikarie, 2-21-1 Shibuya, Shibuya-ku; ⊙11am-8pm; ⨁JR Yamanote line to Shibuya, east exit) The folks behind the D&D Department lifestyle brand and magazine are expert scavengers, searching Japan's nooks and crannies for outstanding examples of artisanship – be it ceramics from Ishikawa or linens from Fukui. An ever-changing selection of finds is on sale.

Shibuya Publishing & Booksellers   Books

(SPBS; Map p246; ☑03-5465-0588; www.shibuyabooks.co.jp; 17-3 Kamiyama-chō, Shibuya-ku; ⊙11am-11pm Mon-Sat, to 10pm Sun; ⨁JR Yamanote line to Shibuya, Hachikō exit) Come browse the selection of art, food and travel magazines and small-press offerings at this indie bookshop, open late among the bars of Shibuya's Kamiyamachō *shōtengai* (market street). There's a small selection of books in English, as well as other stuff like totes and accessories from Japanese designers.

Tsukikageya   Fashion & Accessories

(月影屋; Map p246; www.tsukikageya.com; 1-9-19 Tomigaya, Shibuya-ku; ⊙noon-8pm Thu-Mon, closed irregularly; ⑤Chiyoda line to Yoyogi-kōen, exit 2) Forget cute. Natsuki Shigeta designs *yukata* (cotton kimonos) for men, women and babies with a punk-rock slant that pair with wild accessories. The shop is all but hidden in the back of an apartment complex; enter from the alley behind and look for the jewellery vending machine out front.

Tower Records   Music

(タワーレコード; Map p246; ☑03-3496-3661; http://tower.jp/store/Shibuya; 1-22-14 Jinnan, Shibuya-ku; ⊙10am-11pm; ⨁JR Yamanote line to Shibuya, Hachikō exit) Yes, Tower lives – in Japan at least! This eight-storey temple of music has a deep collection of Japanese and world music. Even if you're not into buying, it can be a great place to browse and discover local artists. There are lots of listening stations.

Mega Donki
Variety

(MEGAドンキ; Map p246; ☑03-5428-4086; 28-6 Udagawa-chō, Shibuya-ku; ⏰24hr; 🚉JR Yamanote line to Shibuya, Hachikō exit) You could show up in Tokyo completely empty-handed and this huge, new outpost of all-night, bargain retailer 'Don Quijote' would have you covered. There are groceries, toiletries, electronics and clothes – along with all sorts of random stuff, including the best selection of unusual flavoured Kit-Kat chocolates we've seen. Don't miss the giant moray eel in the tank at the entrance.

Loft
Department Store

(ロフト; Map p246; ☑03-3462-3807; www.loft. co.jp; 18-2 Udagawa-chō, Shibuya-ku; ⏰10am-9pm; 🚉JR Yamanote line to Shibuya, Hachikō exit) This emporium of homewares, stationery, gadgets and accessories specialises in all that is cute and covetable. The 1st floor, which stocks seasonal stuff and gifts, is great for souvenir hunting.

🄶 Ebisu & Meguro

Kapital
Fashion & Accessories

(キャピタル; Map p246; ☑03-5725-3923; www. kapital.jp; 2-20-2 Ebisu-Minami, Shibuya-ku; ⏰11am-8pm; 🚉JR Yamanote line to Ebisu, west exit) Cult brand Kapital is hard to pin down, but perhaps a deconstructed mash-up of the American West and the centuries-old Japanese aesthetic of *boro* (tatty) chic comes close. Almost no two items are alike; most are unisex. The shop itself is like an art installation. The staff, not snobby at all, can point you towards the other two shops nearby.

Okura
Fashion & Accessories

(オクラ; Map p246; ☑03-3461-8511; www. hrm.co.jp; 20-11 Sarugaku-chō, Shibuya-ku; ⏰11.30am-8pm Mon-Fri, 11am-8.30pm Sat & Sun; 🚉Tōkyū Tōyoko line to Daikanyama) Okura may seem out of place in trendy Daikanyama (the shop looks like a farm-house), but it is actually a neighbourhood landmark. It's full of artsy original clothing items, almost all of which are made from

Takeshita-dōri (p49)

PIUS LEE/SHUTTERSTOCK ©

☆ **Tokyo's Top Malls**

Coredo Muromachi (p162)

Ginza Six (p161)

KITTE (p162)

Tokyo Midtown (p160)

From left: KITTE (p162); kimono; shopper in Nakano Broadway (p155)

natural textiles and dyed a deep indigo blue. Note: there's no sign out the front, but the building stands out.

Daikanyama T-Site
Books

(代官山T-SITE; Map p246; ☑03-3770-2525; http://real.tsite.jp/daikanyama/; 17-5 Sarugaku-chō, Shibuya-ku; ☺7am-2am; 🚈Tōkyū Tōyoko line to Daikanyama) Locals love this stylish shrine to the printed word, which has a fantastic collection of books on travel, art, design and food, including many books in English on Japan. The best part is that you can sit at the in-house Starbucks and read all afternoon – if you can get a seat.

Minä Perhonen
Fashion & Accessories

(Map p246; ☑03-6826-3770; www.mina-perhonen.jp; Daikanyama Hillside Terrace, 18-12 Sarugaku-chō, Shibuya-ku; ☺11am-8pm; 🚈Tōkyū Tōyoko line to Daikanyama) Minä Perhonen, from designer Minagawa Akira, is one of Japan's most successful womenswear labels, known for its instantly classic prints in soft, flattering colours; luxurious fabrics; and loose silhouettes that are both sufficiently sophisticated and easy to wear. This is the brand's flagship shop.

Vase
Fashion & Accessories

(Map p246; ☑03-5458-0337; www.vasenakameguro.com; 1-7-7 Kami-Meguro, Meguro-ku; ☺noon-8pm; ⑤Hibiya line to Naka-Meguro, main exit) A perfect example of one of Naka-Meguro's tiny, impeccably curated boutiques, Vase stocks avant-garde designers and vintage pieces, and also hosts the occasional trunk show. It's in a little white house set back from the Meguro-gawa (with the name on the post box).

...research
General Store
Sports & Outdoors

(Map p246; www.sett.co.jp; 1-14-11 Aobadai, Meguro-ku; ☺noon-7pm; ⑤Hibiya line to Naka-Meguro, main exit) ...research General Store sells original made-in-Japan outdoor wear and gear for the most stylish of mountain hermits (or what designer Kobayashi Setsumasa calls 'anarcho-mountaineers' and 'saunter punks'). There's plenty in here to appeal to the more sedentary too, like T-shirts and tableware.

Cow Books
Books

(Map p246; www.cowbooks.jp/english.html; 1-14-11 Aobadai, Meguro-ku; ☺1-9pm Tue-Sun; ⑤Hibiya

MAHATHIR MOHD YASIN/SHUTTERSTOCK ©

line to Naka-Meguro, main exit) Cow Books is a Naka-Meguro institution, a secondhand bookstore specialising in counter-culture works, rare first editions, small print runs and experimental writing. Most titles are in Japanese, but there is usually a small selection of English-language and art books; the atmosphere is universal.

🔒 Roppongi & Around

Japan Traditional Crafts
Aoyama Square
Arts & Crafts

(伝統工芸 青山スクエア; 📞03-5785-1301; www.kougeihin.jp; 8-1-22 Akasaka, Minato-ku; ⏰11am-7pm; ⑤Ginza line to Aoyama-itchōme, exit 4) Supported by the Japanese Ministry of Economy, Trade and Industry, this is as much a showroom as a shop, exhibiting a broad range of traditional crafts from around Japan, including lacquerwork boxes, woodwork, cut glass, textiles and pottery. There are some exquisite heirloom pieces here, but also beautiful items at reasonable prices.

Toraya
Food & Drinks

(とらや; 📞03-3408-4121; https://global. toraya-group.co.jp; 4-9-22 Akasaka, Minato-ku; ⏰8.30am-7pm Mon-Fri, 9.30am-6pm Sat & Sun, tearoom 11am-6.30pm, to 5.30pm Sat & Sun; ⑤) Founded in the 16th century in Kyoto, Toraya's traditional confectionery has long been patronised by the Imperial Court, giving it a cachet that other sweet-makers can only dream about. This is its impressive flagship store, reopened in 2018. It specialises in *yōkan,* a jelly made from red bean paste, but also sells other seasonal sweets, all beautifully packaged.

Souvenir
from Tokyo
Gifts & Souvenirs

(スーベニアフロムトーキョー; Map p252; 📞03-6812 9933; www.souvenirfromtokyo.jp; basement, National Art Center Tokyo, 7-22-2 Roppongi, Minato-ku; ⏰10am-6pm Sat-Mon, Wed & Thu, to 8pm Fri; ⑤Chiyoda line to Nogizaka, exit 6) There's always an expertly curated and ever-changing selection of home-grown design bits and bobs that make for unique souvenirs at this shop.

Harajuku (p46)

Tokyo Midtown   Mall

(東京ミッドタウン; Map p252; www.tokyo-midtown.com; 9-7 Akasaka, Minato-ku; ⊘11am-9pm; ⓈŌedo line to Roppongi, exit 8) This sleek complex, where escalators ascend alongside waterfalls of rock and glass, brims with sophisticated shops. Most notable is the selection of homewares and lifestyle boutiques, including **The Cover Nippon** and **Wise-Wise**, which carry works by Japanese designers and artisans, on the 3rd floor of the Galleria section.

🔒 Ginza & Tsukiji

Okuno Building   Arts & Crafts

(奥野ビル; Map p250; 1-9-8 Ginza, Chūō-ku; ⊘most galleries noon-7pm; ⓈYūrakuchō line to Ginza-itchōme, exit 10) This 1932 apartment block (cutting edge for its time) is a retro time capsule, its seven floors packed with some 40 tiny boutiques and gallery spaces. Climbing up and down the Escher-like staircases, or using the antique elevator, you'll come across mini-exhibitions that change weekly.

Akomeya   Food

(アコメヤ; Map p250; ☎03-6758-0271; www.akomeya.jp; 2-2-6 Ginza, Chūō-ku; ⊘shop 11am-8pm Sun-Thu, to 9pm Fri & Sat, restaurant 11am-10pm; ⓈYūrakuchō line to Ginza-itchōme, exit 4) Rice is at the core of Japanese cuisine and drink. This stylish store sells not only many types of the grain but also products made from it (such as sake), a vast range of quality cooking ingredients, and a choice collection of kitchen, home and bath items.

Itōya   Arts & Crafts

(伊東屋; Map p250; ☎03-3561-8311; www.ito-ya.co.jp; 2-7-15 Ginza, Chūō-ku; ⊘10.30am-8pm Mon-Sat, to 7pm Sun; ⓈGinza line to Ginza, exit A13) Explore the nine floors (plus several more in the nearby annex) of stationery at this famed, century-old Ginza establishment. There are everyday items (such as notebooks and greeting cards) and luxuries (fountain pens and Italian leather agendas). You'll also find *washi* (handmade paper), *tenugui* (beautifully hand-dyed thin cotton towels) and *furoshiki* (wrapping cloths).

Takumi
Arts & Crafts

(たくみ; Map p250; ☎03-3571-2017; www.
ginza-takumi.co.jp; 8-4-2 Ginza, Chūō-ku; ◷11am-
7pm Mon-Sat; ⑤Ginza line to Shimbashi, exit
5) You're unlikely to find a more elegant
selection of traditional folk crafts, including
toys, textiles and ceramics from around
Japan. Ever thoughtful, this shop also
encloses information detailing the origin
and background of the pieces if you make
a purchase.

Dover Street
Market Ginza
Fashion & Accessories

(DSM; Map p250; ☎03-6228-5080; http://
ginza.doverstreetmarket.com; 6-9-5 Ginza,
Chūō-ku; ◷11am-8pm; ⑤Ginza line to Ginza, exit
A2) A department store as envisioned by
Kawakubo Rei (of Comme des Garçons),
DSM has seven floors of avant-garde
brands, including several Japanese labels
and everything in the Comme des Garçons
line-up. The quirky art installations alone
make it worth the visit.

Ginza Six
Mall

(Map p250; ☎03-6891-3390; http://ginza6.
tokyo; 6-10-1 Ginza, Chūō-ku; ◷10am-10pm;
⑤Ginza line to Ginza, exit A2) This splashy mall
opened in 2017. There are shops from top
international and local brands, of course,
but also a branch of artsy Tsutaya Books
(p162), a 4000-sq-metre rooftop garden
with great views and changing contemporary art installations. On the ground floor,
tourist information centre Terminal Ginza
can arrange shipping and luggage storage.

Mitsukoshi
Department Store

(三越; Map p250; ☎03-3562-1111; http://mitsu
koshi.mistore.jp/store/ginza; 4-6-16 Ginza, Chūō-
ku; ◷10.30am-8pm, restaurant fl 11am-11pm;
⑤Ginza line to Ginza, exits A7 & A11) One of
Ginza's grande dames, Mitsukoshi embod-
ies the essence of the Tokyo department
store. Don't miss the basement food hall.
The homewares selection on the 7th floor is
good for ceramics and other artisan pieces.

Matsuya
Department Store

(松屋; Map p250; ☎03-3567-1211; www.mat
suya.com; 3-6-1 Ginza, Chūō-ku; ◷10am-8pm,

Jimbōchō
Book Town

This compact district has more than
170 new and secondhand booksellers,
covering a huge array of genres.

Komiyama Shoten (小宮山書店; Map
p254; ☎03-3291-0495; www.book-komi
yama.co.jp; 1-7 Kanda-Jimbōchō, Chiyoda-ku;
◷11am-6.30pm Mon-Sat, to 5.30pm Sun;
⑤Hanzōmon line to Jimbōchō, exit A7), in
business since 1939, stocks an incred-
ible selection of art and photography
books, posters and prints with some
very famous Japanese and international
artists represented. Every spare inch of
wall is given over to gallery space.

Ohya Shobō (大屋書房; Map p254;
☎03-3291-0062; www.ohya-shobo.com; 1-1
Kanda-Jimbōchō, Chiyoda-ku; ◷10am-6pm
Mon-Sat; ⑧Hanzōmon line to Jimbōchō, exit
A7) is a splendid old shop specialising in
ukiyo-e (woodblock prints), both old and
newly printed (from ¥2000). There are
antique books and maps, too. The staff
are friendly and can help you with whatever you're looking for. All purchases are
tagged with a small origami crane.

As befitting a neighbourhood full of
bookstores, Jimbōchō also has lots of
cafes for holing up with a favourite book.
Check out Sabōru (p143).

restaurant fl 11am-10pm; 🛜; ⑤Ginza line to Ginza, exit 12A) One of Ginza's top department
stores is packed with designer brands.
Look out for the section on the 7th floor
showcasing household products chosen by

Kappabashi Kitchenware Town

Kappabashi-dōri (合羽橋通り; Map p254; www.kappabashi.or.jp; ⊘most shops 10am-5pm Mon-Sat; ⑤Ginza line to Tawaramachi, exit 3) is the country's largest wholesale restaurant-supply and kitchenware district. Gourmet accessories include bamboo steamer baskets, lacquer trays, neon signs and *chōchin* (paper lanterns). It's also where restaurants get their freakishly realistic plastic food models. Excellent knife store Kama-asa (p166) is here.

the Japan Design Committee, a group of leading designers, architects and critics.

Morioka Shoten & Co   Books
(森岡書店 銀座店; Map p250; ☎03-3535-5020; Suzuki Bldg, 1–28–15 Ginza, Chūō-ku; ⊘1-8pm Tue-Sun; ⑤Asakusa or Hibiya line to Higashi-Ginza, exit A7) This tiny bookshop showcases a single title a week, be it a novel, a cook book or an art tome, alongside an exhibition. However, the real reason for coming here is to admire the wonderful art deco architecture of the 1929 Suzuki Building, with its warm red-brick and decorative tile facade.

Ginza Tsutaya Books   Books
(銀座蔦屋書店; Map p250; ☎03-3575-7755; https://store.tsite.jp/ginza; 6th fl, Ginza Six, 6-10-1 Ginza, Chūō-ku; ⊘10am-10.30pm; ⑤Ginza line to Ginza, exit A2) This big, beautiful bookstore has a well-curated selection of art, architecture, design and travel books. English titles are mixed in with the Japanese ones,

arranged by genre. There's also a cafe and changing art shows.

Uniqlo   Fashion & Accessories
(ユニクロ; Map p250; ☎03-6252-5181; www.uniqlo.com; 5-7-7 Ginza, Chūō-ku; ⊘11am-9pm; ⑤Ginza line to Ginza, exit A2) This now-global brand has made its name by sticking to the basics and tweaking them with style. Offering inexpensive, quality clothing, this is the Tokyo flagship store with 11 floors and items you won't find elsewhere.

❻ Marunouchi & Nihombashi

KITTE   Mall
(Map p250; ☎03-3216-2811; www.jptower-kitte.jp; 2-7-2 Marunouchi, Chiyoda-ku; ⊘shops 11am-9pm Mon-Sat, to 8pm Sun, restaurants to 11pm, to 10pm Sun; ℞JR lines to Tokyo, Marunouchi south exit) This well-designed shopping mall at the foot of JP Tower incorporates the restored original facade of the Tokyo Central Post Office. It is notable for its atrium, around which is arrayed a quality selection of craft-oriented Japanese-brand shops selling homewares, fashion, accessories and lifestyle goods.

Coredo Muromachi   Mall
(コレド室町; Map p250; www.mitsui-shopping-park.com/urban/muromach; 2-2-1 Nihombashi-Muromachi, Chūō-ku; ⊘most shops 10am-9pm; ⑤Ginza line to Mitsukoshimae, exit A4) Spread over three buildings, this stylish development houses many shops from famous gourmet food purveyors, as well as reliable places to eat and drink. In Coredo Muromachi 3 there are elegant fashion and homewares boutiques, including a branch of Muji.

Mitsukoshi   Department Store
(三越; Map p250; ☎03-3241-3311; www.mitsukoshi.co.jp; 1-4-1 Nihombashi-Muromachi, Chūō-ku; ⊘10am-7pm; ⑤Ginza line to Mitsukoshimae, exit A2) Mitsukoshi's venerable Nihombashi branch was Japan's first department store. It's a grand affair with an entrance guarded

by bronze lions and a magnificent statue of Magokoro, the goddess of sincerity, rising up from the centre of the ground floor. For the full effect, arrive at 10am for the bells and bows that accompany each day's opening.

Good Design Store Tokyo by Nohara
Gifts & Souvenirs

(Map p250; ☑03-5220-1007; http://gdst. nohara-inc.co.jp; 3rd fl, KITTE, 2-7-2 Marunouchi, Chiyoda-ku; ☺11am-9pm, until 8pm Sun; ⓡJR lines to Tokyo, Marunouchi south exit) A fab selection of products that have won Japan's Good Design Award are showcased at this lifestyle boutique. It's divided into sections – the front garden, the living, dining and hobby rooms – with nifty, desirable buys scattered throughout.

Muji
Homewares

(無印良品; Map p250; ☑03-5208-8241; www. muji.com/jp/flagship/yurakucho/en; 3-8-3 Marunouchi, Chiyoda-ku; ☺10am-9pm; ⓡJR Yamanote line to Yūrakuchō, Kyōbashi exit) The flagship store of the famously understated brand sells elegant, simple clothing,

accessories, homewares and food. There are scores of outlets across Tokyo, but the Yūrakuchō store, renovated in 2017, is the largest with the biggest range.

Takashimaya
Department Store

(高島屋; Map p250; ☑03-6273 1467; www. takashimaya.co.jp/tokyo/store_information; 2-4-1 Nihombashi, Chūō-ku; ☺10.30am-7.30pm; ⓢGinza line to Nihombashi, Takashimaya exit) The design of Takashimaya's flagship store (1933) tips its pillbox hat to New York's Gilded Age with marble columns, chandeliers and uniformed female elevator operators announcing each floor in high-pitched sing-song voices.

Bic Camera
Electronics

(ビックカメラ; Map p250; ☑03-5221-1111; www. biccamera.co.jp; 1-11-1 Yūrakuchō, Chiyoda-ku; ☺10am-10pm; ⓡJR Yamanote line to Yūrakuchō, Kokusai Center exit) Cameras are just the start of the electronic items and much more (toys, sake, medicine, cosmetics, wine) sold in this mammoth discount store occupying a block. Shopping here is like being inside a very noisy computer game,

Gachapon figures on display inside Akihabara Station

Top Tokyo Souvenirs

Cool Clothes

Bring back some Tokyo style from avant-garde boutiques such as Kapital (p157) and Babaghuri (pictured above; p166).

Kitchen & Homewares

Shop for chef's knives at Kama-asa (p166) and artisan homewares at Yanaka Matsunoya (pictured above; p165).

Furoshiki

These colourful patterned cloths can be knotted into totes and reusable wrappings. Try Musubi (p48) or Itōya (p160).

Gourmet Goods

Pick up green tea, jars of seasoned miso paste and more at gourmet shops such as Akomeya (p160) and Chabara (pictured above; p165).

Cute Characters

Shop for mascots of Japanese pop culture (such as Hello Kitty and Pikachu) at KiddyLand (pictured above; p48) and Pokémon Center Mega Tokyo (p155).

but it's worth enduring for the discounts and the tax-free deals available to tourists.

ⓐ Kanda & Akihabara

Y. & Sons Fashion & Accessories
(Map p254; ☎03-5294-7521; www.yandsons.com; 2-17-2 Soto-Kanda, Chiyoda-ku; ⊙11am-8pm Thu-Tue; ⓇJR Chūō line to Ochanomizu, Ochanomi-zu-bashi exit) Every once in a while in Tokyo, you'll spot a gentleman in a silk-wool kimono and a fedora, looking as if he's stepped out of the 1900s. Bespoke tailor Y. & Sons would like to see this more often. Custom kimonos with obi (sash) start at around ¥65,000 and take two weeks to complete; international shipping is available.

2k540 Aki-Oka Artisan Arts & Crafts
(アキオカアルチザン; Map p254; ☎03-6806 0254; www.jrtk.jp/2k540; 5-9-23 Ueno, Taitō-ku; ⊙11am-7pm Thu-Tue; ⓇGinza line to Suehi-rochō, exit 2) This ace arcade under the JR tracks (its name refers to the distance from Tokyo Station) offers an eclectic range of stores selling Japanese-made goods – everything from pottery and leatherwork to cute aliens, a nod to Akihabara from a mall that is more akin to Kyoto than Electric Town. The best for colourful crafts is **Nippon Hyakkuten** (日本百貨店; http://nippon-dept.jp).

Chabara Food
(ちゃばら; Map p254; www.jrtk.jp/chabara; 8-2 Kanda Neribei-chō, Chiyoda-ku; ⊙11am-8pm; ⓇJR Yamanote line to Akihabara, Electric Town exit) This under-the-train-tracks shopping mall focuses on artisan food and drinks from across Japan, including premium sake, soy sauce, sweets, teas and crackers – all great souvenirs and presents.

ⓐ Ueno & Yanaka

Geidai Art Plaza Arts & Crafts
(Map p254; ☎050-5525-2102; www.artplaza. geidai.ac.jp; Tokyo University of the Arts, 12-8 Ueno-kōen, Taitō-ku; ⊙10am-6pm Tue-Sun; ⓇJR lines to Ueno, Ueno-kōen exit) On the campus of Tokyo's top arts university this shop, opened in 2018, showcases creative pieces in a range of media by the institute's staff, students and graduates. It's well worth a browse and if you can't afford an original work, there are plenty of affordable things such as books, comics and specially de-signed biscuits.

Yanaka Matsunoya Homewares
(谷中松野屋; Map p254; ☎03-3823-7441; www. yanakamatsunoya.jp; 3-14-14 Nishi-Nippori, Arakawa-ku; ⊙11am-7pm Mon & Wed-Fri, from 10am Sat & Sun; ⓇJR Yamanote line to Nippori, west exit) At the top of Yanaka Ginza (p55), Matsunoya sets out its stall with an at-tractive range of mainly household goods – baskets, brooms and canvas totes, for example – simple in beauty and form, and handmade by local artisans.

Art Sanctuary Allan West Art
(繪処アラン・ウエスト; Map p254; ☎03-3827-1907; www.allanwest.jp; 1-6-17 Yanaka, Taitō-ku; ⊙1.30-4.30pm Mon-Wed, Fri & Sat, from 3pm Sun; ⓈChiyoda line to Nezu, exit 1) FREE In this masterfully converted garage, long-time Yanaka resident Allan West paints gorgeous screens and scrolls in the traditional Japa-nese style, making his paints from scratch just as local artists have done for centuries. Smaller votive-shaped paintings start at ¥5000; the screens clock in at a cool ¥6 million.

Mita Sneakers Shoes
(ミタスニーカーズ; Map p254; ☎03-3832-8346; www.mita-sneakers.co.jp; Ameyoko Center Bldg, 4-7-8 Ueno, Taitō-ku; ⊙11am-7.30pm Mon-Fri, from 10am Sat & Sun, closed 3rd Wed of month; ⓇJR Yamanote line to Ueno, central exit) Ameya-yokochō (p55) is widely known as the place to pick up bargain kicks; but among sneaker heads, it's better known as the home of Mita Sneakers, which sells limited-edition made-in-Japan shoes and exclusive collaboration items from the big brands (Adidas, Puma et al).

Flea Markets

Tokyo's best market is the long-running, twice-monthly **Ōedo Antique Market** (大江戸骨董市; Map p250; ☎03-6407-6011; www.antique-market.jp; 3-5-1 Marunouchi, Chiyoda-ku; ⏲9am-4pm 1st & 3rd Sun of month; 🚉JR Yamanote line to Yūrakuchō, Kokusai Forum exit). Held in the courtyard of Tokyo International Forum in Marunouchi, the event draws hundreds of vendors who sell everything from old ceramics and kimono to kitsch plastic figurines and vintage movie posters.

Over the first weekend of the month, hipster flea market **Raw Tokyo** (Map p246; www.rawtokyo.jp; 5-53-7 Jingūmae, Shibuya-ku; ⏲11am-5pm 1st weekend of the month; ⓈGinza line to Omote-sandō, exit B2) joins the Farmer's Market @UNU (p146), bringing with it a DJ booth, live painting, young designers hoping for a break, vintage troves and food trucks.

Note that markets may be cancelled due to rain or conflicting events; check the websites before setting out. For an updated schedule of all the city's flea markets, see www.frma.jp (in Japanese). Though bargaining is permitted, it is considered bad form to drive too hard a bargain.

Pottery, Ōedo Antique Market

TRAVELASIA/GETTY IMAGES ©

Asakusa & Ryōgoku

Kama-asa Homewares

(Map p254; ☎03-3841-9355; www.kama-asa.co.jp; 2-24-1 Matsugaya, Taitō-ku; ⏲10am-5.30pm; ⓈGinza line to Tawaramachi, exit 3) 🌿 A Japanese knife is not only a highly practical and prized piece of kitchenware, it can also be extremely beautiful in its design. Admire an excellent range at this upmarket store that has been in business since 1908. There are English- and French-speaking staff on hand, and there's a good range of other kitchen implements, including steel pans.

Babaghuri Fashion & Accessories

(☎03-3820-8825; www.babaghuri.jp; 3-1-7 Kiyosumi, Koto-ku; ⏲11am-7pm irregular holidays; ⓈŌedo line to Kiyosumi-shirakawa, exit A3) This chic local fashion and household goods brand was created by German-born designer Jurgen Lehl, who passed away in 2014. Made from renewable, natural or recycled materials, the rustically beautiful clothes, pottery, tableware and linens sold here are displayed like artworks.

Marugoto Nippon Food & Drinks

(まるごとにっぽん; Map p254; ☎03-3845-0510; www.marugotonippon.com; 2-6-7 Asakusa, Taitō-ku; ⏲10am-8pm; ⓈGinza line to Tawaramachi, exit 3) Think of this as a small centre, showcasing the best of Japan's speciality food and drink (ground floor) and arts and crafts (2nd floor). The 3rd floor showcases the products and attractions of different Japanese regions on a regularly changing basis.

Yoshitoku Dolls Arts & Crafts

(吉徳人形; Map p254; ☎03-3863-4419; www.yoshitoku.co.jp; 1-9-14 Asakusabashi, Taitō-ku; ⏲9am-5.45pm Mon-Fri; 🚉JR Sobu line to Asakusabashi, east exit) Founded in 1711, this traditional Japanese doll manufacturer is the place to come to see the exquisite craftsmanship of these ornamental figurines, ranging from geisha in beautiful kimono and samurai in full armour to the elaborate sets of dolls displayed during Hina Matsuri in March. The shop stocks many other craft products, too.

Bengara Arts & Crafts

(べんがら; Map p254; ☎03-3841-6613; www.bengara.com; 1-35-6 Asakusa, Taitō-ku; ⏲10am-6pm Mon-Fri, to 7pm Sat & Sun, closed 3rd Thu

Yanaka Ginza (p55)

of the month; §Ginza line to Asakusa, exit 1) *Noren* are the curtains that hang in front of shop doors. This store sells beautiful ones, made of linen and coloured with natural dyes (such as indigo or persimmon) or decorated with ink-brush paintings. There are smaller items too, such as pouches and book covers, made of traditional textiles.

Fujiya   Arts & Crafts
(ふじ屋; Map p254; ☑03-3841-2283; 2-2-15 Asakusa, Taitō-ku; ◷10am-6pm Thu-Tue; §Ginza line to Asakusa, exit 1) Fujiya specialises in *tenugui:* dyed cloths of thin cotton that

can be used as tea towels, handkerchiefs, gift wrapping (the list goes on – they're surprisingly versatile). Here they come in both traditional and humorous modern designs.

Kurodaya   Stationery
(黒田屋; Map p254; ☑03-3844-7511; 1-2-5 Asakusa, Taitō-ku; ◷10am-7pm Tue-Sun; §Ginza line to Asakusa, exit 3) Since 1856, Kurodaya has been specialising in *washi* (traditional Japanese paper) and products made from paper, such as cards, kites and papier-mâché folk-art figures. It sells its own designs and many others from across Japan.

BAR OPEN

Sake bars, craft beer, international DJs and Japanese whisky

Bar Open

Make like Lady Gaga in a karaoke box; see the city from a sky-high bar, cocktail in hand; stumble upon a scene stashed away in an anonymous building; or lose track of time in one of the city's storied, late-night dives: that's nightlife, Tokyo style.

Shinjuku, Shibuya and Roppongi are the biggest nightlife districts, but there are bars everywhere — such is the importance of that time-honoured social lubricant, alcohol, in this work-hard, play-hard city. You'll find people out any night of the week, and out late.

In This Section

Opening Hours

Bars generally open as early as 5pm (though some open earlier on weekends). If they close on any day it's usually Sunday (though this varies). There is no official last call, and some places will close early or late depending on the crowd size. Some clubs have events all week but Friday and Saturday are the big nights out. Most open from 11pm but don't really get going until 1am.

Previous page: Golden Gai (p36)

Shinjuku & Ikebukuro
Cocktail dens and eccentric bars, plus plenty of pubs and karaoke parlours (p174)

Asakusa & Ryōgoku
Some fun spots in this historic area (p183)

Kōenji & Kichijōji
Local faves & indie spots (p175)

Kanda & Akihabara
Craft beer and cocktail bars (p182)

Harajuku & Aoyama
Wine bars and late-night cafes (p175)

Marunouchi & Nihombashi
After-work hang-outs & hotel bars (p181)

Roppongi & Around
One big all-night party (p179)

Shibuya & Shimo-Kitazawa
Nightclubs and bohemian haunts; great for music fans (p176)

Ginza & Tsukiji
A classy, though often pricey, place to drink (p181)

Ebisu & Meguro
Boutique sake & cocktail bars (p178)

Tokyo Bay

Costs & Tipping

Tipping is not customary and typically only hotel bars charge a service fee; however, some bars, especially small speciality ones, will level a cover charge of around ¥500–1000. This may not be clearly stated, but if you are served a snack expect a small extra charge (consider it in lieu of a tip).

Useful Phrases

I'll buy you a drink.
1杯おごります。
ip·pai o·go·ri·mas

It's my round next.
次は私の番です。
tsu·gi wa wa·ta·shi no ban des

Cheers!
乾杯！
kam·pai

The Best...

Experience Tokyo's finest drinking establishments

Music Lovers

Sub Store (p175) Hear indie bands perform for free.

Ginza Music Bar (p181) Cocktails paired with vinyl and excellent sound.

Rhythm Cafe (p178) Fun events at a bar run by a record label.

Craft Beer

Beer-Ma Kanda (p182) Bottles by the hundred.

Rise & Win Brewing Co. Kamikatz Taproom (p181) Run by a pioneering brewery in rural Shikoku.

Two Dogs Taproom (p181) Roppongi gathering spot for craft beer and pizza.

Late Nights

Ghetto (p176) Convos until dawn at this Shimo-Kitazawa dive.

Oath (p176) DJs spin late at this favourite underground Shibuya spot.

Beat Cafe (p176) After-hours hang-out destination for musicians and their fans.

Clubs

Circus Tokyo (p176) Underground venue focussing on experimental music.

Contact (p178) Tokyo's current most fashionable club.

Ele Tokyo (p181) Join the smart set for a night out in Roppongi.

Drinks with a View

Two Rooms (p175) Cool views and a cool crowd, plus an outdoor terrace.

Asahi Sky Room (p115) Spectacular sunset views over the Sumida River.

Peter: the Bar (p182) Views over the Imperial Palace (and an excellent happy hour).

Cocktails

BenFiddich (pictured; p174) Original cocktails made using freshly ground spices and herbs.

Cocktail Works (p182) Award-winning mixologist and artisanal gin.

Bar Trench (p179) Ebisu-based pioneer in Tokyo's new cocktail scene.

☆Lonely Planet's Top Choices

Gen Yamamoto (p179) Enjoy exquisite cocktails in a space inspired by a traditional Japanese teahouse.

Popeye (p183) The most beers on tap in Tokyo.

Lonely (p37) Classic Golden Gai bar in business for over half a century.

Zoetrope (p174) Premium whiskies at this Shinjuku hole-in-the-wall.

New York Bar (p115) The definitive high-altitude Tokyo night spot.

Cool Interiors

Samurai (p175) Jazz haunt with 2500 *maneki-neko* (beckoning cats).

Ginza Lion (pictured; p181) Traditional beer hall with a gorgeous art deco design.

Mother (p178) A surreal (and cosy!) hideaway in bohemian Shimo-Kitazawa.

✪ Shinjuku & Ikebukuro

For a classic Shinjuku Golden Gai experience, see p36.

BenFiddich   Cocktail Bar

(ベンフィディック; Map p253; ☎03-6279-4223; 9th fl, 1-13-7 Nishi-Shinjuku, Shinjuku-ku; ⏱6pm-3am Mon-Sat; 🚈JR Yamanote line to Shinjuku, west exit) BenFiddich is dark and tiny, with vials of infusions on the shelves and herbs hung to dry from the ceiling. The English-speaking barman, Kayama Hiroyasu, in a white suit, moves like a magician. There's no menu, so just tell him what you like and he'll concoct something delicious (we like the gimlet with herbs). Expect to pay around ¥2000 per drink.

There's no sign on the street, but it's the building in between the karaoke parlour and the curry shop. You'll see the wooden door when you exit the elevator.

Zoetrope   Bar

(ゾートロープ; Map p253; ☎03-3363-0162; 3rd fl, 7-10-14 Nishi-Shinjuku, Shinjuku-ku; ⏱5pm-midnight Mon-Sat; 🚈JR Yamanote line to Shinjuku, west exit) A must-visit for whisky fans, Zoetrope has some 300 varieties of Japanese whisky behind its small counter – including hard-to-find bottles from small batch distilleries. It's a one-person show and the owner speaks English well. Cover charge ¥600; whisky by the glass from ¥400 to ¥19,000, though most are reasonably priced (around ¥800 to ¥1200) and there are some good-value tasting flights, too.

Peak Bar   Bar

(ピークバー; Map p253; ☎03-5323-3461; http://restaurants.tokyo.park.hyatt.co.jp/en/pbr.html; 41st fl, Park Hyatt, 3-7-1-2 Nishi-Shinjuku, Shinjuku-ku; ⏱5-11.30pm; 🚇Ōedo line to Tochō-mae, exit A4) The Peak Bar offers soaring views over the city and a generous deal: its three-hour (5pm to 8pm) all-you-can-drink plus unlimited canapés 'Twilight Time' special costs just ¥6000 (tax and service charge included). Okay, that's still a fair amount, but we're talking the Park Hyatt here! Otherwise cocktails start from ¥1950 (plus a 15% service charge). DJs spin Wednesday through Saturday from 6pm. Dress code enforced.

Zoetrope

Samurai
Bar

(サムライ; Map p253; http://jazz-samurai.
seesaa.net; 5th fl, 3-35-5 Shinjuku, Shinjuku-ku;
⏰6pm-1am; 🚃JR Yamanote line to Shinjuku,
southeast exit) Never mind the impressive
record collection, this eccentric jazz *kissa*
(cafe where jazz records are played) is
worth a visit just for the owner's over-
whelming collection of 2500 *maneki-neko*
(beckoning cats). It's on the alleyway
alongside the highway, with a small sign
on the front of the building. There's a ¥300
cover charge (¥500 after 9pm); drinks
from ¥650.

Roof Top Bar & Terrace G
Bar

(📞03-5155-2412; www.granbellhotel.jp/shinjuku/
restaurant/bar/; 13th fl, Shinjuku Granbell Hotel,
2-14-5 Kabukichō, Shinjuku-ku; ⏰5pm-2am Mon-
Sat, to 11pm Sun; 🚇Ōedo line to Higashi-Shinjuku,
exit A1) The drinks and decor here are totally
uninteresting, but we're a sucker for an
open-air rooftop bar – not as common as
you'd think in Tokyo, where the night views
are always divine (even if, in this case, it's
partly of the gentrifying red-light district).
Beer is ¥500 during happy hour (5pm
to 7pm); otherwise drinks start at ¥800.
There's a ¥500 cover charge.

🍶 Kōenji & Kichijōji

Sub Store
Bar

(📞080-3496-3883; https://substore.jimdo.com;
3-1-12 Kita-Kōenji, Suginami-ku; ⏰3pm-midnight
Thu-Mon, 5pm-midnight Wed; 🚃JR Sōbu line to
Kōenji, north exit) Sub Store is many things:
used-vinyl store, sometime art gallery, In-
donesian restaurant (the original Sub Store
is in Jakarta) and, on most weekends, an indie live-music venue. But it's always a great
place to pop in for a beer (from ¥600).

Cocktail Shobō
Bar

(コクテイル書房; http://koenji-cocktail.info;
3-8-13 Kōenji-kita, Suginami-ku; ⏰11.30am-3pm
Wed-Sun, 5-11pm daily; 🚃JR Sōbu line to Kōenji,
north exit) Cocktail Shobō is part used-book
store, part cocktail bar, and 100% a labour
of love in a vintage wooden house where

Drinking Culture

In Japan it's considered bad form to fill
your own glass. Instead, fill the drained
glasses around you and someone will
quickly reciprocate; when they do,
raise your glass slightly with two hands
– a graceful way to receive anything.
'Cheers!' in Japanese is *'Kampai!'*;
glasses are raised though usually not
clinked.

the bar counter doubles as a bookshelf.
Drinks start at just ¥400; the small plates
of Japanese food (¥250 to ¥650) are good
too, but unfortunately the menu is only in
Japanese. During lunch hours, curry and
coffee are served.

Nantoka Bar
Bar

(なんとかバー; www.shirouto.org/nantokabar;
3-4-12 Kōenji-kita, Suginami-ku; ⏰7pm-late; 🚃JR
Sōbu line to Kōenji, north exit) Part of the collective of spaces run by the Kōenji-based
activist group Shirōto no Ran (Amateurs'
Riot), Nantoka Bar is about as uncommer-
cial as a place selling drinks can get: there's
no cover charge, drinks are generous
and cheap, and it's run on any given day
by whoever feels like running it, which is
sometimes no one at all.

🍶 Harajuku & Aoyama

Two Rooms
Bar

(トゥールームス; Map p246; 📞03-3498-0002;
www.tworooms.jp; 5th fl, AO Bldg, 3-11-7 Kita-
Aoyama, Minato-ku; ⏰11.30am-2am Mon-Sat, to

Need to Know

The legal drinking age in Japan is 20. Bars generally don't require photo ID as proof of age, but nightclubs are required to check ID cards (of everyone, no matter how far past 20 you look, so have your passport ready). The city has been cracking down on street touts though you may come across them in neighbourhoods like Shinjuku and Roppongi. Not all are employed by shady places (where bills may come inflated), but it's still best to steer clear of them.

PHOTOS FROM/GETTY IMAGES ©

10pm Sun; ⓈGinza line to Omote-sandō, exit B2) Expect a crowd dressed like they don't care that wine by the glass starts at ¥1600. You can eat here too, but the real scene is at night by the bar. The terrace has sweeping views towards the Shinjuku skyline. Call ahead (staff speak English) on Friday or Saturday night to reserve a spot under the stars.

Harajuku Taproom   Pub
(原宿タップルーム; Map p246; ☑03-6438-0450; https://bairdbeer.com/taprooms/harajuku; 2nd fl, 1-20-13 Jingūmae, Shibuya-ku; ◷5pm-midnight Mon-Fri, noon-midnight Sat & Sun; 圓JR Yamanote line to Harajuku, Takeshita exit) Baird's Brewery is one of Japan's most successful and consistently good craft breweries. This is one of three Tokyo outposts, and you can sample more than a dozen of its beers on tap, including the brewery's Harajuku Real Ale (pints ¥1100).

Yakitori (grilled chicken skewers) and Japanese pub-style dishes are served as well.

🚇 Shibuya & Shimo-Kitazawa

Circus Tokyo   Club
(Map p246; www.circus-tokyo.jp; 3-26-16 Shibuya, Shibuya-ku; 圓JR Yamanote line to Shibuya, new south exit) Circus, the Tokyo offshoot of an Osaka club, is aggressively underground: small, out of the way, in a basement (of course), with no decor to speak of and all attention laser-focused on the often experimental music. It's open most Fridays and Saturdays from 11pm, and sometimes other nights; check the schedule online. Cover ¥2000 to ¥3000 and drinks ¥600; ID required.

Ghetto   Bar
(月灯; 1-45-16 Daizawa, Setagaya-ku; ◷8.30pm-late; 圓Keiō Inokashira line to Shimo-Kitazawa, north exit) Ghetto – the name comes from the characters for 'moon' *(ge)* and 'light' *(to)* – is one of the little bars inside Shimo-Kitazawa's iconic (and rickety) Suzunari theatre complex. Each night a different character is behind the counter; on the other side, a mix of local creatives and travellers. By open until late we mean very, very late. No cover charge; drinks from ¥600.

Oath   Bar
(Map p246; www.djbar-oath.com; basement fl, 1-6-5 Dōgenzaka, Shibuya-ku; ◷8pm-5am Mon-Sat; 圓JR Yamanote line to Shibuya, Hachikō exit) Oath is a tiny space covered in gilt and mirrors, dripping with chandeliers and absolutely not taking itself seriously. It's a very popular spot for pre-partying and after-partying, thanks to cheap drinks (¥500), fun DJs and a friendly crowd. Cover charge is ¥1000 (one drink included).

Beat Cafe   Bar
(Map p246; www.facebook.com/beatcafe; basement fl, 2-13-5 Dōgenzaka, Shibuya-ku; ◷8pm-5am; 圓JR Yamanote line to Shibuya, Hachikō exit) Join an eclectic mix of local and international

Clockwise from top: Omoide-yokochō (p124); *shōchū;* Suntory Hibiki whisky

MATTEO COLOMBO/GETTY IMAGES ©

Kabukichō red light district

regulars at this comfortably shabby bar among the nightclubs and love hotels of Dōgenzaka. It's a known hang-out for musicians and music fans; check the website for info on parties (and after-parties). Look for Gateway Studio on the corner; the bar is in the basement. Drinks from ¥500.

Mother   Bar
(マザー; ☑03-3421-9519; www.rock-mother. com; 5-36-14 Daizawa, Setagaya-ku; ⊙5pm-2am Sun-Thu, 5pm-5am Fri & Sat; 圓Odakyū or Keiō Inokashira line to Shimo-Kitazawa, southwest exit) Mother is a classic Shimo-Kitazawa bar with a soundtrack from the '60s and '70s and an undulating, womb-like interior covered in mosaic tile. It does cocktails (from ¥600) with in-house infusions – try the signature 'mori' liquor, served from a glass skull -- and also Okinawan and Southeast Asian food.

Rhythm Cafe   Bar
(リズムカフェ; Map p246; ☑03-3770-0244; http://rhythmcafe.jp; 11-1 Udagawa-chō, Shibuya-ku; ⊙6pm-2am; 圓JR Yamanote line to Shibuya, Hachikō exit) Rhythm Cafe is a fun little spot secreted among the windy streets of

Udagawa-chō. It's run by a record label and known for having offbeat event nights, such as the retro Japanese pop night on the fourth Thursday of the month. Drinks start at ¥600; some events have a cover, but not usually more than ¥1000.

Contact   Club
(コンタクト; Map p246; ☑03-6427-8107; www. contacttokyo.com; basement, 2-10-12 Dōgen-zaka, Shibuya-ku; ⊙Fri-Wed; 圓JR Yamanote line to Shibuya, Hachikō exit) Shibuya's most fashionable club at the time of research, Contact is several storeys under a parking garage. Come after 1am on a Friday or Saturday night to see it in top form. Music may be hip-hop, house or techno – it depends on the night. It has plenty of space for just lounging, too. To enter, you must first sign up for a membership. ID required.

⊙ Ebisu & Meguro

Gem by Moto   Bar
(ジェムバイモト; Map p246; ☑03-6455-6998; 1-30-9 Ebisu, Shibuya-ku; ⊙5pm-midnight Tue-

Fri, 1-9pm Sat & Sun; ®JR Yamanote line to Ebisu, east exit) Tiny Gem has a seriously good selection of interesting sakes from ambitious brewers. Start with one of the Gem originals (brewed in collaboration with the bar) – or let owner Chiba-san select one for you. Sake by the glass runs from ¥650 to ¥5000 (but most are on the more reasonable end). Cover charge ¥800; reservations recommended.

Another 8
Bar

(☎03-6417-9158; http://sakahachi.jp; 1-2-18 Shimo-Meguro, Meguro-ku; ⊗5pm-1am, closed irregularly; ®JR Yamanote line to Meguro, west exit) Choose from a changing selection of over a dozen craft beers and sakes at this popular new hang-out in an old garage on a side street just south of Meguro-dōri. DJs spin here most Friday and Saturday evenings. Drinks from ¥750.

Bar Trench
Cocktail Bar

(バートレンチ; Map p246; ☎03-3780-5291; www.small-axe.net; 1-5-8 Ebisu-nishi, Shibuya-ku; ⊗7pm-2am Mon-Sat, 6pm-1am Sun; ®JR Yamanote line to Ebisu, west exit) One of the pioneers of Tokyo's new cocktail scene, Trench (a suitable name for a bar hidden in a narrow alley) is a tiny place with an air of old-world bohemianism – but that might just be the absinthe talking. The always-changing original tipples are made with infusions, botanicals, herbs and spices. Drinks from ¥1500; cover ¥500.

⊘ Roppongi & Around

Gen Yamamoto
Cocktail Bar

(ゲンヤマモト; Map p252; ☎03-6434-0652; www.genyamamoto.jp; 1-6-4 Azabu-Jūban, Minato-ku; cover charge ¥1000, 4-/6-cocktail menu ¥4700/6700; ⊗3-11pm Tue-Sun; ⑤Namboku line to Azabu-jūban, exit 7) The delicious fruit-based drinks served here use local seasonal ingredients. Yamamoto's tasting menus are design to be savoured, not to get you sozzled (servings are small), and the bar's ambience – eight seats around a bar made from 500-year-old Japanese oak – is reminiscent

⚢ LGBT+ Tokyo

Shinjuku-nichōme (nicknamed 'Nichōme') is Tokyo's gay and lesbian enclave, with hundreds of small bars and dance clubs within a few square blocks.

Aiiro Cafe (アイイロ カフェ; Map p253; ☎03-6273-0740; www.aliving.net; 2-18-1 Shinjuku, Shinjuku-ku; ⊗6pm-2am Mon-Thu, to 5am Fri & Sat, to midnight Sun; ⑤Marunouchi line to Shinjuku-sanchōme, exit C8) The best place to start a night out in Nichōme, thanks to the all-you-can-drink beer for ¥1000 happy-hour special from 6pm to 9pm daily. The bar itself is teeny-tiny, with customers spilling into the streets.

Eagle (Map p253; www.eagletokyo.com; 2-12-3 Shinjuku, Shinjuku-ku; ⊗6pm-1am Sun-Thu, to 4am Fri & Sat; ®JR Yamanote line to Shinjuku, east exit) Friendly staff, happy-hour prices (¥500 drinks from 5pm to 8pm; otherwise they're ¥700) and an iconic mural from proudly out manga artist Inuyoshi.

Arty Farty (アーティファーティ; Map p253; ☎03-5362-9720; www.arty-farty.net; 2nd fl, 2-11-7 Shinjuku, Shinjuku-ku; ⊗8pm-4am Sun-Thu, to 5am Fri & Sat; ⑤Marunouchi line to Shinjuku-sanchōme, exit C8) Welcomes all in the community to come shake a tail feather on its (admittedly small) dance floor. It gets going later in the evening. Weekend events sometimes have a cover charge (¥1000 to ¥2000). Drinks from ¥700.

Tokyo in a Glass

What much of the world calls 'sake' the Japanese call *nihonshū* (the drink of Japan).

Sake is made from rice, water and kōji, a mould that acts as the fermenting agent.

Sake is the best pairing for traditional Japanese cuisine.

Sake is often categorised as sweet (*ama-kuchi*) or dry (*kara-kuchi*).

Dai-ginjō, a high-quality sake, is made from rice kernels with 50% or more of their original volume polished away.

On average the alcohol content of sake is around 15%.

Sake

AY.IMAGES/GETTY IMAGES ©

How to Drink Sake

Sake can be drunk *reishu* (chilled), *jō-on* (at room temperature), *nuru-kan* (warmed) or *atsu-kan* (piping hot), according to the season and personal preference. The top-drawer stuff is normally served chilled. Sake is traditionally presented in a ceramic jug known as a *tokkuri*, and poured into tiny cups known as *o-choko* or *sakazuki*. A traditional measure of sake is one *gō* (一合), which is a little over 180mL or 6oz. In speciality bars, you will have the option of ordering by the glass, which will often be filled to overflowing and brought to you in a wooden container to catch the overflow.

Right: Sake shop display
CAROLYNE PARENT/SHUTTERSTOCK ©

☆ Top Three for Sake

Another 8 (p179) Craft sake and cool atmosphere.

Gem by Moto (p178) New-wave sake bar with a small *kura* (brewery) line-up.

Toyama Bar (p181) Sake specialist from Toyama prefecture.

of a traditional teahouse. We highly recommend the six-cocktail menu.

Two Dogs Taproom
Craft Beer

(Map p252; ☑03-5413-0333; www.twodogs-tokyo.com; 3-15-24 Roppongi, Minato-ku; ⏰11.30am-2.30pm Mon-Fri, 5-11pm Sun & Mon, until midnight Tue & Wed, until 2am Thu-Sat; ⓢHibiya line to Roppongi, exit 3) There are 24 taps devoted to Japanese and international craft beers, including its own Roppongi Pale Ale, at this convivial pub just off the main Roppongi drag. Work your way through a few jars to wash down the tasty and decent-sized pizzas.

Ele Tokyo
Club

(Map p252; ☑03-5572-7535; www.eletokyo.com; Fukao Bldg, 1-4-5 Azabu-Jūban, Minato-ku; women free, men incl 1 drink Thu ¥2000, Fri & Sat ¥3000; ⏰10pm-5am Thu-Sat; ⓢŌedo line to Azabu-jūban, exit 7) Dress to impress to gain entry to this bling-tastic, two-level dance club that's one of the classier late-night joints around Roppongi. It's always free entry for women. You must be over 20 years old and have photo ID.

Rise & Win Brewing Co. Kamikatz Taproom
Craft Beer

(Map p252; ☑03-6441-3800; www.kamikatz.jp; The Workers & Co, 1st fl, 1-4-2 Higashi-azabu, Minato-ku; ⏰noon-3pm Mon-Fri, 6-11pm Mon-Sat; ⓢHibiya line to Kamiyachō, exit 2) This craft-beer brewery is based in a village in Tokushima Prefecture, Shikoku, that has adopted a zero-waste program. The bar features an appealing mishmash of country cabin design, plus a light fixture made from recycled bottles. There's usually six types of beer on tap, including an IPA, a porter and a leuven white; a flight of four costs ¥1400.

❼ Ginza & Tsukiji

Ginza Music Bar
Cocktail Bar

(Map p250; ☑03-3572-3666; www.ginzamusicbar.com; 4F Brownplace, 7-8-13 Ginza, Chūō-ku; cover charge after midnight ¥1000; ⏰6pm-4am Mon-Sat; ⓢGinza line to Shimbashi, exits 1 & 3)

A superb sound system showcases the 3000-plus vinyl collection that ranges from the likes of cool classic jazz to contemporary electronica. There are deep-blue walls and comfy seats in which to enjoy inventive cocktails (starting from ¥1400), such as the *matcha* and wasabi martini.

Ginza Lion
Beer Hall

(銀座ライオン; Map p250; ☑050-5269-7095; https://ginzalion.net; 7-9-20 Ginza, Chūō-ku; ⏰11.30am-11pm, until 10.30pm Sun; ⓢGinza line to Ginza, exit A2) So what if Sapporo's beers are not among the best you can quaff in Tokyo? Dating to 1934, the gorgeous art deco design at Japan's oldest beer hall – including glass mosaic murals – is to die for. The oom-pah-pah atmosphere, with waiters ferrying frothy mugs and plates of Bavarian-style sausages to the tables, is also priceless.

Old Imperial Bar
Bar

(Map p250; Mezzanine, Main Bldg, Imperial Hotel, 1-1-1 Uchisaiwai-chō, Chiyoda-ku; ⏰11.30am-midnight; ⓢHibiya line to Hibiya, exit A13) One of the few parts of the Imperial Hotel to feature some of the designs and materials used in Frank Lloyd Wright's 1923 building (note the architectural drawing behind the cash desk). It's a dimly lit, classy place to enjoy a cocktail (from ¥1580) or a shot of its signature 21-year-old Scotch whisky blend (¥2400).

❼ Marunouchi & Nihombashi

Toyama Bar
Bar

(トヤマバー; Map p250; ☑03-6262-2723; www.toyamakan.jp; 1-2-6 Nihombashi-muromachi, Chūō-ku; ⏰11am-9pm; ⓢGinza line to Mitsukoshi-mae, exit B5) This slick counter bar offers a selection of sakes from 17 different Toyama breweries. A set of three 30mL cups costs a bargain ¥700 (90mL cups from ¥700 each). English tasting notes are available. It's part of the Nihonbashi Toyama-kan (日本橋とやま館), which promotes goods produced in Japan's northern Toyama Prefecture.

Summer Beer Gardens

Summer beer gardens are a Tokyo tradition, typically running late May to early September.

Beer Terrace Sekirei (ビアテラス鶺鴒; ☏03-3746-9419; www.meijikinenkan.gr.jp/english/restaurant_sekirei.html; Meiji Kinenkan, 2-2-23 Moto-Akasaka, Minato-ku; cover charge ¥500; ⏰5-10.30pm Mon-Fri Jun–mid-Sep; ⛴JR Sōbu line to Shinanomachi) Every summer, the neatly clipped lawn of the elegant Meiji Kinenkan (one of the city's most sought-after wedding venues) become Tokyo's classiest beer garden. You can reserve a 'premium table' that seats four for ¥6000; otherwise it's first come, first served for ordinary seating. Food and drink start from a (relatively) reasonable ¥1000.

Forest Beer Garden (森のビアガーデ ン, Mori-no Beer Garden; ☏03-5411-3715; http://mbg.rkfs.co.jp; 14-13 Kasumigaoka-chō, Shinjuku-ku; ⏰5-10pm Mon-Fri, noon-10pm Sat & Sun mid-May–mid-Sep; ⛴JR Sōbu line to Shinanomachi) Following a long-standing Tokyo summer tradition, this corner of Meiji-jingū Gaien becomes a loud and lively beer garden with seating for 1000 around a grand, century-old tree. Reserve ahead for two hours of all-you-can-eat-and-drink barbecue and beer (men/women ¥4200/3900, discounted for kids). Closed in the event of heavy rain. Also look for department stores advertising beer gardens on their rooftops.

Pick up a bottle of anything you like at the attached shop.

Peter: the Bar   Cocktail Bar
(Map p250; ☏03-6270-2763; http://tokyo.peninsula.com/en/fine-dining/peter-lounge-bar; 24th fl, 1-8-1 Yūrakuchō, Chiyoda-ku; ⏰noon-midnight, to 1am Fri & Sat; ⛾Hibiya line to Hibiya, exits A6 & A7) The Peninsula Tokyo hotel's 24th-floor bar has dress-circle views across the Imperial Palace (p98), Hibiya Park and Ginza and a generous happy hour (5pm to 8pm Sunday to Thursday), when drinks – including the bar's signature 'Tokyo Joe' cocktail (gin, *ume* (plum) liqueur, Drambuie and cranberry juice) – and snacks are all ¥800. There's a 15% service charge, but no cover charge.

◎ Kanda & Akihabara

Beer-Ma Kanda   Craft Beer
(びあマ神田; Map p250; ☏03-3527-1900; www.facebook.com/kanda.wbm; 1-6-4 Kajichō, Chiyoda-ku; ⏰4-11pm Mon-Sat, 3-9pm Sun; ⛴JR lines to Kanda, south exit) Down an alley of sketchy-looking drinking dens is this nirvana for craft-beer lovers. It's principally a bottle shop stocking hundreds of different beer brands, all of which you can buy and drink on the premises (corkage ¥200). There's also eight taps of barrel beer available with servings in a range of sizes.

Craft Beer Server Land   Craft Beer
(☏03-6228-1891; Okawa Bldg B1F, 2-9 Kagurazaka, Shinjuku-ku; service charge ¥380; ⏰5pm-midnight Mon-Fri, from noon Sat & Sun; ☏; ⛴JR Sōbu line to Iidabashi, west exit) With some 14 Japanese craft beers on tap, going for a reasonable ¥500/840 a glass/pint, plus good food (the deep-fried eel in batter and chips is excellent), this brightly lit basement bar with wooden furniture and a slight Scandi feel is a winner.

Cocktail Works   Cocktail Bar
(カクテルワークス; Map p254; ☏03-6886-2138; 3-7-13 Ogawamachi, Chiyoda-ku; ⏰6pm-3am Mon-Sat; ⛾Mita line to Jimbōchō, exit 9)

Kamiya Bar

Award-winning mixologist Eiji Miyazawa brings sophisticated style to studenty Jimbōchō with this spacious bar selling cocktails from ¥1400. Gin lovers will be in heaven with some 160-plus versions to choose from, including several local artisan brands.

Hitachino Brewing Lab   Craft Beer
(Map p254; ☑️03-3254 3434; http://hitachino.cc; 1-25-4 Kanda-Sudachō, Chiyoda-ku; ⊗11am-11pm Mon-Sat, until 9pm Sun; ଭChūō or Sōbu lines to Akihabara, Electric Town exit) Sake brewery Kiuchi has been brewing its excellent range of Hitachino Nest craft beers since 1996. At this dedicated outlet you can have a very merry time working your way from the white beer to the sweet stout while gazing across the Kanda-gawa from the terrace seating.

🍴 Asakusa & Ryōgoku

Popeye   Pub
(ポパイ; Map p254; ☑️03-3633-2120; www.lares. dti.ne.jp/~ppy; 2-18-7 Ryōgoku, Sumida-ku; sampler set of 3/10 beers ¥630/1750; ⊗5-11.30pm Mon-Fri, from 3pm Sat; ଭJR Sōbu line to Ryōgoku, west exit) Popeye boasts an astounding 100 beers on tap, including a huge selection of Japanese beers – from Echigo Weizen to Hitachino Nest Espresso Stout. The happy-hour deal (5pm to 8pm, from 3pm on Saturday) offers select brews with free plates of pizza, sausages and other snacks to munch on. It's extremely popular and fills up fast; get here early to grab a seat.

Kamiya Bar   Bar
(神谷バー; Map p254; ☑️03-3841-5400; www.kamiya-bar.com; 1-1-1 Asakusa, Taitō-ku; ⊗11.30am-10pm Wed-Mon; ⑤Ginza line to Asakusa, exit 3) One of Tokyo's oldest Western-style bars, Kamiya opened in 1880 and is still hugely popular. The house drink for over a century has been Denki Bran, a secret mix of brandy, gin, wine, curaçao and medicinal herbs. Order either 'blanc' (30 proof) or the 40 proof 'old' at the counter, then give your tickets to the server.

SHOWTIME

Kabuki, international acts, jazz clubs and traditional dance theatre

Showtime

Many styles of traditional Japanese performing arts can be seen on Tokyo stages, including dramatic kabuki – Japan's signature performing art – and austere nō (an even older form of dance-drama). Earphones or subtitles with an English translation of the plots and dialogue are often available; unfortunately, this isn't the case with contemporary theatre.

Tokyoites have a great appreciation for jazz and classical music and there are fantastic venues for both. If you'd prefer to catch an in-your-face noise performance in a basement club, well, Tokyo has that for you too.

In This Section

Tickets

● The easiest way to get tickets is from a Ticket Pia kiosk. There are convenient locations inside Tower Records (p156) and the Asakusa Culture Tourist Information Center (p73). Its online booking site (http://t.pia.jp) is in Japanese only.

● Purchase tickets for national theatre production online though the Japan Arts Council (www.ntj.jac.go.jp). Kabuki tickets are available at www.kabukiweb.net.

Asakusa Culture Tourist Information Center (p73), designed by Kengo Kuma & Associates

The Best...

Theatre

National Theatre (p190) A grand setting for *nō* (a stylised dance-drama performed on a bare stage), bunraku (puppet theatre) and other classical styles.

Kabukiza (p90) The spot to see kabuki.

Setagaya Public Theatre (p190) Excellent space for contemporary drama and dance.

Suigian (p192) Chic dinner theatre offering a sampler of traditional Japanese performing arts.

Live Music

Shinjuku Pit Inn (p188) Tokyo jazz-scene institution for decades.

WWW (p190) Shibuya live house with a solid line-up of indie acts.

Tokyo Opera City Concert Hall (p188) Legendary acoustics for classical performances.

Oiwake (p193) One of the city's few remaining *minyō izakaya* (pubs where traditional folk music is performed).

Unit (p190) Offering both live gigs and DJs to a stylish crowd.

✪ Shinjuku & Ikebukuro

Shinjuku Pit Inn   Jazz
(新宿ピットイン; Map p253; ☎03-3354-2024; www.pit-inn.com; basement, 2-12-4 Shinjuku, Shinjuku-ku; from ¥3000; ⏰matinee 2.30pm, evening show 7.30pm; ⑤Marunouchi line to Shinjuku-sanchōme, exit C5) This is Tokyo's best jazz spot: intimate, unpretentious and with an always solid line-up of influential, avant-garde, crossover and up-and-coming musicians from Japan and abroad. If you're already a fan of jazz, you'll want to make it a point to visit; and if you're not, Pit Inn is the kind of place that just might win you over.

Tokyo Opera City Concert Hall   Classical Music
(東京オペラシティコンサートホール; ☎03-5353-9999; www.operacity.jp; 3rd fl, Tokyo Opera City, 3-20-2 Nishi-Shinjuku, Shinjuku-ku; ⬛Keiō New line to Hatsudai, east exit) This beautiful, oak-panelled, A-frame concert hall, with legendary acoustics, hosts the Tokyo Philharmonic Orchestra among other well-regarded ensembles; *bugaku* (dance pieces played by court orchestras in ancient Japan) is also sometimes performed here. Free lunchtime organ performances take place monthly, usually on Fridays. Get information and tickets from the box office next to the entrance to the Tokyo Opera City Art Gallery.

New National Theatre   Performing Arts
(新国立劇場, Shin Kokuritsu Gekijō; ☎03-5351-3011; www.nntt.jac.go.jp; 1-1-1 Hon-machi, Shibuya-ku; ⬛Keiō New line to Hatsudai, central exit) This is Tokyo's premier public performing-arts centre, with state-of-the-art stages for drama, opera and dance. The plays are in Japanese, while the operas and ballets are usually visiting international productions. Japanese contemporary dance (including the avant-garde Japanese style known as *butō*) is sometimes performed here, and it happily requires no language ability.

Robot Restaurant   Cabaret
(ロボットレストラン; Map p253; ☎03-3200-5500; www.shinjuku-robot.com; 1-7-1 Kabukichō,

Souvenir masks

Shinjuku-ku; tickets ¥8000; ⊘shows at 5.55pm, 7.50pm & 9.45pm, additional show at 4pm Fri-Sun; 🚃JR Yamanote line to Shinjuku, east exit) This Kabukichō spectacle has hit it big with its vision of 'wacky Japan': bikini-clad women ride around on giant robots against a backdrop of animated screens and enough LED lights to illuminate all of Shinjuku. You can book ahead online (at full price) or save up to ¥2000 per person by purchasing at the venue with a discount flyer (available at Tourist Information Centers and hotels).

✪ Kōenji & Kichijōji

UFO Club
Live Music

(www.ufoclub.jp; basement fl, 1-11-6 Kōenji-Minami, Suginami-ku; Ⓢ Marunouchi line to Higashi-Kōenji, exit 2) Named for the infamous 1960s London spot, Kōenji's UFO Club is committed to keeping the spirit of the era alive: the small basement space, with red-and-black swirling walls, feels like the inside of a lava lamp. Music-wise, expect psychedelic and acid rock from mostly local bands, but really anything goes so long as it's a bit weird.

✪ Harajuku & Aoyama

National Nō Theatre
Theatre

(国立能楽堂, Kokuritsu Nō-gakudō; ☎03-3423-1331; www.ntj.jac.go.jp; 4-18-1 Senda-gaya, Shibuya-ku; adult ¥2700-4900, student ¥1900-2200; 🚃JR Sōbu line to Sendagaya) The traditional music, poetry and dances of nō, Japan's oldest continued mode of performing arts, unfold here on an elegant cypress stage. Each seat has a small screen displaying an English translation of the dialogue. Shows take place only a few times a month and can sell out quickly; purchase tickets online one month in advance.

 Nō

Nō, which emerged in 14th-century Kyoto, is the oldest existent Japanese performing art. Its roots are likely older still: nō is believed to be a pastiche of earlier traditions, including Shintō rites, popular entertainments such as pantomime and acrobatics, and *gagaku* (the traditional music and dance of the imperial court).

Rather than a drama in the usual sense of a story in motion, nō seeks to express a poetic moment by symbolic and almost abstract means: glorious movements, sonorous chorus and music, and subtle expression. Characters speak in the language of the medieval court.

The nō stage is furnished with only a single pine tree. There are two principal characters: the *shite,* who is sometimes a living person but more often a demon or a ghost whose soul cannot rest; and the *waki,* who leads the main character towards the play's climactic moment. Haunting masks, carved from wood, are used to depict female or nonhuman characters.

Some viewers find this all captivating; others (including most Japanese today) find its subtlety all too subtle. As if anticipating this, comic vignettes known as *kyōgen,* using colloquial language, are part of nō plays programs.

In Tokyo, see nō at the National Nō Theatre (p189) and Kanze Nōgakudō (p192).

Nō performer

✪ Shibuya & Shimo-Kitazawa

WWW Live Music

(Map p246; 📞03-5458-7685; https://www-shibuya.jp; 13-17 Udagawa-chō, Shibuya-ku; tickets ¥3000-5000; 🚃JR Yamanote line to Shibuya, Hachikō exit) In a former art-house cinema with the tell-tale tiered floor still intact, this is one of those rare venues where you could turn up just about any night and hear something good. The line-up varies from indie pop to hip-hop to electronica. Upstairs is WWW X, a bigger space.

Setagaya Public Theatre Performing Arts

(世田谷パブリックシアター; 📞03-5432-1515; www.setagaya-pt.jp; 4-1-1 Taishidō, Setagaya-ku; tickets ¥5000-7500; 🚃Tōkyū Den-en-toshi line to Sangenjaya, Carrot Tower exit) Setagaya Public Theatre, comprising a main stage and the smaller, more experimental Theatre Tram, is the city's top venue for contemporary drama and dance. Particularly accessible to non-Japanese speakers is the theatre's series on modern nō (a stylised Japanese dance-drama performed on a bare stage); butō (an avant-garde form of dance) is also sometimes staged here.

Shimo-Kitazawa Three Live Music

(下北沢Three; 📞03-5486-8804; https://shimokitazawathree.tumblr.com; basement fl, 5-18-1 Daizawa, Setagaya-ku; free-¥3500; 🚃Odakyū or Keiō Inokashira line to Shimo-Kitazawa, southwest exit) We love Three's mission to make live music more accessible in Tokyo: it hosts 10 free events a month (otherwise they average around ¥2000). The line-up is pretty random, but the welcoming attitude means there's usually a good crowd, which doesn't take much – capacity is 170. Live shows start around 6pm or 7pm; club events from 11.30pm.

Club Quattro Live Music

(クラブクアトロ; Map p246; 📞03-3477-8750; www.club-quattro.com; 4th & 5th fl, 32-13-4 Udagawa-chō, Shibuya-ku; tickets ¥3000-4000;

🚃JR Yamanote line to Shibuya, Hachikō exit) This small venue attracts a more grown-up, artsy crowd than the club's location – near Shibuya Center-gai (p67) – might lead you to expect. There's no explicit musical focus, but the line-up leans towards indie rock and world music. One drink (¥600) minimum order.

Uplink Cinema

(アップリンク; Map p246; 📞03-6825-5503; www.uplink.co.jp; 37-18 Udagawa-chō, Shibuya-ku; adult/student/senior ¥1800/1500/1100; 🚃JR Yamanote line to Shibuya, Hachikō exit) Watching indies here feels a bit like hanging out in a friend's basement; with just 40 comfy, mismatched seats, Uplink is officially Tokyo's smallest theatre. Uplink screens artsy domestic and foreign films (subtitled in Japanese). On weekdays students pay just ¥1100.

✪ Ebisu & Meguro

Unit Live Music

(ユニット; Map p246; 📞03-5459-8630; www.unit-tokyo.com; 1-34-17 Ebisu-nishi, Shibuya-ku; ticket ¥2500-5000; 🚃Tōkyū Tōyoko line to Daikanyama) This subterranean club stages live music and DJ-hosted events (sometimes staggered on the same night). The solid line-up includes Japanese indie bands, veterans playing to a smaller crowd and overseas artists making their Japan debut. Unit has high ceilings and an intentionally industrial-cool interior (in addition to excellent sound), separating it from Tokyo's grungier live-music spots.

✪ Roppongi & Around

National Theatre Theatre

(国立劇場, Kokuritsu Gekijō; 📞03-3265-7411, box office 03-3230-3000; www.ntj.jac.go.jp; 4-1 Hayabusa-chō, Chiyoda-ku; tickets ¥1700-7000; 🚇Hanzōmon line to Hanzōmon, exit 1) This is the capital's premier venue for traditional performing arts with 1600-seat and 590-seat auditoriums. Performances include

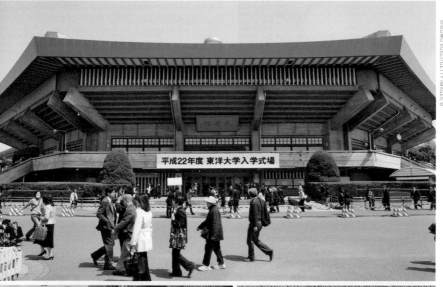

Clockwise from top: Nippon Budōkan (p193), designed by Mamoru Yamada; New National Theatre (p188); poster outside Kabukiza Theatre (p90)

 Butō

Butō is Japan's unique and fascinating contribution to contemporary dance. It was born out of a rejection of the excessive formalisation that characterises traditional forms of Japanese dance and of an intention to return to more ancient roots. Hijikata Tatsumi (1928–86), born in the remote northern province of Akita, is credited with giving the first *butō* performance in 1959; Ōno Kazuo (1906–2010) was also a key figure.

During a performance, dancers use their naked or seminaked bodies to express the most elemental and intense human emotions. Nothing is forbidden in *butō* and performances often deal with taboo topics such as sexuality and death. For this reason, critics often describe *butō* as scandalous, and *butō* dancers delight in pushing the boundaries of what can be considered beautiful in artistic performance. It's also entirely visual, meaning that both Japanese and non-Japanese spectators are on level footing.

Though performers have toured internationally, in Japan *butō* has remained a largely underground scene. It is sometimes performed at the Setagaya Public Theatre (p190). Dairakudakan is one of the more active troupes today. They have a practice and performance space, Studio Kochūten, in Kichijōji. Shows are irregular; info is posted online in English.

Butō performer
KAZUHIRO NOGI/GETTY IMAGES ©

kabuki (a form of stylised Japanese theatre), *gagaku* (music of the imperial court) and *bunraku* (classic puppet theatre). Earphones with English translation are available for hire (¥700, plus ¥1000 deposit). Check the website for performance schedules.

Toho Cinemas Roppongi Hills
Cinema

(TOHOシネマズ 六本木ヒルズ; Map p252; ☏10am-9pm 050-6868-5024; https://tohotheater.jp; Keyakizaka Complex, Roppongi Hills, 6-chōme Roppongi, Minato-ku; adult/student/senior/child ¥1800/1500/1100/1000; ⑤Hibiya line to Roppongi, exit 1C) Besides being one of Tokyo's nicest and biggest cinemas (it has nine screens, some with 3D and 4D capability), Toho's Roppongi Hills theatre screens some popular Japanese new releases with English subtitles. The 3D and 4D screenings cost extra.

✪ Ginza & Tsukiji

Kanze Nōgakudō
Performing Arts

(観世能楽堂; Map p250; ☏03-6274-6579; www.kanze.net; Ginza Six B3, 6-10-1 Ginza, Chūō-ku; ⑤Ginza line to Ginza, exit A2) This venerable group specialising in *nō* dramas relocated to the bowels of the Ginza Six shopping complex in 2017. The theatre seats 48; if you haven't booked in advance and would like a taster, you can check on the day for ¥3000 'happy hour' tickets; one of these gets you an unreserved seat for the performance's last act.

✪ Marunouchi & Nihombashi

Suigian
Performing Arts

(水戯庵; Map p250; ☏03-3527-9378; https://suigian.jp; basement, 2-5-10 Nihombashi-Muromachi, Chūō-ku; seating charge from ¥3800 plus 1 drink or food; ☏11am-11.30pm, until 9pm Sun; ⑤Ginza line to Mitsukoshimae, exit A6) If you would like an up-close and personal taster of traditional Japanese performing arts, including *nō*, *kyōgen* (comic drama) and courtly dances, make a reservation for one of three 40-minute performances that take place here. The small stage is backed by a beautiful painting of a pine tree, and surrounded by an intimate, sophisticated restaurant and bar.

Nippon Budōkan
Live Music

(日本武道館; Map p254; ☑03-3216-5100; www.nipponbudokan.or.jp; 2-3 Kitanomaru-kōen, Chiyoda-ku; ⑤Hanzōmon line to Kudanshita, exit 2) The 14,000-plus-seat Budōkan was originally built for the judo competition of the 1964 Olympics (*budō* means 'martial arts') and will be pressed into service again for the 2020 event. Martial-arts practice and contests are still held here, but the Budōkan is better known as a concert hall: lots of big names, from the Beatles to Beck, have played here.

Cotton Club
Jazz

(コットンクラブ; Map p250; ☑03-3215-1555; www.cottonclubjapan.co.jp; 2nd fl, Tokia, Tokyo Bldg, 2-7-3 Marunouchi, Chiyoda-ku; tickets ¥6000-10,000.; ⊙5-11pm Mon-Fri, 4-10.30pm Sat & Sun; ◙JR lines to Tokyo, Marunouchi south exit) You're more likely to hear contemporary international jazz stars here than musicians harking back to the 1920s New York club it honours. Also on the roster is a medley of interesting Japanese artists such as saxophonist Itō Takeshi. Check the website for schedules and ticket prices.

☺ Kanda & Akihabara

Club Goodman
Live Music

(クラブグッドマン; Map p254; ☑03-3862-9010; www.clubgoodman.com; basement, AS Bldg, 55 Kanda-Sakumagashi, Chiyoda-ku; cover charge ¥100-5500; ◙JR Yamanote line to Akihabara, Shōwa-dōri exit) In the basement of a building with a guitar shop and recording studios, it's no surprise that this live house is a favourite with Tokyo's indie-scene bands and their fans. Entry charge depends on the band playing.

☺ Ueno & Yanaka

Tokyo Bunka Kaikan
Classical Music

(東京文化会館; Map p254; ☑03-3828-2111; www.t-bunka.jp; 5-45 Ueno-kōen, Taitō-ku; ⊙library 1-8pm Tue-Sat, to 5pm Sun, closed irregularly; ◙JR lines to Ueno, Ueno-kōen exit) The Tokyo Metropolitan Symphony Orchestra and the Tokyo Ballet both make regular appearances at this concrete bunker of a building designed by Maekawa Kunio, an apprentice of Le Corbusier. Prices vary wildly; look out for monthly morning classical-music performances that cost only ¥500. The gorgeously decorated auditorium, with cloud-shaped acoustic panels on the wall, has superb acoustics.

Tokyo University of the Arts Performing Arts Center
Classical Music

(東京藝術大学奏楽堂; Map p254; ☑050-5525-2465; www.pac.geidai.ac.jp; 12-8 Ueno-kōen, Taitō-ku; tickets ¥1000-5000) With its stage dominated by a French Garnier Organ and a ceiling that can be moved to create optimum acoustics, the university's intimate hall is a superb spot to take in a classical concert. Check online for the schedule and enquire about the occasional morning concerts, which usually start at 11am and cost ¥1000.

☺ Asakusa & Ryōgoku

Oiwake
Traditional Music

(追分; Map p254; ☑03-3844-6283; www.oiwake.info; 3-28-11 Nishi-Asakusa, Taitō-ku; ¥2000 plus 1 food item & 1 drink; ⊙5.30pm-midnight Tue-Sun; ◙Tsukuba Express to Asakusa, exit 1) Oiwake is one of Tokyo's few *minyō izakaya*, pubs where traditional folk music is performed. It's a homely place, where the waitstaff and the musicians – who play *shamisen* (a banjo-like instrument), hand drums and bamboo flute – are one and the same. Sets start at 7pm and 9pm; children are welcome for the early show. Seating is on tatami.

ACTIVE
TOKYO

Baseball, sumo, amusement parks,
cooking courses and traditional crafts

Active Tokyo

Sumo, steeped in ancient ritual, is Japan's national sport. While it has its devout followers, it's baseball that is the clear fan favourite. Within Tokyo, the Yomiuri Giants and the Yakult Swallows are cross-town rivals. Interest in sports in general is at a high, as Tokyo hosts the Summer Olympics in 2020.

See the city from a different angle through a cycling or kayaking tour. Traditional crafts workshops and cooking courses offer a chance to engage with Japanese culture. Book in advance.

In This Section

Sports Seasons

Sumo Tournaments *(bashō)* are held in Tokyo in January, May and September; see a practice session year-round (except when tournaments take place).

Baseball The season runs March to October.

Soba

The Best...

Spectator Sports

Ryōgoku Kokugikan (p68) Location of the three annual Tokyo sumo *bashō*.

Tokyo Dome (p198) Home to the Yomiuri Giants, Japan's top baseball team.

Jingū Baseball Stadium (p198) The base of Tokyo underdogs Yakult Swallows.

Courses

Wanariya (p200) Indigo-dyeing and handloom-weaving workshops.

Tsukiji Soba Academy (p200) Soba-making lessons from a seasoned pro.

Toyokuni Atelier Gallery (p200) Learn the art of *sumi-e* (ink-wash painting).

Mokuhankan (p201) Make your own woodblock prints.

⊕ Spectator Sports

Tokyo Dome   Baseball
(東京ドーム; Map p254; www.tokyo-dome.co.jp;
1-3 Kōraku, Bunkyō-ku; tickets ¥1700-6200; 🚆JR
Chūō line to Suidōbashi, west exit) Tokyo Dome
(aka 'Big Egg') is home to the Yomiuri Giants. Love 'em or hate 'em, they're the most
consistently successful team in Japanese
baseball. If you're looking to see the Giants
in action, the baseball season runs from the
end of March to the end of October. Tickets
usually sell out in advance; get them early
at www.giants.jp.

Jingū Baseball Stadium   Baseball
(神宮球場, Jingū Kyūjo; Map p246; 📞0180-993-
589; www.jingu-stadium.com; 3-1 Kasumigaoka-
machi, Shinjuku-ku; tickets ¥2200-5000; 🚇Ginza
line to Gaienmae, exit 3) Jingū Baseball Stadium, built in 1926, is home to the Yakult
Swallows, Tokyo's number-two team (but
number-one when it comes to fan loyalty).
Most games start at 6pm. Get tickets from
the booth next to Gate 9, which is open

from 11am to 5pm (or until 20 minutes
after the game ends).

Arashio Stable   Spectator Sport
(荒汐部屋, Arashio-beya; 📞03-3666-7646;
www.arashio.net; 2-47-2 Hama-chō, Nihombashi,
Chūō-ku; ⊗7.30am-10am; 🚇Toei Shinjuku line to
Hamachō, exit A2) FREE Watch the wrestlers
practise through the window between
7.30am and 10am at this friendly sumo
stable. Call the day before to double-check
that practice (keiko) is on – they take
breaks during the March, July and September tournaments; more info is on the
English website.

⊕ Outdoors

Tokyo Great Cycling Tour   Cycling
(Map p250; 📞03-4590-2995; www.tokyocycling.
jp; 1-3-2 Shinkawa, Chūō-ku; tours ¥3000-10,000;
🚇Hibiya line to Kayabachō, exit 3) There's a
fine variety of routes and different themes
offered here to suit everyone from casual
pedallers to more serious cyclists. The
English-speaking staff and guides are very

Thunder Dolphin roller coaster at Tokyo Dome City Attractions (p200)

friendly and professional. You can also rent bikes from ¥2500 a day.

The same company also offers excellent **kayaking tours** (the longest route takes you on a fascinating 10km circuit including the Sumida, Kanda and Nihombashi Rivers) and **running tours** around the palace and along the Sumida-gawa.

ZAC
Kayaking

(📞03-6671-0201; www.zacsports.com; adult/child ¥5500/4500; Ⓢ Shinjuku line to Higashi-ōshima, Komatsugawa exit) Choose either day or night to go on these 1½-hour kayaking tours of Kyunaka-gawa (actually a canal) way out east of Ryūgoku. It's a wonderful way to get an alternative view of the city, plus some light exercise. If there is just one person on the tour, add ¥1000 to the pricing.

🎡 Amusement Parks

Tokyo
Disney Resort
Amusement Park

(東京ディズニーリゾート; 📞domestic calls 0570-00-8632, from overseas +81-45-330-5211; www.tokyodisneyresort.jp; 1-1 Maihama, Urayasu-shi, Chiba-ken; 1-day ticket for 1 park adult/child ¥7400/4800, after 6pm ¥4200; ⊙varies by season; 🚉JR Keiyō line to Maihama, south exit) Tokyo Disney Resort includes Tokyo Disneyland, modelled after the one in California, and also Tokyo DisneySea, an original theme park with seven 'ports' evoking locales real and imagined (the Mediterranean and 'Mermaid Lagoon', for example). DisneySea targets a more grown-up crowd, but still has many attractions for kids. Both resorts get extremely crowded, especially on weekends and during summer holidays; you'll have to be strategic with your Fast-Passes. Book admission tickets online to save time.

Tokyo Joypolis
Amusement Park

(東京ジョイポリス; http://tokyo-joypolis.com; 3rd-5th fl, DECKS Tokyo Beach, 1-6-1 Daiba, Minato-ku; adult/child ¥800/500, all-rides passport ¥4300/3300, passport after 5pm ¥3300/2300; ⊙10am-10pm; 🚉Yurikamome line

🚲 Cycling in the City

Tokyo is by no means a bicycle-friendly city. Bike lanes are almost nonexistent and you'll see no-parking signs for bicycles everywhere. (Ignore these at your peril: your bike could get impounded, requiring a half-day excursion to the pound and a ¥3000 fee.) Despite all this you'll see locals on bikes everywhere.
Cogi Cogi (www.cogicogi.jp; 24hr ¥2400) Bike-sharing system with ports around the city, including some hostels. There are instructions in English, but it's a little complicated to use. You'll need to download an app, register a credit card and have wi-fi connection on the go to sync with the ports.

Hipster bicycle manufacturer **Tokyobike Rentals Yanaka** (Map p254; 📞03-5809-0980; www.tokyobikerentals.com; 4-2-39 Yanaka, Taitō-ku; 1st day ¥3000, additional day ¥1500; ⊙10am-7.30pm Wed-Mon; 🚉JR Yamanote line to Nippori, west exit) rents seven- and eight-speed city bikes for the day – great for exploring Ueno and Yanaka. Book ahead online. Helmet and locker rentals (¥500 each) are available too.

Some accommodations have bikes to lend, sometimes for free or for a small fee.

to Odaiba Kaihin-kōen, north exit) This indoor amusement park is full of virtual-reality attractions and thrill rides, such as the video-enhanced Halfpipe Tokyo; there are rides for little ones, too. Separate admission and individual ride tickets (¥500 to ¥800) are available, but if you plan to ride more than a few, the unlimited 'passport' makes sense.

Sky Circus
Amusement Park

(スカイサーカス; ☑️03-3989-3457; www.sky circus.jp; Sunshine 60, 3-1-1 Higashi-Ikebukuro, Toshima-ku; observatory ticket adult/child ¥1200/600, attractions extra; ☺10am-10pm; 🚉JR Yamanote line to Ikebukuro, east exit) One of Tokyo's better virtual-reality parks, Sky Circus has an aerial roller-coaster that snakes between Ikebukuro's skyscrapers (Swing Coaster; ¥400) and a cannon attraction that sends you bouncing around a futuristic version of Tokyo's more famous attractions (Tokyo Bullet Flight; ¥600). Basic instructions are given in English. If you are prone to motion sickness you will feel it, possibly acutely.

You have to first buy a ticket to the 60th-floor observatory – which is nice in its own right – from the ticket counter in the basement of Sunshine 60 (part of Sunshine City). You can get your hand stamped for in-and-out entry all day. Attraction tickets can be bought on the 60th floor. Last ticket sales are at 8.50pm.

To ride the attractions, children must be over seven years of age and taller than 130cm; grown-ups no bigger than 2m and 100kg.

Tokyo Dome City Attractions
Amusement Park

(東京ドームシティアトラクションズ; Map p254; ☑️03-5800-9999; www.tokyo-dome.co.jp; 1-3-61 Kōraku, Bunkyō-ku; day pass adult/child/teenager ¥3900/2500/3400; ☺10am-9pm; 👶; 🚉JR Chūō line to Suidōbashi, west exit) The top attraction at this amusement park next to Tokyo Dome (p198) is the Thunder Dolphin (¥1030), a roller coaster that cuts a heart-in-your-throat course in and around the tightly packed buildings of downtown. There are plenty of low-key, child-friendly rides as well. You can buy individual-ride tickets, day passes, night passes (valid from 5pm) and a five-ride pass (¥2600).

 ## Courses

Wanariya
Traditional Craft

(和なり屋; Map p254; ☑️03-5603-9169; www. wanariya.jp; 1-8-10 Senzoku, Taitō-ku; indigo dyeing/weaving from ¥1920/1980; ☺10am-7pm irregular holidays; 🚇Hibiya line to Iriya, exit 1) A team of young and friendly Japanese runs this indigo-dyeing and traditional *hataori* (handloom-weaving) workshop. In under an hour you can learn to dye a T-shirt or a tote bag or weave a pair of coasters. It's a fantastic opportunity to make your own souvenirs. Book at least three days in advance.

Tsukiji Soba Academy
Cooking

(築地そばアカデミー; Map p250; http://soba. specialist.co.jp; Hins Minato #004, 3-18-14 Minato, Chūō-ku; up to 3 people from ¥30,000, per additional person ¥10,000; 🚇Yūrakuchō line to Shintomichō, exit 7) Good-natured English-speaking chef Inoue Akila is a master of soba – noodles made from nutty buckwheat flour. He has taught chefs who have gone on to win Michelin stars for their versions of this classic Tokyo dish. Classes are held in a compact kitchen overlooking the Sumida-gawa.

Additional vegetarian and gluten-free menus available for an extra fee.

Toyokuni Atelier Gallery
Arts & Crafts

(豊國アトリエ; Map p254; ☑️090-4069-8410; www.nekomachi.com; 3-1-13 Kanda-Jimbōchō, Chiyoda-ku; 1hr class ¥2000; ☺gallery noon-5pm Tue-Thu & Sat & Sun, classes 1pm, 3pm or 5pm; 🚇Shinjuku line to Jimbōchō, exit A1) Get a taster of *sumi-e*, the delicate art of ink painting on *washi* (Japanese handmade paper), at this gallery displaying the artworks of master ink painter Honda Toyokuni. The one-hour class is taught by his English-speaking, affable son Yuta, and is highly recommended for budding artists of all ages. Reservations are essential.

Mokuhankan
Traditional Craft

(木版館; Map p254; ☑️070-5011-1418; www. mokuhankan.com; 1-41-8 Asakusa, Taitō-ku;

Ikebana (Japanese flower arrangement)

per person ¥2000; ⊘10am-5.30pm Wed-Mon; 🚇Tsukuba Express to Asakusa, exit 5) Try your hand at making *ukiyo-e* (woodblock prints) at this studio run by expat David Bull. Hour-long 'print parties' are great fun and take place daily; sign up online. There's a shop here too, where you can buy vintage prints as well as Bull's and Jed Henry's humorous *Ukiyo-e Heroes* series – contemporary prints featuring video-game characters in traditional settings.

Buddha Bellies   Cooking
(Map p254; 📞080-5001-9395; www.buddha belliestokyo.jimdo.com; classes ¥5500-10,000; ⑤Chiyoda line to Yushima, exit 3) English-speaking professional sushi chef and sake sommelier Ayuko and her husband lead small hands-on classes in sushi, *bentō* (boxed lunch), udon and *wagashi* (Japanese sweets) making. Classes are held at Ayuko's home close to Yushima Station (she'll meet you at exit 3) and run usually from 11am, lasting 2½ hours. Book early.

Vegetarian, vegan and halal menus are also available.

Kitchen Kujo Tokyo   Cooking
(Map p254; 📞03-5832-9452; www.kujo.tokyo; 1-2-10 Yanaka, Taitō-ku; classes ¥6000-12,000; ⊘classes 10.30am or 1.30pm, bar 6-10.30pm Mon-Sat; ⑤Chiyoda line to Nezu, exit 2) The Kobayashi family and their translator and ramen chef Jun offer an interesting variety of cooking and culture classes at this handy studio devoted to cooking with organic products. Learn how to make tofu, miso, vegan ramen and curry rice with guest instructor Curryman (who dresses in a wacky costume). Also available are calligraphy, tea-ceremony and yoga classes.

Ohara School of Ikebana   Ikebana
(小原流いけばな; Map p246; 📞03-5774-5097; www.ohararyu.or.jp; 5-7-17 Minami-Aoyama, Minato-ku; classes ¥4000; ⑤Ginza line to Omote-sandō, exit B1) This well-regarded, modern ikebana school teaches 90-minute introductory flower-arrangement classes in English every Thursday at 10am and 1pm, and at 10.30am on the first and third Sunday of the month. Sign up online by 3pm the Tuesday before (the earlier the better, as spaces are limited).

REST YOUR HEAD

Top tips for the best accommodation

Rest Your Head

As in any major city, accommodation will take up a major chunk of your Tokyo budget. But here's the good news: there are plenty of attractive budget and midrange options, and levels of cleanliness and service are generally high everywhere. You can play it safe with a standard hotel or change it up with a more local option, such as a ryokan (traditional inn with Japanese-style bedding) or a capsule hotel. Tokyo is huge, so be sure to factor in travel time and costs when deciding where to stay.

In This Section

Rates

Hostels, capsule hotels and ryokan typically have fixed rates; for hotels of all classes, rates can vary tremendously, and discounts significantly below rack rates can be found online. Note that prices tend to increase on weekends. Sales tax applies to hotel rates. There is also a city-wide 'accommodation tax' (per person and per night) of ¥100 on rooms over ¥10,000 and ¥200 on rooms over ¥15,000.

Ryokan (traditional Japanese inn)

The Best...

Reservations

It's really best to reserve in advance; on many weekends Tokyo hotels are near full capacity and the best properties book out early. At smaller inns or ryokan, walk-ins can fluster staff (or staff might not be present); hostels are better prepared for this. The busiest periods include the first week of January, Golden Week (29 April to 5 May) and August.

Useful Websites

Often it is cheapest to book online directly with the accommodation.

Jalan (www.jalan.net) Popular local discount accommodation site.

Japanese Inn Group (www.japaneseinn group.com) Bookings for ryokan and other small, family-run inns.

Lonely Planet (lonelyplanet.com/Japan/Tokyo/hotels) Reviews, recommendations and bookings.

Apartment Rentals

Apartment rentals are strictly regulated in Tokyo (and Japan in general). Very few places are currently able to meet the requirements to qualify. Those that appear on AirBnB have completed the proper registration process. **Housing Japan** (https://housingjapan.com) can also arrange legal short-term stays. Options may increase in the near future, as more and more operators are able to get their paperwork through the approval process.

 # Accommodation Types

Business Hotels

Functional and economical, 'business hotels' have compact rooms, usually with semidouble beds (140cm across; roomy for one, a bit of a squeeze for two) and tiny en-suite bathrooms. If cost performance is your chief deciding factor – and you don't plan to spend much time in your room – then a business hotel is your best bet. They're famous for being deeply unfashionable, though many chains have updated their look in recent years. Expect to pay from ¥10,000 to ¥15,000 (or ¥15,000 to ¥20,000 for double occupancy). In major hubs, front desk staff should speak some English.

Capsule Hotels

Capsule hotels offer a space the size of a single bed, with just enough headroom for you to sit up – like a bunk bed with more privacy. Older capsule hotels have large communal baths (in which case visitors with visible tattoos are not allowed to stay); newer ones, geared more towards international travellers, often just have showers. Prices range from ¥3500 to ¥5000. Floors and facilities are gender-segregated; some close for a few hours per day for cleaning.

Hostels

Tokyo excels at hostels: they're clean and well managed. Staff typically speak good English and are often very helpful. Some hostels put on cultural activities and social events for guests. Laundry facilities are common; some but not all hostels have cooking facilities. Expect to pay about ¥3000 for a dorm and ¥8000 for a private room (double occupancy), and possibly extra for amenities like towels.

Luxury Hotels

Name-brand luxury hotels have big rooms full of mod-cons and luxe amenities, but the biggest perk of all is the English-language concierge service. Many luxury hotels are atop high-rise buildings and offer fantastic city views; one downside is that some are in rather inconvenient locations. Prices vary wildly but average around ¥50,000 for a double room.

Ryokan

Ryokan (traditional Japanese inns) offer a traditional experience, with tatami (tightly woven floor matting) and futons (traditional quilt-like mattress that is rolled up and stowed away during the day) on the floor instead of beds. Many have 'family rooms' that can sleep four or five. Some have rooms with private baths, but one of the pleasures of staying in a traditional inn is the spacious communal bath. At inns with frequent foreign guests, these communal baths can often be used privately. Note that ryokan often charge per person (from around ¥5000) rather than per room.

Where to Stay

Neighbourhood	Atmosphere
Shinjuku & Ikebukuro	Excellent transit connections, food and nightlife options; very crowded around station areas. Cheaper options are clustered around the red-light district.
Kōenji & Kichijōji	Cheaper than central Tokyo and with a local vibe. Far from main sights; riding the crowded Chūō line everyday can be a drag.
Harajuku & Aoyama	Sights, restaurants and shops galore; very limited sleeping options.
Shibuya & Shimo-Kitazawa	Shibuya is a major transport hub with lots to see and do, but gets crowded and hectic.
Ebisu & Meguro	Good transit access, bars and restaurants, with fewer crowds; scant options near major stations.
Roppongi & Around	Art museums by day, bar scene at night; noisy after dark with some seedy pockets.
Ginza & Tsukiji	Ginza's shops and restaurants at your doorstep. Congested; few inexpensive options compared to other districts.
Marunouchi & Nihombashi	Convenient for all sights and for travel out of the city; business district with sky-high prices and quiet weekends.
Kanda & Akihabara	Central, with reasonable prices and good transit access. Can feel dead at night.
Ueno & Yanaka	Great for ryokans, sightseeing and easy airport access; some options may be deep within residential neighbourhoods.
Asakusa & Ryōgoku	Atmospheric old city feel, great budget options and backpacker vibe; quieter at night and far from more central areas.
Odaiba & Tokyo Bay	Proximity to family-friendly attractions; otherwise inconvenient, expensive and isolated.

Traditional painting depicting samurai battle

In Focus

Shibuya Crossing (p66)

Tokyo Today

Tokyo has reinvented itself countless times in the four centuries since its founding. Following decades of economic stagnation and a shrinking workforce, two milestones – the start of a new imperial era and the 2020 Summer Olympics – mark a turning point for the city. Does Tokyo have what it takes to pull off another reincarnation?

A New Era Begins

It caught everyone off guard when Emperor Akihito announced abruptly in 2016 – on TV no less – that he wished to abdicate. The last abdication was in 1817, which was back in the days of the shogun. The modern constitution had no provision for what to do in this situation. For over a year, lawmakers debated whether or not Akihito, Japan's 125th emperor (according to the Imperial House Agency's record-keeping), should even be allowed to abdicate. Finally, a bill was passed that would allow the sitting emperor, just this once, to retire, at the end of April 2019.

When Crown Prince Naruhito ascends the chrysanthemum throne, the Heisei era will end and a new one will begin. Of course, the starts and ends of Japan's historic periods – in modern times determined by the passing of emperors – depend on nature, yet they really

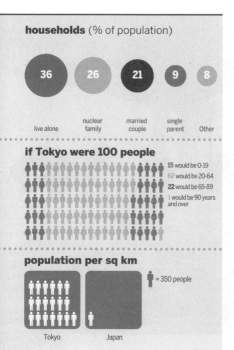

households (% of population)

36 — live alone
26 — nuclear family
21 — married couple
9 — single parent
8 — Other

if Tokyo were 100 people

15 would be 0-19
62 would be 20-64
22 would be 65-89
1 would be 90 years and over

population per sq km

≈ 350 people

Tokyo   Japan

do seem to effectively bracket the culture's shifting moods. The Heisei era has become symbolic of economic stagnation and uncertainty. In the current, unstable global climate, everyone can't help but wonder, what changes will the new era bring?

The Olympics are Here!

To understand just how much hosting the 2020 Olympics means to Tokyo, you have to look back to the 1964 Summer Olympics. The first Games to be held in Asia, the 1964 Olympics marked Tokyo's big comeback after the city was all but destroyed in WWII. The powers that be hope that the 2020 Games will again be symbolic, reaffirming Tokyo's position in the pantheon of the world's great cities, following nearly three decades of economic malaise and the faltering of its export giants (such as Sony).

Ever conscious of its image, the city has been undertaking dramatic changes to prepare for an influx of foreign visitors and media attention. There are all those shiny new skyscrapers, but also a ramped-up effort to make the city more accessible and open. Many major attractions and train stations, for example, now have wheelchair-accessible, gender-neutral toilets. Long seen as a smokers' city, Tokyo recently enacted the country's strictest antismoking laws to date. English signage is everywhere.

Which is not to say there aren't things to grumble about: the high cost of it all, of course, but also, in the rush to build anew – and to live up to the city's international image as a vision of the future – the erasure of older pockets of Tokyo. The relocation of the city's central wholesale market from Tsukiji to Toyosu, for example, was contested vehemently by both market workers and local community members until the very end.

The City of the Future?

Japan's population is famously shrinking; the latest estimates see a decline of 20 million (roughly one sixth of the total population) in the next 25 years. The birth rate for the capital hovers at around 1.1, the lowest in the nation (the national average is 1.4); however, Tokyo's population is expected to remain relatively steady, drawing more and more people from increasingly depopulated rural areas. But like everywhere in Japan, the demographics will skew older. Japan as a whole has long been wary of immigration, but Tokyo's foreign population is growing: it stands now at just over 3%. But here's where the numbers get interesting (and problematic): roughly 10% of twenty-somethings in Tokyo are foreign-born. The majority are from Asian countries (Chinese make up 40% of Tokyo's foreign population) and many are on student or so-called 'trainee' visas – with no path to permanent residency. The city is increasingly relying on foreign help to fill labour gaps, but is making no effort to promote integration. A reckoning seems inevitable.

Meiji-jingū (p38)

History

Tokyo is one of the world's great cities. In the four centuries since its founding the city has played many roles: samurai stronghold, imperial capital and modern metropolis. Its latest identity as a city of the future – as it is portrayed in manga (Japanese comics), anime (Japanese animation) and think pieces – is just another example of Tokyo's protean nature.

400 BC
Wet-rice farming cultures begin supplanting older neolithic hunter-gatherer cultures around Japan.

794
The capital is moved to Heian-kyō (later renamed Kyoto), which would be the centre of Japanese politics for a millennium.

12th century
Monks travel to China for study and return with Ch'an (Zen) Buddhism, which would have a huge cultural impact.

Yomeimon Gate, where Shogun Tokugawa Ieyasu (p214) is buried

SEAN PAVONE/SHUTTERSTOCK ©

Early History

For most of Japan's first thousand or so years, power was concentrated in the imperial capital, Kyoto. Here noble families vied for influence, upstart warriors challenged authority and Buddhist sects instigated cultural shifts. Tokyo, meanwhile, was a sleepy backwater. Then, and for most of its history, it was called Edo, meaning 'estuary' – which was fitting, given its location on the tidal flats at the mouth of the Sumida-gawa (Sumida River).

Early on, the imperial court was the ultimate authority. As the young empire sought to expand its territory over the archipelago, it enlisted warriors to assert dominion over outlying territories. Eventually these warriors began to covet power for themselves. This led to a new arrangement in the 12th century: the emperor continued to rule in title but a new figure, the shogun (generalissimo), would have the real authority. The feudal era had begun.

In truth though, the shoguns struggled just as the emperors had. Provincial warlords (called *daimyō*) were still needed to carry out orders and keep the peace in areas far from

1543	**1603**	**1657**
Portuguese, the first Westerners, arrive by chance in Japan, bringing firearms and Christianity.	Shogun Tokugawa Ieyasu establishes his government in Edo (present-day Tokyo).	Great Meireki Fire devastates Edo, killing over 100,000 people and destroying two-thirds of the city.

Cinema, Shinjuku

★ **Tokyo on Film**

Shoplifters (Kore-eda Hirokazu; 2018)

Your Name (Shinkai Makoto; 2016)

Terrace House (Fuji TV & Netflix; 2012–present)

Akira (Ōtomo Katsuhiro; 1988)

Tokyo Story (Ozu Yasujirō; 1953)

the capital; the more successful they became, the bigger a threat to cohesion they posed. By the 15th century, the *daimyō* had carved Japan into a patchwork of fiefdoms. Castles and fortresses were erected around the country (including one by a warrior poet named Ōta Dōkan in Edo). A series of powerful *daimyō* contested (violently; guns were now in the picture) for rule of the land. Finally, after much bloodshed and betrayal, one emerged victorious: Tokugawa Ieyasu.

The Tokugawa Shoguns

Tokugawa Ieyasu (1543–1616) was the ambitious son of a minor warlord in what is present-day Aichi prefecture (near Nagoya). With his power base lying far to the east of the capital, he chose to break with tradition, establishing his government not in Kyoto but in Edo. Within a half-century, the minor castle town would become Japan's largest city; in another hundred years it would be the largest city in the world.

Like previous shoguns, Ieyasu left the emperor alone; but unlike his predecessors, he established a dynasty that would manage to rule Japan with a fairly consistent iron fist for the next 250 years. They required *daimyō* and their retainers to spend every second year in Edo, where their families were kept permanently as hostages. This dislocating policy also bankrupted many a fiefdom as the processions to and from the provinces required expensive pageantry (which in turn bolstered Edo's economy). Society was made rigidly hierarchical, comprising (in descending order of importance) samurai, farmers, artisans and merchants. Class dress, living quarters and even speech were strictly codified; inter-class movement was prohibited. Though classed at the bottom, in reality, merchants could be fabulously wealthy (thanks to all that *daimyō* spending).

But the most striking feature of Tokugawa rule was its policy of *sakoku* (closure to the outside world). The shogunate feared foreign agitation (especially from Catholic missionaries) and expelled all Westerners (save for a handful of Protestant Dutch confined to an island off the coast of Nagasaki with whom trade was permitted) in the early 17th century.

1707
Mt Fuji erupts, spewing ash over Edo 100km to the northeast. The stratovolcano remains active but with a low risk of eruption.

1721
Edo's population grows to 1.1 million; meanwhile, London's population is roughly 650,000.

1868
The Meiji Restoration initiates a new period of constitutional monarchy, with Tokyo as its capital.

Overseas travel for Japanese was banned (as well as the return of those already overseas).

Meiji Restoration

By the turn of the 19th century, the stagnating Tokugawa regime was losing its grip. It is questionable how much longer it might have held on but, as it happened, external forces were to hasten its demise. In 1853 and again the following year, US Commodore Matthew Perry steamed into Edo-wan (now Tokyo Bay) with a show of gunships and demanded Japan open up to trade and provisioning.

The humiliating acquiescence that followed fanned existing flames of antigovernment sentiment into outright rebellion. A series of military clashes resulted in the abdication of the last shogun, Yoshinobu (1837–1913) in 1867. In 1868 authority was restored to the teenage emperor Mutsuhito (1852–1912, later known as Meiji) and a new government was formed in his name. The role of shogun, and the whole feudal system, was abolished. The emperor moved to Edo, which was renamed Tokyo (Eastern Capital).

The Great Kantō Earthquake

At noon on 1 September 1923, a magnitude 7.9 earthquake struck Japan just south of Tokyo in Sagami Bay. More damaging were the fires that spread through the city as a result, lasting some 40 hours and killing an estimated 142,000 people. Until the earthquake, Tokyo retained much of old Edo's layout, with the Sumida-gawa as its central artery and the population concentrated in the old merchant's quarters in the river delta – and it was these areas that went up in flames.

Tokyo started rebuilding immediately, but its landscape would be altered permanently: many Shitamachi residents whose homes and businesses had been destroyed chose to resettle in what was then the westernmost fringe of Tokyo, in districts such as Shibuya and Shinjuku that were provincial by comparison. From this point onward, the city's centre – both literally and figuratively – would be pulled increasingly to the west.

Above all, the new leaders of Japan feared colonisation by the West and moved quickly to modernise (in the image of the West), embarking on a grand project of industrialisation and militarisation. With *sakoku* over, a great exchange began between Japan and the West began: Japanese scholars were dispatched overseas while Western scholars were invited to teach in Japan's nascent universities. By 1889 the country had a constitution, modelled after the government frameworks of England and Prussia.

The Meiji Restoration also brought about far-reaching social changes. The four-tier class system was scrapped; after centuries of having everything prescribed for them, citizens were now free to choose their occupation and place of residence. In the coming decades, hundreds of thousands would come to Tokyo from the provinces, to try their luck in a city that now dazzled with electric lights, street cars and white-collar jobs.

1923	1944–45	1964
Great Kantō Earthquake kills more than 140,000 and destroys an estimated 300,000 houses.	Allied air raids during WWII destroy large swaths of the city, including the Imperial Palace.	The Tokyo Summer Olympics mark Japan's postwar reintegration into the international community.

World War II

The early 20th century was, devastating earthquake aside, a time of great optimism in Tokyo. Old feudal-era loyalties finally buckled and party politics flourished for the first time. Western fashions and ideas, initially the domain of only the elite, began to trickle down to the emergent middle class. Cafes and dance halls flourished. Women began to work in offices, department stores and factories, enjoying a new freedom and disposable income.

But there were sinister undercurrents: the nation's newfound confidence was tied to its displays of military might on the world stage. Japan had won victories over China (1894–95) and Russia (1904–05) and embarked on modern, Western-style empire building with its annexation of Taiwan (1895), then Korea (1910) and Micronesia (1914). In 1931, the Japanese military manufactured a conflict with China and then installed a puppet government in Manchuria. Nationalist fervour was quickly replacing democratic ideals.

Japan signed a pact with Germany and Italy in 1940; a year later, the country drew the US into WWII with an attack on Pearl Harbor. At first Japan scored rapid successes, pushing its battlefronts across to India, down to the fringes of Australia and into the mid-Pacific, confiscating territories that were until then colonised by the European powers. But the decisive Battle of Midway in 1942 turned the tide against Japan and in the end the war was disastrous. Incendiary bombing in 1944 and 1945 destroyed half of Tokyo. In one night alone some 100,000 people were killed – more than were killed by the atomic bombing of Hiroshima – as fires swept through densely populated neighbourhoods of wooden homes.

The emperor formally surrendered on 15 August 1945 and American forces, under the command of General Douglas MacArthur, occupied the country. Japan was obligated to give up its territorial claims in Korea and China, and adopt a new constitution that dismantled the political power of the emperor, denounced war and banned a Japanese military.

Postwar Period

In the early postwar years, conditions in Tokyo remained dire: food was scarce and unemployment was high; many relied on black markets to survive. However, in the 1950s Japan took off on a trajectory of phenomenal growth that has been called miraculous. (Many historians say Japan's role as a forward base for the USA in the Korean War was the catalyst for this.) The 1964 Tokyo Summer Olympics are seen by many as a turning point in the nation's history – the moment when Japan finally recovered from the devastation of WWII to emerge as a fully fledged member of the modern world economy.

Growth continued at a breakneck pace, peaking in the late '80s, when wildly inflated real-estate prices and stock speculation fuelled what is now known as the 'bubble economy'. Based on the price paid for the most expensive real estate in the late 1980s, the land value of Tokyo exceeded that of the entire US. In 1991 the bubble burst, sending the economy into a protracted slump. The 1990s were christened the 'Lost Decade', but that has since turned into two, and probably three, as the economy continues to slump along, despite government intervention.

1995	2011	2016
Doomsday cult Aum Shinrikyō releases sarin gas on the Tokyo subway, killing 12 and injuring more than 5000.	Massive earthquake and tsunami in northeastern Japan kills nearly 20,000 and cripples a Fukushima nuclear power plant.	Tokyo elects its first female governor, Koike Yuriko; Emperor Akihito (b 1933) announces his wish to retire.

Cosplayers at Comiket (p13)

Pop Culture

From giant robots to saucer-eyed schoolgirls to ubiquitous kitties, Japanese pop culture is a phenomenon that has reached far around the world. Tokyo is the country's pop-production centre; meanwhile, neighbourhoods such as Akihabara incubate subcultures that are gaining more and more influence over the culture at large.

Manga

Whole generations have come of age reading classic manga, such as Tezuka Osamu's *Tetsuwan Atom* (Astro Boy; 1952–68) and *Black Jack* (1973–83); Toriyama Akira's *Dragon Ball* (1984–95); and Kishimoto Masashi's *Naruto* (1999–2014). Osamu (1928–89) is often known as *manga no kamisama* (the god of manga) for having brought a level of artistry and profundity to the form, raising it above mere pulp. (Astro Boy is a humanoid robot with empathic powers and a champion of robots' rights.) Osamu was also the first to draw characters with big eyes; though this look has come to define Japanese manga and anime, Osamu was in fact influenced by early Disney works (such as *Bambi*) and the 1930s US cartoon character Betty Boop (animation's first pin-up).

Pop Culture Districts

Akihabara (Akiba) is considered the locus of *otaku* (geek) subculture, but there are other areas, too: Nakano, just west of Shinjuku, has a reputation as a more low-key, underground Akiba – the original Mandarake Complex (p112) is here. Ikebukuro, north of Shinjuku, has many of the same anime and manga stores that you see in Akihabara, but they're full of goods that girl geeks love. Gundam fans should head to Odaiba to see 'life-sized' Unicorn Gundam (p81). There are also the temporary communities that come together around events such as Comiket.

Some series have been going on so long as to transcend generations: the titular character of *Doraemon* (1969–96; Fujiko Fujio), who is a blue robot cat from the future, is so iconic he's sometimes called Japan's Mickey Mouse. The best-selling manga of all time is Oda Eiichirō's *One Piece*, nominally about a band of misfit pirates. First serialised in 1997, it's still going – meaning one lucky generation might just get to grow old with their favourite manga.

Anime

Anime has a synergistic relationship with manga: many anime series are adapted from manga (*Full Metal Alchemist, Death Note* and *Jojo's Bizarre Adventure* are great examples; and of course there's a *One Piece* animated series). There are also hugely popular original anime series, such as *Mobile Suit Gundam* (1979–1980) and *Neon Genesis Evangelion* (1995–1996), which have since spawned larger media franchises, including manga series feature-length movies. Both *Mobile Suit Gundam* and *Neon Genesis Evangelion* belong to the genre of anime and manga called 'mecha', meaning they feature robots.

While anime, like film, can be about anything really, the form has proven to be particularly outstanding at world building and imbuing posthumans and machines with a certain pathos. Other classics include Ōtomo Katsuhiro's *Akira* (1988), psychedelic fantasy set in a future Tokyo (actually 2019); Ōishii Mamoru's *Ghost in the Shell* (1995), with a sci-fi plot worthy of Philip K Dick involving cyborgs, hackers and the mother of all computer networks; and the works of Kon Satoshi (1963–2010), the Hitchcockian *Perfect Blue* (1997), the charming *Tokyo Godfathers* (2003) and the sci-fi thriller *Paprika* (2006).

Studio Ghibli (www.ghibli.jp) is Japan's most critically acclaimed and commercially successful producer of animated movies. Its films include *Nausicaä of the Valley of the Winds* (1984), *My Neighbor Totoro* (1988) and the Oscar-winning *Spirited Away* (2001), all directed by Miyazaki Hayao. In 2016 Miyazaki announced he was coming out of retirement to make one last film, to be called *How Do You Live?* Based on a 1930s novel of the same name, it will likely be released in 2020 or 2021.

Otaku Culture

Otaku is the word used to describe superfans of manga and anime. (It has since evolved into a general modifier for any kind of superfan; a *densha* (train) *otaku*, for example, is a trainspotter). *Otaku* are famous consumers, proving their affection through their collection of merch; but theirs is also a subculture rich in creation and humour. A popular phenomenon is *dōjinshi*, amateur manga, which are often parodies or fan fictions of established series (and sometimes involving romantic or sexual scenes not found in the original). There are also those fans who go to great lengths to transform themselves into their favourite characters – an art known as cosplay (a portmanteau for costume play).

Kaiseki (Japanese haute cuisine)

Food & Drink

At its heart, Japanese food is highly seasonal, drawing on fresh local ingredients coaxed into goodness with a light touch. But it's also far more varied than you might imagine: it's not just sushi and sake, it's also gut-busting ramen and fiery shōchū (distilled liquor). In Tokyo you can sample all the best Japan has to offer, from the classics to the trendsetting.

Dining Out Like a Local

When you enter a restaurant in Japan the staff will likely all greet you with a hearty *'Irass-hai!'* (Welcome!) In all but the most casual places, where you just seat yourself, the wait-staff will next ask you *'Nan-mei sama?'* (How many people?) Indicate the answer with your fingers, which is what the Japanese do. You may also be asked if you would like to sit at a *zashiki* (low table on the tatami), at a *tēburu* (table) or the *kauntā* (counter). Once seated you will be given an *o-shibori* (hot towel), a cup of tea or water (this is free) and a menu.

There are two ways to order: *omakase* (chef's choice) and *okonomi* (your choice). It's common for high-end restaurants to offer nothing but *omakase* – the equivalent of a chef's tasting course, usually with two or three options of different value. (Pricier doesn't neces-sarily mean more food; it often means more luxurious ingredients.) Most other restaurants

Japanese Spirits

Sake, aka *nihonshū* (日本酒) is the obvious drink choice, but there are spirits worth sampling, too. *Shōchū* (焼酎) is a clear, distilled spirit usually made from potato or barley. It is potent (alcohol content of around 30%) and thus usually served diluted with hot water *(oyu-wari)* or mixed in a cocktail – the combination of *shōchū*, soda water and lemon juice known as a 'lemon sour' is popular.

Japan produces some of the finest whiskies in the world and Tokyo has a growing number of dedicated bars where travellers can sample the best of the major makers Suntory and Nikka, as well as from cult faves and small-batch producers such as Chichibu. Keep a lookout on bar counters for gin from Kyoto's new craft distillery Ki No Bi.

will hand you a menu and expect you to choose what you like. If there's no English menu (and you're game) you can ask for the server's recommendation *(O-susume wa nan desu ka?)* and give the okay to whatever he or she suggests.

When your food arrives, it's the custom to say *'Itadakimasu'* (literally 'I will receive' but closer to 'bon appétit' in meaning) before digging in. All but the most extreme type-A chefs will say they'd rather have foreign visitors enjoy their meal than agonise over getting the etiquette right. Still, there's nothing that makes a Japanese chef grimace more than out-of-towners who overseason their food – a little soy sauce and wasabi go a long way.

Often a bill is placed discreetly on your table after your food has been delivered. If not, catch your server's eye with a *sumimasen* (excuse me) and ask for the check by saying, *o-kaikei kudasai*. Payment, even at high-end places, is often settled at a counter near the entrance, rather than at the table.

Tokyo Food Scene

Tokyo foodies take pride in what they like to think of as their 'boutique' dining scene. Rather than offering long menus of elaborate dishes, many of the best restaurants make just a few things – and sometimes even just one! Sushi shops make sushi; tempura shops make tempura. A restaurant that does too much might be suspect: how can it compare to a speciality shop that has been honing its craft for three generations?

Tokyo has very few actual local specialities; its strength lies in its variety. You can get anything here, and get it done to perfection: all the Japanese staples, such as tempura, *tonkatsu* (deep-fried pork cutlets), *yakitori* (chicken grilled on skewers), soba (buckwheat noodles) and *okonomiyaki* (savoury pancake); regional dishes from all over Japan, including Kyoto-style *kaiseki* (Japanese haute cuisine); and a wide spread of international cuisines.

But if there is one dish that Tokyo can truly claim, it's *nigiri-zushi,* the style of sushi most popular around the world today: those bite-sized slivers of seafood hand-pressed onto pedestals of rice. It's a dish that originated in the urban culture of Edo (the old name for Tokyo) and is sometimes still called 'Edo-mae' sushi (as in the style of Edo). Dietary restrictions notwithstanding, a good sushi meal should be at the top of your Tokyo bucket list.

Tokyoites' twin passions for novelty and eating out mean that the city is also a hotbed for experimentation. Trends come and go, but one that has stuck around – and spread roots – is the city's home-grown farm-to-table movement. Increasingly, owner-chefs are working directly with rural producers to source ingredients, which might be used in orthodox-style Japanese cooking or creatively, to add a new twist to a classic dish or a fresh take on an imported one.

Which brings us to Tokyo's two hottest dining trends right now: nouveau ramen, creativity distilled in a bowl of noodles and the best budget gourmet experience around; and neo-bistros, a format that has afforded chefs more leeway for innovation than classic Japanese cooking allows (or at least that's their current feeling). Increasingly, Japanese cuisine is a global one – borrowing this and contributing that – and Tokyo, naturally, is at the forefront.

Recommended Reading

○ *Sake Confidential: A Beyond-the-Basics Guide to Understanding, Tasting, Selection and Enjoyment* (John Gauntner; 2014)

○ *What's What in Japanese Restaurants: A Guide to Ordering, Eating and Enjoying* (Robb Satterwhite; 2011)

○ *Washoku* (Elizabeth Andoh; 2005)

Izakaya

Izakaya (居酒屋) translates as 'drinking house'; it's the Japanese equivalent of a pub. An evening at an *izakaya* is dinner and drinks all in one: food is ordered for the table a few dishes at a time along with rounds of beer or sake. While the vibe is lively and social, it's perfectly acceptable to go by yourself and sit at the counter. If you don't want alcohol, it's fine to order a soft drink instead, but it would be strange to not order at least one drink.

An orthodox *izakaya* is family-run with menu items, such as *shio-yaki-zakana* (塩焼魚; a whole fish grilled with salt), designed to go with sake. There are also large, cheap chains, popular with students, that often have some Western pub-style dishes (like chips), and stylish chef-driven *izakaya* with creative menus. A night out at an average izakaya should run from ¥3000 to ¥5000 per person, depending on how much you drink; a bit more for a more gourmet one.

Classic starters to get you going, that most *izakaya* will have, include: *sashimi moriawase* (刺身盛り合わせ; a selection of sliced sashimi), *edamame* (枝豆; salted and boiled fresh soy beans) and *moro-kyū* (もろきゅう; sliced cucumbers and chunky barley miso). If you're struggling with what to order, tell the server or chef *'Omakase shimasu'* (please decide for me) and they'll most likely bring you a succession of the restaurant's greatest hits and some seasonal specialities. It's probably a good idea to set a price cap, for example: *'Hitori de san-zen-en'* (one person for ¥3000).

Shokudō

Shokudō (食堂) are casual, inexpensive eateries that serve homey meals – similar to what might be called a greasy-spoon cafe or a diner in the United States. You'll find them around every train station and in popular tourist areas. Meals typically cost ¥800 to ¥1500 per person. Many have plastic food displays in the windows, which makes ordering simple. One thing to get at a *shokudō* is a *teishoku* (定食), a meal set with one main dish (such as grilled fish), rice, miso soup and pickles. Other likely menu items include various *donburi* (どんぶり or 丼; large bowls of rice with meat or fish piled on top) and *katsu* (カツ) dishes, where the main is crumbed and deep fried, as in *tonkatsu* (豚カツ or とんかつ; deep-fried pork cutlets) and *ebi-katsu* (海老カツ; breaded and fried prawns).

Reservations & Etiquette

If you have your heart set on eating at a particular restaurant, you'll want to make a reservation. This is especially true for dinner, but if you want to take advantage of a fancy restaurant's lunch special, you'll want to book – if you can, that is: some restaurants only take bookings for dinner, or for the first seating or not at all. Groups larger than four are required to book ahead at some places. Confusing, yes – even for Tokyoites. Some places have introduced online reservation systems (though it might only be in Japanese). Check restaurant websites for email addresses (most Japanese can read and write English better than they speak it). Open Table (www.opentable.com/tokyo-restaurants) has a small presence in Japan.

The big advantage of staying in a top-tier hotel is having a concierge who can do all the hard work for you. At some exclusive restaurants, a well-connected concierge may be your only hope. Tokyo restaurants have a real fear of no-shows and there is a prevailing belief that foreign tourists are more prone to flaking. Whether this is actually true or an urban myth is unclear, but a handful of restaurants will only take reservations from a concierge. If you speak Japanese and have a local phone number you might be able to get around this. This goes without saying, but do show up. If you have to cancel, call the day before; otherwise, you may be expected to pay a no-show fee.

If you're planning to frequent just casual places, pay no mind to any of the above. You'll be fine, though you might have to queue for a bit at a popular ramen shop or wait for a table if you're a bigger party. Solo travellers, meanwhile, are in the best position: often you can squeeze into a counter seat at an otherwise fully packed restaurant.

Tokyo restaurants are often very small and run on a tight margin (hence the fear of no-shows; a missing party of four at a 12-seat restaurant is a big loss). Lunch is one of the city's great bargains; however, restaurants can only offer cheap lunch deals because they anticipate high turnover. Spending too long sipping tea after finishing your meal might earn you dagger eyes from the kitchen. In general, as long as you're not negatively influencing the bottom line, restaurants have a high tolerance for tourist gaffes. If you're enjoying the food, they're happy. The only really offensive thing you can do is to stick your chopsticks upright in a bowl of rice or pass food from one pair of chopsticks to another – both are reminiscent of Japanese funereal rites.

Dietary Restrictions

Given that most Tokyo restaurants are small, dietary restrictions can be hard to accommodate. They'll try, but in many cases your options will be defined by how strictly you adhere to restrictions; for example, unless explicitly noted otherwise, your vegetable tempura is going to be fried in the same oil as the prawns. Dishes can also be deceiving: many that look ostensibly vegetarian are prepared with *dashi* (fish stock); pork is often used in curry roux. Always state your restrictions up front when making a reservation, to give the restaurant more time to prepare.

Happy Cow (www.happycow.net) is a great resource for restaurants that prepare strictly vegetarian and vegan dishes; also check Tourist Information Centres for the Tokyo VegeMap (vegemap.org). For certified halal restaurants, see Halal Gourmet Japan (www.halalgourmet.jp); the city also publishes a travel guide for Muslims, which lists restaurants and is available at most Tourist Information Centres. Gluten free is particularly challenging, as there is little awareness of coeliac disease in Japan and many kitchen staples, such as soy sauce, contain wheat (and even restaurant staff may not be aware of this). The Gluten-Free Expats Japan! Facebook group is a good resource.

Snow at Kaiunbashi Bridge and First National Bank by Kobayashi Kiyochika, Mori Art Museum (p106)

SHIMIZU CORPORATION TOKYO ©

Arts

Tokyo has an arts scene that is broad, dynamic and scattered – much like the city itself. Highlights include visiting the museums whose collections include some of the most celebrated works of classical Japanese art; seeing ukiyo-e (woodblock prints) and kabuki, Tokyo's signature arts; and gawking at the fascinating creations of Japan's 20th-century architects.

Classical Arts

Japan has a long artistic tradition of painting, metalwork, lacquerware, textiles and pottery. Early on, and during periods of openness, Japan imported styles, techniques and themes from its nearest Asian neighbours, China and Korea. During times of retreat, Japan's artists refined these techniques, filtered styles through local sensibilities and tweaked themes to correspond with the times and materials at hand.

Traditional paintings – adorning folding screens, sliding doors and hanging scrolls – are done in black ink or mineral pigments on *washi* (Japanese handmade paper). Over the centuries, painting modes have included colourful, highly stylised scenes of courtly life *(yamato-e)*; monochromatic suggestions of craggy mountains executed with a few lively brushstrokes *(sumi-e)*; or flattened compositions of seasonal motifs, boldly outlined against

Bookstore, Jimbōchō (p161)

★ Tokyo in Print

Moshi Moshi (Banana Yoshimoto; 2010)

Convenience Store Woman (Murata Sayaka; 2016)

Coin Locker Babies (Murakami Ryū; 1980)

After Dark (Murakami Haruki; 2004)

a backdrop of solid gold leaf (works of the Kano school). Today, *nihonga* (Japanese-style painting) may reference any of the above.

Metalwork includes bronze statues of Buddhist deities and ritual elements as well as tea kettles and intricately designed hand guards for swords. Lacquerware – sometimes black, sometimes red and sometimes inlaid with mother-of-pearl or sprinkled with gold leaf – appears on boxes for storing sutras or writing implements and serving trays. Japan's skilled weavers, dyers and embroiders come together to create the lavish kimono historically worn by the nobility and the actors on the *nō* (stylised dance-drama performed on a bare stage) and kabuki (a form of stylised Japanese theatre) stages.

Pottery can be rough earthenware or delicate enamelled porcelain. Ceramics made for the tea ceremony often appeared dented or misshapen, with drips of glaze running down the side – and were prized all the more for their imperfections.

The Tokyo National Museum (p52) and the Suntory Museum of Art (p106) are the best places to see classical artworks in Tokyo.

Art of the Floating World

The Edo period (1603–1868) was one of prolonged isolation and great creative experimentation – especially in the wealthy capital, Edo (premodern Tokyo). This is when two of Japan's most recognisable art forms emerged: kabuki and *ukiyo-e* (woodblock prints).

'Ukiyo' was a play on words: spelt with one set of Chinese characters, it meant the 'fleeting world', our tenuous, temporary abode on earth and a pivotal concept in Japanese Buddhism for centuries. Change the first character, however, and you get the homophone, the 'floating world', which was used to describe the urban pleasure quarters of the Edo period (1603–1868). In this topsy-turvy world, the social hierarchies dictated by the Tokugawa shoganate were inverted: money meant more than rank, kabuki actors were the arbitrators of style and courtesans were the most accomplished of artists.

Ukiyo-e were literally pictures of the floating world, capturing famed beauties, pleasure boats and outings under the cherry blossoms. They were also postcards from the world beyond; at a time when rigid laws prevented much of the populace from travelling, woodblock prints presented compelling scenes from around Japan. The famous *ukiyo-e* artists, Katsushika Hokusai (1760–1849) and Utagawa Hiroshige (1797–1858) are best known, respectively, for their series *Thirty-six Views of Mount Fuji* and *The Fifty-three Stations of the Tōkaidō*.

The vivid colours, novel composition and flowing lines of *ukiyo-e* caused great excitement in the West in the late 19th century, sparking a vogue that one French art critic dubbed *japonisme*. The best place in Tokyo to see *ukiyo-e* is the Ukiyo-e Ōta Memorial Museum of Art (p49); the Tokyo National Museum (p52) also has some on display.

19th- & 20th-Century Modernism

When Japan opened up to the world in the late 19th century, new forms and ideas came spilling in – oil painting, figurative sculpture, the novel – which was exciting, but also fraught. A painting tradition with a 1000-year history was flattened into the catch-all term *nihonga* (Japanese-style painting) as a foil to the new *yōga* (Western-style painting). Making art now meant either a rejection or an embrace of Western influence, a choice that was hard to divorce from politics.

This shift raised a number of questions: should the old styles stay just that? And, if not, how could they possibly evolve organically without addressing the elephant (Western influence) in the room? Could works in Western mediums ever transcend mere imitation? Some critics argue that these same questions haunt the arts to this day. In the 1950s and '60s avant-garde movements sought a clean break from the weight of all this history, and strove to create something new entirely. The National Museum of Modern Art (p101) traces the history of visual art in Japan from the Meiji Restoration onwards.

Literature and film, with their narrative qualities, were perhaps the best mediums in which to parse the profound disorientation that had settled upon Japan by the early 20th century. Novels such as Sōseki Natsume's *Kokoro* (1914) and Kawabata Yasunari's *Yukiguni* (Snow Country; 1935–37) address the conflict between Japan's nostalgia for the past and its rush towards the future, between its rural heartland and its burgeoning metropolises. These are themes still explored today: just watch recent anime hit *Your Name*.

Contemporary Architecture

Japan's contemporary architects continue to explore both modernism and postmodernism, while mining Japan's architectural heritage. Among the more influential ones are Tadao Ando (b 1941), Itō Toyō (b 1941) and Kengo Kuma (b 1954). Andō's works tend to be grounded and monumental, yet unobtrusive, with no unnecessary flourishes; he works in modern materials such as concrete and steel. Itō's designs are lighter and more conceptual, meditating on the ideas of borders between inside and outside, public and private. Kengo is famous for his use of wood, employing cutting-edge computer drafting technology to that age-old staple of Japanese construction. He's behind the new National Stadium for the 2020 Tokyo Summer Olympics.

Tokyo Pop & Beyond

Love him or hate him, Murakami Takashi (b 1962) brought Japan back into an international spotlight it hadn't enjoyed since 19th-century collectors went wild for *ukiyo-e*. His work makes fantastic use of the flat planes, clear lines and decorative techniques associated with *nihonga*, while lifting motifs from the lowbrow subculture of manga (Japanese comics). As much an artist as a clever theorist, Murakami proclaimed in his 'Superflat' manifesto that his work picked up where Japanese artists left off after the Meiji Restoration – and might just be the future of painting, given that most of us now view the world through the portals of two-dimensional screens.

Today's younger artists, working in diverse mediums, have had trouble defining themselves in the wake of 'Tokyo Pop' – as the highly exportable art of the '90s came to be known. They have also to contend with what it means to make art in a post-Fukushima world. The Mori Art Museum (p106) stages exhibitions of established contemporary artists from both Japan and abroad. Galleries worth checking out include those at Complex 665 (p107) and 3331 Arts Chiyoda (p113). For exhibition recommendations, see Tokyo Art Beat (www.tokyoartbeat.com).

SIMON DUBREUIL/500PX ©

Traditional Culture

Over the centuries, Japan's two most prominent belief systems, Shintō and Buddhism, shaped the country's culture. Together (they were not mutually exclusive), they profoundly influenced Japan's art and architecture, ritual and daily life. While few today consider themselves religious, Shintō and Buddhism's influence remains visible – even in contemporary Tokyo.

Shintō & Shrines

Shintō, or 'the way of the gods', is the native religion of Japan. Its innumerable *kami* (gods) are located mostly in nature (in trees, rocks, waterfalls and mountains, for example), but also in the mundane objects of daily life, like hearths and wells. According to Japanese mythology, the celebrated sun goddess, Amaterasu, was the ancestress of the emperor. Historically, extraordinary people could be recognised as *kami* upon death, such as the Emperor Meiji who, along with is wife, is enshrined at Meiji-jingū (p38).

Kami can be summoned through rituals of dance and music into the shrines the Japanese have built for them, where they may be beseeched with prayers (for a good harvest or a healthy pregnancy, maybe, and in modern times for success in business or school exams). Sumo was once part of shrine festivities.

Shintō's origins are unknown. For ages it was a vague, amorphous set of practices and beliefs; however, in the late 19th and early 20th centuries, it was reconfigured by the imperialist state into a national religion centred on emperor worship. This ended with Japan's defeat in WWII, when Emperor Hirohito himself publicly renounced his divinity. Today just 3% of Japanese affiliate themselves to Shintō, but what exactly they believe is unclear.

Still, there are customs so ingrained in Japanese culture that many continue to perform them, regardless of belief. Shrines are still the place to greet the New Year in a rite called *hatsu-mōde;* to celebrate the milestones of childhood, during festivals such Seijin-no-hi and Shichi-go-san; and the place where the lovelorn come to pray for a match. At the very least, many would say, doing such things can't hurt.

Temple or Shrine?

Centuries of coexistence means Buddhist temples and Shintō shrines resemble each other architecturally. The easiest way to tell the two apart is by the gate. Shrine have *torii* (a style of gate specific to Shintō shrines), usually composed of two upright pillars, joined at the top by two horizontal crossbars, the upper of which is normally slightly curved. In contrast, a temple *mon* (main entrance gate, also used in palaces and estates) is often a much more substantial affair, constructed of several pillars or casements, joined at the top by a multitiered roof.

In Tokyo there are grand, monumental shrines, such as Meiji-jingū, but also countless small ones, sometimes no bigger than a doll's house. They're maintained by local communities, who take up collections for their upkeep and leave fresh offerings, such as fruit, flowers or sake. The shrines are located at auspicious points, based on ancient geomancy, and for that reason aren't moved – even if it means constructions have to go up around them.

Matsuri: Traditional Festivals

Shrines continue to hold their annual *matsuri* during which local *kami* are welcomed into a portable shrine (called a *mikoshi*) and paraded through the streets, accompanied by much ceremony, chanting and merrymaking. The Sanja Matsuri is the city's biggest event and draws huge crowds; but there are small neighbourhood festivals, too. They're mostly held between May and September.

Catching a *matsuri* is like stepping back in time: participants come dressed straight out of the Edo period (1603–1868), with some men wearing just short coats and *fundoshi* (the loincloths worn by sumo wrestlers). Many spectators arrive in colourful cotton kimono (called *yukata*). And while the younger generation normally shows little interest in traditional culture, everyone loves a *matsuri*. (Bonus: festivals have street-food vendors.)

Buddhism & Temples

It is said that Shintō is concerned with this life and Buddhism with the afterlife. So while shrines perform weddings, temples perform funeral rites and memorial services. The Buddhist festival of O-Bon, in midsummer, is when the souls of departed ancestors are believed to pay a short visit. Families return to their hometowns to sweep gravestones, an act called *ohaka-mairi,* and welcome them. Only a third of Japanese today identify as Buddhist, but even non-believers might feel it ominous to skip such rituals.

In Tokyo, O-Bon traditions include Kōenji's Awa Odori, a folk dance parade, and lantern festivals. Temple bells ring out the end of the year on 31 December, during a rite called Joya-no-kane.

COWARDLION/SHUTTERSTOCK ©

Survival Guide

Directory A–Z

Accessible Travel

- Tokyo is making steps to improve universal access (called 'barrier free' here), but still gets mixed reviews from travellers. Newer buildings have wheelchair-access ramps and more and more subway stations have elevators (look for signs on the platform, as not all exits have elevators). Hotels from the higher end of midrange and above usually have a 'barrier-free' room or two (book well in advance).

- Accessible Japan (www.accessible-japan.com) is a great resource.

- Download Lonely Planet's free *Accessible Travel* guide from http://lptravel.to/AccessibleTravel.

Customs Regulations

- Japan has typical customs allowances for duty-free items; see Visit Japan Customs (www.customs.go.jp) for more information.

- Some prescription medications that may be legal in your home country may be controlled substances in Japan (such as the ADHD medication Adderall). See the Ministry of Health, Labour & Welfare's website (www.mhlw.go.jp/english/policy/health-medical/pharmaceuticals/01.html) for more details.

Electricity

100V/50Hz/60Hz

Emergency

Ambulance & Fire	☎119
Police	☎110
Medical Information English Hotline (9am-8pm)	☎03-5285-8181

Health

The level of care is high, though few hospitals and clinics have doctors and nurses who speak English. Larger hospitals are your best bet.

Clinics

Primary Care Tokyo (プライマリーケア東京; ☎03-5432-7177; http://pctclinic.com; 3rd fl, 2-1-16 Kitazawa, Setagaya-ku; consultation fee ¥8640; ⏰9am-12.30pm Mon-Sat, 2.30-6pm Mon-Fri, closed 1st & 3rd Wed; ⚇Keiō Inokashira line to Shimo-Kitazawa, south exit) Appointments accepted and recommended, but walk-ins will be seen.

Tokyo Medical & Surgical Clinic (東京メディカルアンドサージカルクリニック; ☎03-3436-3028; www.tmsc.jp; 2nd fl, 32 Shiba-kōen Bldg, 3-4-30 Shiba-kōen, Minato-ku; consultations from ¥12,960; ⏰8.30am-5.30pm Mon-Fri, to noon Sat; ⑤Hibiya line to Kamiyachō, exit 1) Appointments required; however, walk-ins needing urgent care will be accepted. Has in-house English-speaking specialists. Pricier than most.

Emergency Rooms

St Luke's International Hospital (聖路加国際病院; Seiroka Kokusai Byōin; ☎appointments 03-3527-9527, general 03-3541-5151, international department 03-5550-7166; http://hospital.luke.ac.jp; 9-1 Akashi-chō, Chūō-ku; ⏰international department

8.30am-5pm Mon-Fri; ⑤Hibiya line to Tsukiji, exits 3 & 4)

Tokyo's most foreigner-friendly hospital, with English-speaking doctors and translation services provided.

Medications

Pharmacies in Japan do not carry foreign medications, so it's a good idea to bring your own. In a pinch, reasonable substitutes can be found, but the dosage may be less than what you're used to.

Insurance

Basic emergency coverage is adequate. Note that Japanese hospitals only take Japanese health insurance, so you will need to pay in full and get reimbursed. Worldwide travel insurance is available at www.lonelyplanet.com/travel-insurance. You can buy, extend and claim online any time – even if you're already on the road.

Book Your Stay Online

For more accommodation reviews by Lonely Planet authors, check out http://hotels.lonelyplanet.com/tokyo. You'll find independent reviews, as well as recommendations on the best places to stay. Best of all, you can book online.

Internet Access

● Free wi-fi can be found on subway platforms, at convenience stores, major attractions and shopping centres – though signals are often weak. Look for the sticker that says 'Japan Wi-Fi'. Download the Japan Connected (www.ntt-bp.net/jcfw/en.html) app to avoid having to log in to individual networks; if you are unable to connect, try clearing your cache.

● Pocket wi-fi devices, which can be used by multiple devices, can be rented from the airport. Some services, such as Japan Wireless (www.japan-wireless.com), will ship to your hotel.

Legal Matters

● Japanese police have extraordinary powers compared with their Western counterparts. If you find yourself in police custody, insist that you will not cooperate in any way until allowed to make a call to your embassy. Police will speak almost no English; insist that a *tsuyakusha* (interpreter) be summoned; police are legally bound to provide one before proceeding with any questioning.

● It is a legal requirement to have your passport on you at all times. Though checks are not common, if you are stopped by police and caught without it, you could be hauled off to a police station to wait until someone fetches it for you.

● Japan takes a hard-line approach to narcotics possession, with long sentences and fines even for first-time offenders.

LGBT+ Travellers

● Gay and lesbian travellers are unlikely to encounter problems in Tokyo. There are no legal restraints on same-sex sexual activities in Japan apart from the usual age restrictions. Some travellers have reported being turned away or grossly overcharged when checking into love hotels with a partner of the same sex. Otherwise, discrimination is unusual. One note: Japanese people, regardless of their sexual orientation, do not typically engage in public displays of affection.

● Tokyo has a small but very lively gay quarter, Shinjuku-nichōme; outside this and a handful of other places, however, the gay scene is all but invisible. For more recommendations in Tokyo, see Utopia Asia (www.utopia-asia.com).

● **Akta Community Centre** (✆03-3226-8998; http://akta.jp; 301 Nakae Bldg No 2, 2-15-13 Shinjuku, Shinjuku-ku;

⊘6-10pm Thu-Mon; 凡JR Yamanote line to Shinjuku, east exit) offers free HIV tests, counselling and any other information you might need.

Money

○ These days pretty much everywhere in Tokyo accepts credit cards, but it's still a good idea to keep at least several thousand yen on hand for the few places that don't. Visa is the most widely accepted card, followed by MasterCard, American Express and Diners Club. Foreign-issued cards should work fine.

○ Most Japanese bank ATMs do not accept foreign-issued cards. Seven Bank ATMs at 7-Eleven convenience stores and Japan Post Bank ATMs at post offices accept most overseas cards and have instructions in English. Seven Bank ATMs are accessible 24 hours a day. Be aware that many banks place a limit on the amount of cash you can withdraw in one day (often around US$300).

○ Major banks and post office main branches can usually exchange US, Canadian and Australian dollars, pounds sterling, euros, Swiss francs, Chinese yuan and Korean won. Note that you receive a better exchange rate when withdrawing cash from ATMs than when exchanging cash in Tokyo.

Practicalities

Magazines *Time Out Tokyo* (www.timeout.com/tokyo), *Tokyo Weekender* (www.tokyoweekender.com) and *Metropolis* (www.metropolisjapan.com) are free English-language mags with city info.

Newspapers *Japan Times* (www.japantimes.co.jp) is a long-running English-language daily.

Smoking From October 2019, smoking in Tokyo will be banned inside all bars and restaurants that employ staff (other than family) unless they can provide an air-tight smoking area. For some time now, smoking has been banned in public spaces, including city streets and train stations, except for within designated smoking areas.

Weights & Measures The metric system is used along with some traditional Japanese measurements.

Opening Hours

Note that some outdoor attractions (such as gardens) may close earlier in the winter, so always check the website ahead. Standard opening hours:

Banks 9am to 3pm (some to 5pm) Monday to Friday

Bars Around 6pm to late

Boutiques Noon to 8pm, irregularly closed

Cafes Vary enormously; chains 7am to 10pm

Department stores 10am to 8pm

Museums 9am or 10am to 5pm; often closed Monday

Post offices 9am to 5pm Monday to Friday; larger ones have longer hours and open Saturday

Restaurants Lunch 11.30am to 2pm, dinner 6pm to 10pm; last orders taken about half an hour before closing

Public Holidays

If a national holiday falls on a Monday, most museums and restaurants that normally close on Mondays will remain open and close the next day instead.

New Year's Day (Ganjitsu) 1 January

Coming-of-Age Day (Seijin-no-hi) Second Monday in January

National Foundation Day (Kenkoku Kinen-bi) 11 February

Emperor's Birthday (Tennō-no-Tanjōbi) 23 February

Spring Equinox (Shumbun-no-hi) 20 or 21 March

Shōwa Day (Shōwa-no-hi) 29 April

Constitution Day (Kempō Kinem-bi) 3 May

Green Day (Midori-no-hi) 4 May

Children's Day (Kodomo-no-hi) 5 May

Marine Day (Umi-no-hi) Third Monday in July

Tokyo Addresses

Tokyo is difficult to navigate even for locals. Only the biggest streets have names, and they don't figure into addresses; instead, addresses are derived from districts *(ku)*, blocks (*chōme*, pronounced cho-may) and building numbers. Smartphones with navigation apps have been a real boon.

Mountain Day (Yama-no-hi)
11 August

Respect-for-the-Aged Day
(Keirō-no-hi) Third Monday in September

Autumn Equinox (Shūbun-no-hi) 23 or 24 September

Health & Sports Day (Taiiku-no-hi) Second Monday in October

Culture Day (Bunka-no-hi)
3 November

Labour Thanksgiving Day
(Kinrō Kansha-no-hi)
23 November

Safe Travel

○ The biggest threat to travellers in Tokyo is the city's general aura of safety. It's wise to keep up the same level of caution and common sense that you would back home. Of special note are reports that drink-spiking continues to be a problem in Roppongi (resulting in robbery, extor-

tion and, in extreme cases, physical assault).

○ Twenty-four-hour staffed *kōban* (police boxes) are located near most major train stations.

Telephone

The country code for Japan is 81; Tokyo's area code is 03, although some outer suburbs have different area codes.

Mobile Phones

○ Japan operates on the 3G network, so compatible phones should work in Tokyo.

○ Prepaid data-only SIM cards for unlocked smartphones are widely available and can be purchased at kiosks in the arrival halls at both Narita and Haneda airports and also from dedicated desks at major electronics retailers like Bic Camera and Yodobashi Camera.

○ Many mid- to high-end hotels in Tokyo offer complementary Handy phones, which you can use free of charge for data and calls. For a list of properties that provide this service, see www.handy.travel.

Public Phones

○ Public phones do still exist and they work almost 100% of the time; look for them around train stations.

Ordinary public phones are green; those that allow you to call abroad are grey and are usually marked 'International & Domestic Card/Coin Phone'.

○ Local calls cost ¥10 per minute; note that you won't get change on a ¥100 coin. The minimum charge for international calls is ¥100, which buys you a fraction of a minute. Reverse-charge (collect) international calls can be made by dialling ☏0051.

Time

Tokyo local time is nine hours ahead of Greenwich Mean Time (GMT). Japan does not observe daylight saving time.

Toilets

○ Free toilets, typically clean and with toilet paper, can be found in most train stations; convenience stores often have toilets you can use, too.

○ The most common words for toilet in Japanese are トイレ (pronounced 'toire') and お手洗い ('o-te-arai'); 女 (female) and 男 (male) will also come in handy.

○ Some restrooms still have squat toilets; Western-style toilets are often marked with the characters 洋式 (*yōshiki*) on the stall door.

'Washlets', increasingly common, are heated-seat thrones that wash and dry your intimate areas at the touch of a button.

○ Larger attractions, train stations, department stores and shopping centres usually have at least one wheelchair-accessible, gender-neutral toilet.

○ Separate toilet slippers are usually provided in establishments where you take off your shoes at the entrance; they are typically just inside the toilet door.

Tourist Information

Note that Tourist Information Centers (TICs) cannot make accommodation bookings.

Tokyo Tourist Information Center (☏03-5321-3077; info@ tokyo-tourism.jp; 1st fl, Tokyo Metropolitan Government Bldg 1, 2-8-1 Nishi-Shinjuku, Shinjuku-ku; ◷9.30am-6.30pm; ⑤Ōedo line to Tochōmae, exit A4) Booking counters for tours, money-exchange machines, wi-fi, and a shop with a range of souvenirs. Additional branches in Keisei Ueno Station, Haneda Airport and Shinjuku Bus Terminal.

JNTO Tourist Information Center (☏03-3201-3331; www. jnto.go.jp; 1st fl, Shin-Tokyo Bldg, 3-3-1 Marunouchi, Chiyoda-ku; ◷9am-5pm; ☏; ⑤Chiyoda line to Nijūbashi-mae, exit 1) Run by the Japan

National Tourism Organisation, this TIC has information on Tokyo and beyond. There are also branches in Narita Airport terminals 1 and 2.

Visas

Citizens of 68 countries, including Australia, Canada, Hong Kong, Korea, New Zealand, Singapore, USA, UK and almost all European nations will be automatically issued a *tanki-taizai* (temporary visitor visa) on arrival. Typically this visa is good for 90 days.

For a complete list of visa-exempt countries, consult www.mofa.go.jp/j_info/ visit/visa/short/novisa. html#list.

Women Travellers

○ Tokyo is a relatively safe city for women travellers, though basic common sense still rules. Foreign women are occasionally subjected to some forms of verbal harassment or prying questions. Physical attacks are very rare, but have occurred.

○ Note that some budget hotels that target foreign travellers are in areas where prostitution occurs (such as Kabukichō); women, especially solo travellers, are more likely to be harassed in such places.

○ Several train companies have introduced women-only cars during rush hour to protect female passengers from *chikan* (men who grope women and girls on packed trains). There are signs (usuaily in pink) on the platform indicating where you can board these cars.

Transport

Arriving in Tokyo

Tokyo has two international airports. Narita Airport, in neighbouring Chiba Prefecture, is the primary gateway to Tokyo; most budget flights end up here. Haneda Airport, closer to the city centre, is now seeing an increasing number of international flights; this is also where most domestic flights arrive. Flying into Haneda means quicker and cheaper access to central Tokyo. Both airports have smooth, hassle-free entry procedures and are connected to the city centre by public transport.

Flights, tours and cars can be booked online at lonelyplanet.com/bookings.

Narita Airport

Narita Airport (NRT, 成田空港; ☎0476-34-8000; www.narita-airport.jp; ☎) has three terminals, with Terminal 3 handling low-cost carriers. All terminals have tourist information desks.

Only Terminals 1 and 2 have train stations; all terminals are accessible via coach lines. A free shuttle bus runs between Terminal 2 and Terminal 3 approximately every five minutes (4.30am to 11.20pm); otherwise it is a 15-minute walk between the two terminals. Free shuttles also run be-

tween all terminals every 15 minutes (8am to 8pm) and every 30 minutes (7am to 8am and 8pm to 9.30pm).

Bus

Access Narita (www.access narita.jp; ¥1000) Discount buses depart roughly every 20 minutes (7.30am to 10.45pm) for Tokyo Station and Ginza (one to 1¼ hours). There's no ticket counter at the airport; just go directly to bus stop 31 at Terminal 1, stops 2 or 19 at Terminal 2, or stop 2 at Terminal 3 and pay on board. Luggage is restricted to one suitcase of less than 20kg.

Friendly Airport Limousine (www.limousinebus.co.jp/en) Direct, reserved-seat buses (¥3100) depart from all Narita Airport terminals for major hotels and train stations in Tokyo. Schedules vary by route; **Shinjuku Bus Terminal** (バスタ新宿, Busuta Shinjuku; ☎03-6380-4794; www.shinjuku-busterminal.co.jp; 4th fl, 5-24-55 Sendagaya, Shibuya-ku; ☎; 🚉JR Yamanote line to Shinjuku, new south exit) is the most frequent destination, with buses running 7am and 11pm. The journey takes 1½ to two hours depending on traffic. At

the time of writing, discount round-trip 'Welcome to Tokyo Limousine Bus Return Voucher' tickets (¥4500) were available for foreign tourists; ask at the ticket counter at the airport. Purchase tickets from kiosks in the arrivals hall; travellers are allowed two bags up to 30kg each.

Train

Both Japan Railways (JR) and the independent Keisei line run between central Tokyo and Narita Airport terminals 1 and 2. Tickets can be purchased in the basement of either terminal, where the entrances to the train stations are located.

Keisei Skyliner (www.keisei.co.jp/keisei/tetudou/skyliner/us) The quickest service into Tokyo runs nonstop to Nippori (¥2470, 36 minutes) and Ueno (¥2470, 41 minutes) stations, on the city's northeast side, where you can connect to the JR Yamanote line or the subway (Ueno Station only). Trains run roughly twice an hour, 7.30am to 11pm. The Skyliner & Tokyo Subway Ticket, which combines a one-way or round-trip ticket on the Skyliner and a one-, two- or three-day subway pass, is a good deal.

Keisei Main Line Limited-express trains (*kaisoku kyūkō*; ¥1030, 71 minutes to Ueno) follow the same route as the Skyliner, but make stops. This is a good budget option. Trains run every 20 minutes during peak hours.

Narita Express (www.jreast.co.jp/e/nex) N'EX trains depart Narita approximately every half-hour between 7.45am

---

Baggage Shipment

Baggage couriers provide next-day delivery of your large luggage from Narita and Haneda airports to any address in Tokyo (around ¥2000 per large bag), so you don't have to haul it on the trains. Look for kiosks in the arrival terminals. If you plan on taking advantage of this service, make sure to put the essentials you'll need for the next 24 hours in a small bag. For more information and a list of courier counters, see www.jnto.go.jp/hands-free-travel.

and 9.45pm for Tokyo Station (¥3020, 53 minutes) and Shinjuku (¥3190, 80 minutes); the latter also stops at Shibuya (¥3190; 75 minutes). At the time of writing, foreign tourists could purchase return N'EX tickets for ¥4000 (valid for 14 days; ¥2000 for under 12s). Check online or enquire at the JR East Travel Service centres at Narita Airport for the latest deals.

Taxi

Fixed-fare taxis run ¥20,000 to ¥22,000 for most destinations in central Tokyo, plus tolls (about ¥2000 to ¥2500). There's a 20% surcharge between 10pm and 5am. Credit cards accepted.

Haneda Airport

Haneda Airport (HND, 羽田空港; ☑international terminal 03-6428-0888; www.haneda-airport.jp; ☎) has two domestic terminals and one international terminal. Note that some international flights arrive at awkward night-time hours, between midnight and 5am, when only sporadic buses to central Tokyo will be running.

Bus

Purchase tickets at the kiosks at the arrivals hall.

Friendly Airport Limousine (www.limousinebus.co.jp/en) Coaches connect Haneda with major train stations and hotels in Shibuya (¥1030), Shinjuku (¥1230), Roppongi (¥1130), Ginza (¥930) and others; fares double between midnight and 5am. Travel times vary wildly,

---

Climate Change & Travel

Every form of transport that relies on carbon-based fuel generates CO_2, the main cause of human-induced climate change. Modern travel is dependent on aeroplanes, which might use less fuel per kilometre per person than most cars but travel much greater distances. The altitude at which aircraft emit gases (including CO_2) and particles also contributes to their climate change impact. Many websites offer 'carbon calculators' that allow people to estimate the carbon emissions generated by their journey and, for those who wish to do so, to offset the impact of the greenhouse gases emitted with contributions to portfolios of climate-friendly initiatives throughout the world. Lonely Planet offsets the carbon footprint of all staff and author travel.

---

taking anywhere from 30 to 90 minutes depending on traffic. Buses for Shinjuku depart every 30 to 40 minutes (5am to 11.30pm) and at 12.20am, 1am, 1.40am and 2.20am; departures for other areas are less frequent.

Train & Monorail

Note that the international and domestic terminals have their own stations; when travelling to the airport, the international terminal is the second to last stop.

Keikyū Airport Express (www.haneda-tokyo-access.com/en) Trains depart several times an hour (5.30am to midnight) for Shinagawa (¥410, 12 minutes), where you can connect to the JR Yamanote line.

Tokyo Monorail (www.tokyo-monorail.co.jp/english) Leaves approximately every 10 minutes (5am to midnight) for Hamamatsuchō Station (¥490, 15 minutes), which is a stop on the JR Yamanote line. Good for

---

travellers staying near Ginza or Roppongi.

Taxi

Fixed fares from designated airport taxi stands include: Ginza (¥5900), Shibuya (¥6600), Shinjuku (¥7100), Ikebukuro (¥8900) and Asakusa (¥7200), plus highway tolls (around ¥800). There's a 20% surcharge between 10pm and 5am. Credit cards accepted.

Getting Around

Boat

Tokyo Cruise (水上バス, Suijō Bus; ☎0120-977-311; http://suijobus.co.jp) Water buses run up and down the Sumida-gawa (Sumida River) roughly twice an hour between 10am and 6pm connecting Asakusa with Hama-rikyū Onshi-teien (¥980, 35 minutes) and Odaiba (¥1260, 70 minutes). Tickets

Train & Subway Passes

Prepaid rechargeable Suica and Pasmo cards (they're essentially the same; JR issues Suica and the subway issues Pasmo) work on all city trains and subways and allow you to breeze through the ticket gates without having to work out fares or transfer tickets.

Purchase one from any touch-screen ticket-vending machine in Tokyo (including those at Haneda and Narita airports). A ¥500 deposit and a minimum charge of ¥2000 is required (¥1000 for Pasmo); the deposit is refunded when you return the pass to any ticket window.

The only reason not to get a Suica or Pasmo is to take advantage of Tokyo Metro's 24-hour unlimited ride pass (adult/child ¥600/300). Note that this is only good on the nine subway lines operated by Tokyo Metro; purchase at any ticket machine at a Tokyo Metro subway station.

can be purchased immediately before departure, if available, at any pier.

Taxi

◦ All cabs run by the meter. Fares start at ¥410 for the first 1km, then rise by ¥80 for every 237m you travel (or for every 90 seconds spent in traffic). There's a surcharge of 20% between 10pm and 5am (including fixed-fare taxis from the airport). Most (but not all) taxis take credit cards.

◦ Drivers rarely speak English, though fortunately most taxis now have navigation systems. It's a good idea to have your destination written down in Japanese, or better yet, a business card with an address.

◦ Train stations and hotels have taxi stands where you are expected to queue. Otherwise, you can hail a cab from the street, by standing on the curb and sticking your arm out. A red indicator sign means the taxi is free; green means it's taken.

Train & Subway

◦ Tokyo's extensive rail network includes JR (Japan Rail) lines; 13 subway lines, nine of which are operated by Tokyo Metro (www.tokyo metro.jp) and four by Toei (www.kotsu.metro.tokyo. jp); and private commuter lines that depart in every direction for the suburbs.

◦ Major transit hubs include Tokyo, Shinagawa, Shibuya, Shinjuku, Ikebukuro and Ueno stations. Trains and subways run 5am to midnight. Lines are colour-coded, making navigation fairly simple.

◦ Fares start at ¥133/170/180 for JR/ Tokyo Metro/Toei and go up depending on how far you travel. Unfortunately, journeys that require transfers between lines run by different operators cost more than journeys that use only one operator's lines.

◦ Purchase paper tickets or top up train passes at the touch-screen ticket-vending machines outside station ticket gates. These have an English function.

◦ Figure out the best route to your destination using the Navitime for Japan Travel app (www.navi timejapan.com); you can download routes to be used offline, too.

◦ Most train and subway stations have several different exits. Try to get your bearings and decide where to exit while still on the platform; look for the yellow signs that indicate which stairs lead to which exits. If you're not sure which exit to take, look for street maps of the area usually posted near the ticket gates, which show the locations of the exits.

Language

Japanese pronunciation is easy for English speakers, as most of its sounds are also found in English. Note though that it's important to make the distinction between short and long vowels, as vowel length can change the meaning of a word. The long vowels (**ā, ē, ī, ō, ū**) should be held twice as long as the short ones. All syllables in a word are pronounced fairly evenly in Japanese. If you read our pronunciation guides as if they were English, you'll be understood.

To enhance your trip with a phrasebook, visit **lonelyplanet.com**.

Basics

Hello.	こんにちは。	kon·ni·chi·wa
Goodbye.	さようなら。	sa·yō·na·ra
Yes.	はい。	hai
No.	いいえ。	ī·e
Please.	ください。	ku·da·sai
Thank you.	ありがとう。	a·ri·ga·tō
Excuse me.	すみません。	su·mi·ma·sen
Sorry.	ごめんなさい。	go·men·na·sai

What's your name?

お名前は	o·na·ma·e wa
何ですか?	nan des ka

My name is ...

私の	wa·ta·shi no
名前は…です。	na·ma·e wa ... des

Do you speak English?

英語が	ē·go ga
話せますか?	ha·na·se·mas ka

I don't understand.

わかりません。	wa·ka·ri·ma·sen

Accommodation

Where's a ...?	…はど こですか?	... wa do·ko des ka
campsite	キャンプ場	kyam·pu·jō
guesthouse	民宿	min·shu·ku
hotel	ホテル	ho·te·ru
inn	旅館	ryo·kan

Do you have a ... room?	…ルームは ありますか?	...·rū·mu wa a·ri·mas ka
single	シングル	shin·gu·ru
double	ダブル	da·bu·ru

How much is it per ...?	…いくら ですか?	... i·ku·ra des ka
night	1泊	ip·pa·ku
person	1人	hi·to·ri

air-con	エアコン	air·kon
bathroom	風呂場	fu·ro·ba
window	窓	ma·do

Eating & Drinking

I'd like to reserve a table for (two).

(2人)の 予約をお 願いします。	(fu·ta·ri) no yo·ya·ku o o·ne·gai shi·mas

I'd like (the menu).

(メニュー) をお願いします。	(me·nyū) o o·ne·gai shi·mas

I don't eat (red meat).

(赤身の肉) は食べません。	(a·ka·mi no ni·ku) wa ta·be·ma·sen

That was delicious!

おいしかった。	oy·shi·kat·ta

Please bring the bill.

お勘定 をください。	o·kan·jō o ku·da·sai

Emergencies

Help!	たすけて!	tas·ke·te
Go away!	離れろ!	ha·na·re·ro
Call the police!	警察を呼んで!	kē·sa·tsu o yon·de
Call a doctor!	医者を呼んで!	i·sha o yon·de
I'm lost.	迷いました。	ma·yoy·mash·ta

I'm ill.

私は病 気です。	wa·ta·shi wa byō·ki des

Where are the toilets?

トイレは どこですか?	toy·re wa do·ko des ka

Transport & Directions

Where's the ...?

…はどこ ですか?	... wa do·ko des ka

What's the address?

住所は何 ですか?	jū·sho wa nan des ka

Can you show me (on the map)?

(地図で)教えて くれませんか?	(chi·zu de) o·shi·e·te ku·re·ma·sen ka

When's the next (bus)?

次の(バス)は 何時ですか?	tsu·gi no (bas) wa nan·ji des ka

Behind the Scenes

Acknowledgements

Illustrations p56–57 by Michael Weldon.

Cover photograph: Asakusa district, Sean Pavone/Alamy©

This Book

This third edition of Lonely Planet's *Best of Tokyo* guidebook was researched and written by Rebecca Milner, Thomas O'Malley and Simon Richmond. The previous edition was also written by Rebecca. This guidebook was produced by the following:

Destination Editors Laura Crawford, James Smart

Senior Product Editor Kate Chapman

Regional Senior Cartographer Diana Von Holdt

Product Editors Sandie Kestell, Hannah Cartmel

Book Designer Jessica Rose

Assisting Editors Lauren O'Connell, Kristin Odijk, Charlotte Orr, Maja Vatrić

Cover Researcher Brendan Dempsey-Spencer

Thanks to Ronan Abayawickrema, Naoko Akamatsu, Claire Rourke

Send Us Your Feedback

We love to hear from travellers – your comments keep us on our toes and help make our books better. Our well-travelled team reads every word on what you loved or loathed about this book. Although we cannot reply individually to postal submissions, we always guarantee that your feedback goes straight to the appropriate authors, in time for the next edition. Each person who sends us information is thanked in the next edition, the most useful submissions are rewarded with a selection of digital PDF chapters.

Visit lonelyplanet.com/contact to submit your updates and suggestions or to ask for help. Our award-winning website also features inspirational travel stories, news and discussions.

Note: We may edit, reproduce and incorporate your comments in Lonely Planet products such as guidebooks, websites and digital products, so let us know if you don't want your comments reproduced or your name acknowledged. For a copy of our privacy policy visit lonelyplanet.com/privacy.

Index

TAKASHI IMAGES/SHUTTERSTOCK ©

Tokyo Maps

Harajuku, Aoyama, Shibuya & Ebisu

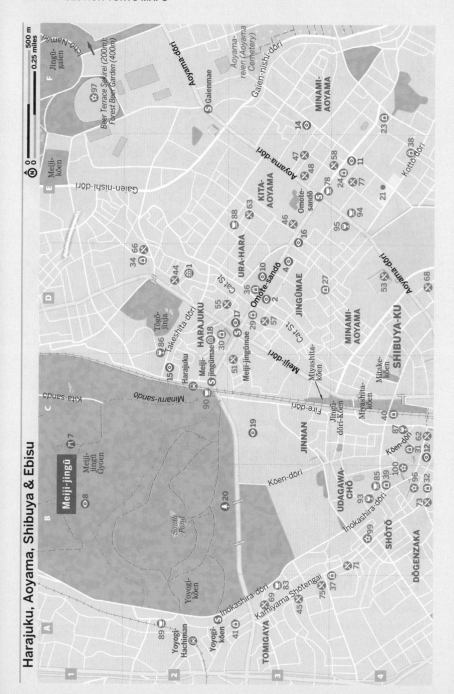

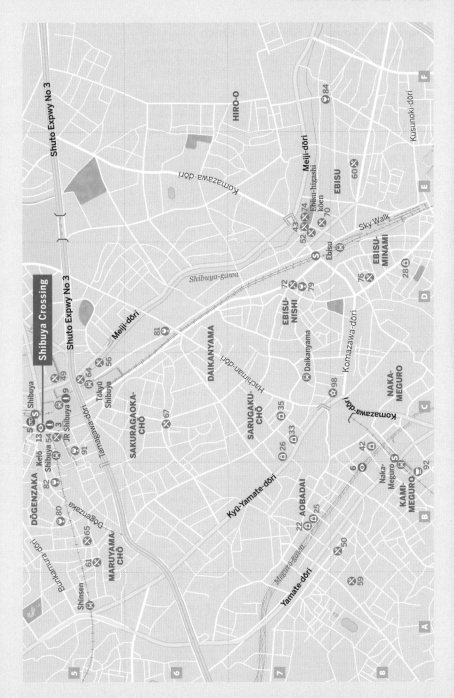

Harajuku, Aoyama, Shibuya & Ebisu

◉ Sights
1	Design Festa	D2
2	Dior Omote-sandō	D3
	Espace Louis Vuitton Tokyo	(see 4)
3	Hachikō Statue	C5
4	Louis Vuitton Omote-sandō	D3
5	Mag's Park	C5
6	Meguro-gawa	B8
7	Meiji-jingū	C1
8	Meiji-jingū Gyoen	B1
9	Myth of Tomorrow	C5
10	Omotesandō Hills	D3
11	Prada Aoyama	E4
12	Shibuya Center-gai	C4
13	Shibuya Crossing	C5
14	SunnyHills Minami-Aoyama	F3
15	Takeshita-dōri	C2
16	Tod's Omote-sandō	E3
17	Tokyu Plaza	D3
18	Ukiyo-e Ōta Memorial Museum of Art	D2
19	Yoyogi National Stadium	C3
20	Yoyogi-kōen	B2

◉ Activities, Courses & Tours
21	Ohara School of Ikebana	E4

◉ Shopping
22	...research General Store	B7
23	Arts & Science	F4
24	Comme des Garçons	E4
25	Cow Books	B7
	d47 design travel store	(see 49)
26	Daikanyama T-Site	C7
27	House @Mikiri Hassin	D3
28	Kapital	D8
29	KiddyLand	D3
30	Laforet	D2
31	Loft	C4
32	Mega Donki	B4
33	Minä Perhonen	C7
34	Musubi	D2
35	Okura	C7
36	Pass the Baton	D3
	Raw Tokyo	(see 53)
37	Shibuya Publishing & Booksellers	A4
38	Sou-Sou	E4
39	Tokyu Hands	B4
40	Tower Records	C4
41	Tsukikageya	A3
42	Vase	C8

◉ Eating
43	Afuri	E7
44	Agaru Sagaru Nishi-iru Higashi-iru	D2
45	Ahiru Store	A3
46	Anniversaire Café	E3
47	Aoyama Kawakami-an	E3
	Camelback	(see 45)
48	Commune 2nd	E3
49	d47 Shokudō	C5
50	Delifucious	B8
51	Eatrip	C3
52	Ebisu-yokochō	E7
53	Farmer's Market @UNU	D4
54	Food Show	C5
55	Gomaya Kuki	D2
56	Gyūkatsu Motomura	C5
57	Harajuku Gyōza-rō	D3
58	Higashiya Man	E4
59	Higashi-Yama	A8
60	Ippo	E8
61	Kaikaya	B5
62	Katsu Midori	C4
63	Maisen	E3
64	Maru Bengara	C5
65	Matsukiya	B5
66	Mominoki House	D2
67	Nagi Shokudō	C6
68	Narukiyo	D4
69	Nata de Cristiano	A3
70	Ouca	E7
	Out	(see 68)
71	Pignon	B4
72	Rangmang Shokudō	D7
73	Sagatani	B4
74	Udon Yamachō	E7
75	Uoriki	A3
76	Yakiniku Champion	D8
77	Yanmo	E4

◉ Drinking & Nightlife
78	Aoyama Flower Market Teahouse	E3
79	Bar Trench	D7
80	Beat Cafe	B5
81	Circus Tokyo	D6
82	Contact	B5
83	Fuglen Tokyo	A3
84	Gem by Moto	F7
85	Gen Gen An	B4
86	Harajuku Taproom	D2
87	Karaoke Rainbow	C4
88	Koffee Mameya	E3
89	Little Nap Coffee Stand	A2
90	Mori no Terrace	C2
91	Oath	C5
92	Onibus Coffee	B8
93	Rhythm Cafe	B4
94	Sakurai Japanese Tea Experience	E4
95	Two Rooms	E4

◉ Entertainment
96	Club Quattro	B4
97	Jingū Baseball Stadium	F1
98	Unit	C8
99	Uplink	B4
100	WWW	B4

Marunouchi, Nihombashi, Ginza & Tsukiji

Marunouchi, Nihombashi, Ginza & Tsukiji

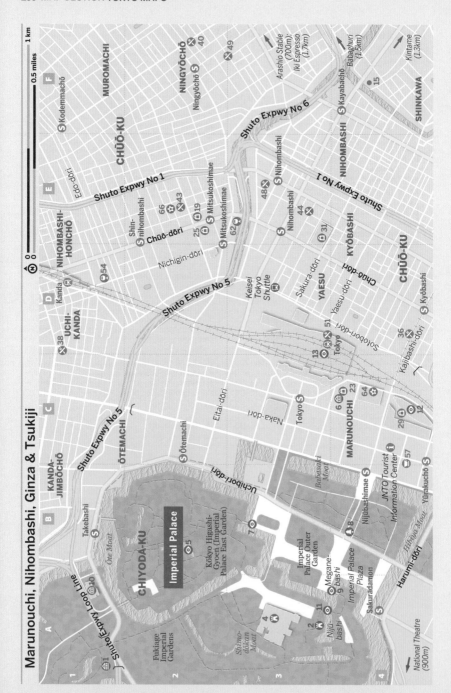

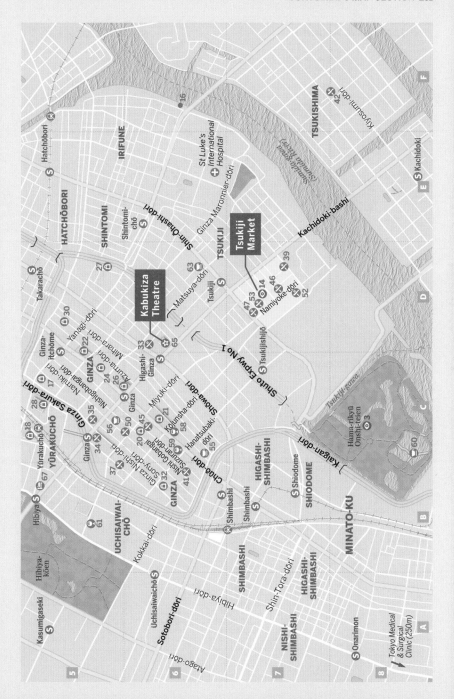

Roppongi & Around

Roppongi & Around

⊙ Sights
1	21_21 Design Sight	B1
2	Complex 665	B2
3	Mori Art Museum	A3
4	National Art Center Tokyo	A2
5	Roppongi Hills	B3
6	Suntory Museum of Art	B1
7	Tokyo City View	A2
	Tokyo Midtown Design Hub	(see 6)
8	Tokyo Tower	D3

🔒 Shopping
	Souvenir from Tokyo	(see 4)
9	Tokyo Midtown	B2

⊗ Eating
10	Bricolage Bread & Co	A3

11	Honmura-An	B2
12	Jōmon	B2
13	Kikunoi	B1
14	Sougo	B2
15	Tofuya-Ukai	D3

⊙ Drinking & Nightlife
16	Ele Tokyo	B3
17	Gen Yamamoto	B3
18	Pasela Resorts	B2
19	Rise & Win Brewing Co. Kamikatz Taproom	D3
20	Two Dogs Taproom	B2

⊙ Entertainment
21	Toho Cinemas Roppongi Hills	A3

Shinjuku

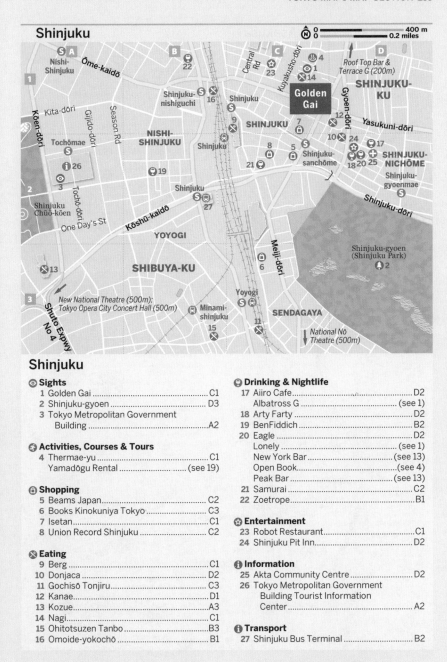

Shinjuku

◎ Sights
1 Golden Gai	C1
2 Shinjuku-gyoen	D3
3 Tokyo Metropolitan Government Building	A2

✛ Activities, Courses & Tours
| 4 Thermae-yu | C1 |
| Yamadōgu Rental | (see 19) |

⬤ Shopping
5 Beams Japan	C2
6 Books Kinokuniya Tokyo	C3
7 Isetan	C1
8 Union Record Shinjuku	C2

✕ Eating
9 Berg	C1
10 Donjaca	D2
11 Gochisō Tonjiru	C3
12 Kanae	D1
13 Kozue	A3
14 Nagi	C1
15 Ohitotsuzen Tanbo	B3
16 Omoide-yokochō	B1

◐ Drinking & Nightlife
17 Aiiro Cafe	D2
Albatross G	(see 1)
18 Arty Farty	D2
19 BenFiddich	B2
20 Eagle	D2
Lonely	(see 1)
New York Bar	(see 13)
Open Book	(see 4)
Peak Bar	(see 13)
21 Samurai	C2
22 Zoetrope	B1

✿ Entertainment
| 23 Robot Restaurant | C1 |
| 24 Shinjuku Pit Inn | D2 |

ⓘ Information
| 25 Akta Community Centre | D2 |
| 26 Tokyo Metropolitan Government Building Tourist Information Center | A2 |

ⓘ Transport
| 27 Shinjuku Bus Terminal | B2 |

Ueno, Akihabara & Asakusa

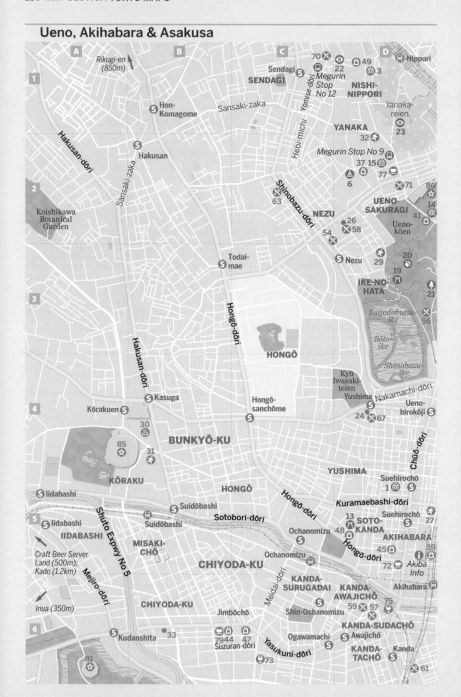

ARAKAWA-KU

SENZOKU

TAITŌ-KU

NEGISHI

Ogubashi-dōri

Ōtakebashi-dōri

Shōwa-dōri

Kokusai-dōri

Kototoi-dōri

Kototoi-dōri

66 ⊗

Uguisudani

9

8 17

18

Tokyo National Museum

Kototoi-dōri

⊙ 34

ASAKUSA

UENO

KITA-UENO

82

Kototoi-dōri

64 69

Sensō-ji

Megurin Stop No 2

UENO

Ueno

Kappabashi Hon-dōri

Shuto Expwy No 1

Tsukuba Express Asakusa

4

16

84

HIGASHI-UENO

MATSUGAYA

42

52

46 55

7 10

Umamichi-dōri

Edo-dōri

3

43

68

28

25

40

Ueno

Inarichō

62

53

38

Tōbu Asakusa

Keisei Ueno

Asakusa-dōri

ASAKUSA

12

76 65

HIGASHI-UENO

KAMINARI-MON

87 Asakusa

36

Tawaramachi

Asakusa-dōri

Asakusa

2

Ueno-Okachimachi

Naka-Okachimachi

Shin-Okachimachi

KOTOBUKI

4

Okachimachi

Kasuga-dōri

KOMAGATA

Dembōin-dōri

Komagata-bashi

HIGASHI-KOMAGATA

TAITŌ-KU

Kuramae

Shuto Expwy No 6

Kasuga-dōri

35

Shōwa-dōri

KURAMAE

74

Kuramae

ASAKUSABASHI

Asakusabashi

Kuramae-bashi

60

YOKOAMI

Kuramaebashi-dōri

SUMIDA-KU

50

Akihabara

Ryōgoku Kokugikan

11

80

Kanda-gawa

MUROMACHI

51

Tokyo Mizube Cruising Line Ryōgoku Pier

83

Yokoami-kōen

Ryōgoku

5

6

Iwamotochō

Ryōgoku-bashi

Ryōgoku

IWAMOTO-CHŌ

BAKUROCHŌ

Ryōgoku-bashi

78

Ryōgoku

RYŌGOKU

Keiyō-dōri

Bakuroyokoyama

Ueno, Akihabara & Asakusa

Symbols & Map Key

Look for these symbols to quickly identify listings:

- ◎ Sights
- ⊗ Eating
- ✚ Activities
- ◐ Drinking
- ⊜ Courses
- ★ Entertainment
- ☞ Tours
- 🔒 Shopping
- ✪ Festivals & Events
- ❶ Information & Transport

Find your best experiences with these Great For... icons.

 Art & Culture

 History

 Beaches

 Local Life

 Budget

 Nature & Wildlife

Cafe/Coffee

 Photo Op

Cycling

 Scenery

Detour

 Shopping

Drinking

 Short Trip

Entertainment

 Sport

Events

 Walking

Family Travel

Winter Travel

Food & Drink

These symbols and abbreviations give vital information for each listing:

- 🍃 Sustainable or green recommendation
- **FREE** No payment required

- ☎ Telephone number
- 🚌 Bus
- ⏱ Opening hours
- ⛴ Ferry
- Ⓟ Parking
- 🚊 Tram
- ⊖ Nonsmoking
- 🚆 Train
- ❄ Air-conditioning
- 🈺 English-language menu
- @ Internet access
- 🌱 Vegetarian selection
- 🛜 Wi-fi access
- 👫 Family-friendly
- 🏊 Swimming pool

Sights

- 🏖 Beach
- 🐦 Bird Sanctuary
- 🛕 Buddhist
- 🏰 Castle/Palace
- ✝ Christian
- ☯ Confucian
- 🕉 Hindu
- ☪ Islamic
- 卐 Jain
- ✡ Jewish
- 🗿 Monument
- 🏛 Museum/Gallery/ Historic Building
- 🏚 Ruin
- ⛩ Shinto
- 🪯 Sikh
- ☯ Taoist
- 🍇 Winery/Vineyard
- 🐾 Zoo/Wildlife Sanctuary
- ◎ Other Sight

Points of Interest

- © Bodysurfing
- ⛺ Camping
- ☕ Cafe
- 🛶 Canoeing/Kayaking
- • Course/Tour
- 🤿 Diving
- 🍸 Drinking & Nightlife
- 🍴 Eating
- 🎭 Entertainment
- ♨ Sento Hot Baths/ Onsen
- 🛍 Shopping
- ⛷ Skiing
- 🛏 Sleeping
- 🤿 Snorkelling
- 🏄 Surfing
- 🏊 Swimming/Pool
- 🚶 Walking
- 🏄 Windsurfing
- ◎ Other Activity

Information

- 🏦 Bank
- 🏛 Embassy/Consulate
- ➕ Hospital/Medical
- @ Internet
- 👮 Police
- ✉ Post Office
- 📞 Telephone
- 🚻 Toilet
- ❶ Tourist Information
- • Other Information

Geographic

- 🏖 Beach
- ⋈ Gate
- ⛺ Hut/Shelter
- 🚨 Lighthouse
- 🔭 Lookout
- ▲ Mountain/Volcano
- 🌴 Oasis
- 🌳 Park
-)(Pass
- 🧺 Picnic Area
- 💧 Waterfall

Transport

- ✈ Airport
- Ⓑ BART station
- ⊗ Border crossing
- 🅣 Boston T station
- 🚌 Bus
- ➕ Cable car/Funicular
- 🚲 Cycling
- ⛴ Ferry
- Ⓜ Metro/MRT station
- 🚝 Monorail
- Ⓟ Parking
- ⛽ Petrol station
- Ⓢ Subway/S-Bahn/ Skytrain station
- 🚕 Taxi
- ➕ Train station/Railway
- Tram
- Ⓤ Underground/ U-Bahn station
- • Other Transport

Our Story

A beat-up old car, a few dollars in the pocket and a sense of adventure. In 1972 that's all Tony and Maureen Wheeler needed for the trip of a lifetime – across Europe and Asia overland to Australia. It took several months, and at the end – broke but inspired – they sat at their kitchen table writing and stapling together their first travel guide, *Across Asia on the Cheap*. Within a week they'd sold 1500 copies. Lonely Planet was born.

Today, Lonely Planet has offices in Franklin, London, Melbourne, Oakland, Dublin, Beijing and Delhi, with more than 600 staff and writers. We share Tony's belief that 'a great guidebook should do three things: inform, educate and amuse'.

Our Writers

Rebecca Milner

California-born, living in Tokyo since 2002. Co-author of Lonely Planet guides to Tokyo and Japan. Freelance writer covering travel, food and culture. Published in the *Guardian,* the *Independent,* the *Sunday Times Travel Magazine,* the *Japan Times* and more.

Thomas O'Malley

A British writer based in Beijing, Tom is a world-leading connoisseur of cheap eats, dive bars, dark alleyways and hangovers. He has contributed travel stories to everyone from the BBC to *Playboy,* and reviews hotels for the *Telegraph.* Under another guise, he is a comedy scriptwriter. Follow him by walking behind at a distance.

Simon Richmond

Journalist and photographer Simon Richmond has specialised as a travel writer since the early 1990s and first worked for Lonely Planet in 1999 on its Central Asia guide. He's long since stopped counting the number of guidebooks he's researched and written for the company, but countries covered include Australia, China, India, Iran, Japan, Korea, Malaysia, Mongolia, Myanmar (Burma), Russia, Singapore, South Africa and Turkey.

STAY IN TOUCH LONELYPLANET.COM/CONTACT

AUSTRALIA The Malt Store, Level 3, 551 Swanston St, Carlton, Victoria 3053 03 8379 8000, fax 03 8379 8111

IRELAND Digital Depot, Roe Lane (off Thomas St), Digital Hub, Dublin 8, D08 TCV4, Ireland

USA 124 Linden Street, Oakland, CA 94607 510 250 6400, toll free 800 275 8555, fax 510 893 8572

UK 240 Blackfriars Road, London SE1 8NW 020 3771 5100, fax 020 3771 5101

 twitter.com/ lonelyplanet facebook.com/ lonelyplanet instagram.com/ lonelyplanet   youtube.com/ lonelyplanet lonelyplanet.com/ newsletter